IRANIANS IN TEXAS

IRANIANS IN TEXAS

Migration, Politics, and Ethnic Identity

Mohsen M. Mobasher

University of Texas Press ◆ Austin

Copyright © 2012 by the University of Texas Press
All rights reserved
Printed in the United States of America
First edition, 2012

Requests for permission to reproduce material from this work
should be sent to:

Permissions
University of Texas Press
P.O. Box 7819
Austin, TX 78713-7819
www.utexas.edu/utpress/about/bpermission.html

The paper used in this book meets the minimum requirements
of ANSI/NISO Z39.48-1992 (R1997) (Permanence of Paper). ∞

Designed by Ayham Ghraowi

Library of Congress Cataloging-in-Publication Data

Mobasher, Mohsen M., 1962–
        Iranians in Texas : migration, politics, and ethnic identity /
Mohsen M. Mobasher. — 1st ed.
                p.   cm.
        Includes bibliographical references and index.
        ISBN 978-0-292-72859-2 (cloth : alk. paper)
        ISBN 978-0-292-73708-2 (e-book)
        1. Iranian Americans—Texas. 2. Iranians—Texas.
3. Immigrants—Texas. 4. Political refugees—Texas. 5. Iran—Politics
and government—20th century. I. Title.
        F395.I5M63   2012
        305.891'550764—dc23   2011031400

Dedicated to the loving memory of my father, Morteza, and my brother Majeed for their endless support; my dear mother, Fatemeh Tabatabaie, for enduring seven painful years of separation and for her relentless push for a reunion; my brother Mojtaba for his solitary fortitude in managing our family affairs in Iran; and my sister, Maryam, for her infinite love and effort in reconstructing our family in exile.

Contents

Preface

In 1978–1979, millions of Iranian men and women from all social backgrounds marched through the streets of Tehran to end the fifty-year reign
of the Pahlavi dynasty. During and after the 1978–1979 revolutionary upheavals, for various political and social reasons a great number of individuals and families from diverse socioeconomic and religious backgrounds
left Iran and settled mainly in Europe, Canada, and the United States.
This book presents the experience of Iranian immigrants in the United
States since the Iranian revolution in the context of the ongoing political
tension between Iran and the United States precipitated by the Iranian
government's taking of fifty-two Americans as hostages for 444 days in
1979. I chose the Iranian revolution and the hostage crisis as my point of
departure for three reasons. First, with the exception of a massive migration of a large number of Iranians to India in the seventh century (Ansari
1992), the revolution of 1978–1979 was the only time in Iranian history
to witness an enormous number of people uprooted and forced to live in
exile. Second, the Iranian revolution and the U.S.-Iranian hostility generated by the hostage crisis has not only shaped the ebb and flow of Iranians'
immigration to the United States during the past thirty years but also influenced the attitudes of Iranian expatriates toward the United States and
their relations with American people. Finally, the Iranian revolution and
hostage crisis marked a radical negative shift in American public opinion
toward Iran, Iranians, and Muslims.

The hostage crisis and its subsequent sanctions against Iran and Iranian immigrants shook the foundation of social life for Iranians in the United States both individually and collectively. Suddenly, thousands of Iranians in the United States were stigmatized and viewed as enemies because of political actions by their government. Widespread hostility, prejudice, and ongoing discrimination against Iranian immigrants in retaliation for the political behavior of the Islamic Republic of Iran since the hostage crisis marginalized many Iranians, retarded and minimized their integration into American society, and pushed them to conceal their Iranian national identity and to construct a new, less threatening ethnic identity. Furthermore, these political forces and the prevailing stereotyped and politicized portrayals of Iranian immigrants and the extensive overt discrimination against them slowed down the assimilation of Iranians thus restraining them from full participation in American society and contributed to a wide range of institutional crises and personal dilemmas.

In focusing on U.S.-Iranian relations during the past half-century, this book is grounded in two major theoretical perspectives. First, unlike many migration scholars who emphasize the role of human capital as well as cultural beliefs and practices of migrants in the host society, in this book I emphasize the political nature of immigration, underscoring the powerful impact of political relations between migrant-sending and migrant-receiving countries on the integration and incorporation of immigrants. As research has shown, the mode of entry as well as the social, political, and economic conditions of the host society at the time of a migrant's arrival are the key factors that shape the experience of an immigrant in the United States. Equally important, the degree of stability or social change in the migrants' society of origin has a profound impact on their community and lifestyle in the host society.

The second theoretical thrust of the book is to show the impact of exclusionary and discriminatory practices of the United States' immigration policy on the formation and perpetuation of the Iranian family in exile, ethnic identity formation among Iranian immigrants, and their attitudes toward American society. The cumulative effect of the Iranian revolution, the hostage crisis, and the political rupture between the United States and Iran and its impact on the integration of Iranian immigrants in the United States have not yet been subject to comprehensive analysis. Despite the increased interest in Iranian immigrants in diaspora by social scientists in recent years, there is a lack of theoretical work that focuses on both the sending and receiving political ends of the migration process for Iranians. Moreover, given the theoretical significance of contexts of reception and the policies of the receiving government in the incorporation of newcomers, there has yet to be a book-length study of the impact of U.S.–Iranian conflict, negative persistent media stereotypes, and discrimination and prejudice against Iranians since the hostage crisis on integration and incorporation of Iranian immigrants in the United States. This book is a major step in that direction.

In my attempt to show the consequences of the political clash between Iran and United States and integration of Iranian immigrants in exile I draw primarily on theoretical works of such prominent figures as Max Weber, C. Wright Mills, Edward Said, Erving Goffman, Robert Merton, Robert Park, Edna Bonacich, and Jeffrey Alexander. I endeavor to synthesize the literature on cultural racism, stigma, cultural trauma, host hostility, marginality, and ambivalence. By combining and synthesizing the works of theorists with different orientations, I do not intend to develop a "metatheory" of ethnic relations and integration that would be applicable to all immigrant populations but rather to combine propositions from different perspectives in a complementary way in order to explain the situation of Iranians in the United States.

This book is both descriptive and explanatory and is written for general readers who desire to gain a better understanding of migration politics and the impact of political forces on the integration of immigrants into American society. It is based on ten years of periodic data collection including formal and informal interviews with first- and second-generation Iranian immigrants, two surveys, and systematic participant observation in three Iranian communities (Houston, Dallas, and Austin) in Texas. My first goal in this book is to describe who Iranian immigrants are, why they have come to this country, what kinds of dilemmas they confront, how they perceive Americans, and how they feel about their own community in exile. In my description, I attempt to echo the diverse voices of Iranian immigrants and reflect their innermost subjective feelings, dilemmas, and paradoxes. Through extensive quotations, I invite the reader into Iranian immigrants' private world of personal identity, cultural pride, religious experience, marginality, ambivalence, and clash of cultures that is often hidden from ordinary eyes in the public domain of everyday life. But of equal importance, I also attempt to explain what the sources of these dilemmas are and why first- and second-generation Iranian immigrant men and women feel the way they do about Americans and their own co-ethnics.

The tone of anger, bitterness, and discontent with American society and culture reflected in parts of this book derives from the actual voices of hundreds of Iranian men and women who participated in this project—

not from my authorial voice. I have simply gathered their individual views and attempted to echo them collectively and systematically in a single manuscript. To be sure, there are major demographic differences between Iranians in Texas and other parts of the country in size, entrepreneurial activities, ethnic associations, ethnoreligious diversity, and community organization. But there is a striking similarity across Iranian communities in American cities, and most Iranians confront the same challenges and are affected by the same social and political forces in Iran and the United States. Veiling national or religious identity among many Iranians, for example, lies not so much with the characteristics of Iranian communities in Texas or California as with the inevitable political and social forces in Iran and the United States within which Iranian migration has occurred. Most people probably think of an immigrant community as a small territory or clustered ethnic neighborhood in a large city composed of people with common ethnic or national origins, ethnic businesses, and native signs where a homogeneous, nostalgic people speak their native language. By Iranian community I refer not to bounded neighborhoods where Iranians live and interact with one another. On the contrary, by Iranian community I refer to a nonterritorial field of people manifesting a collective consciousness, experiencing the same collective traumas, and confronting the same collective social issues. Within this rather amorphous, postmodern field, social networking and interaction are facilitated by shared identification with language, religious tradition, subethnicity, political orientation, occupation, and lifestyle.

I approach my topic from the perspectives of anthropology and sociology. I am not a historian or a political scientist and intend neither to examine the political development of U.S.-Iranian relations in the past half-century nor the roots of the Iranian revolution in 1978 and its social and political outcomes. It is beyond the scope of this book to engage in any political analysis of postrevolutionary Iran. I have carefully refrained from making any judgments about political actions of the Iranian government. A half-century ago C. Wright Mills in his seminal work *The Sociological Imagination* (1959) noted that many of the personal troubles individuals endure in their private lives are rooted in historical changes, structural transformations, and institutional contradictions that transcend the local environments of the individuals. Therefore, to have a better understanding of major "public issues," Mills adds, social scientists need to look beyond the character of individuals and their immediate environments and trace the links between individual biography and world history. Whatever the specific problems or points of interests and however limited or broad,

Mills wrote, it is central for social analysts in any society to examine the intricate connection and interplay between biography and history and to ask questions about the structure of that particular society and its components, its place in human history, and the mechanisms by which it is changing and the varieties of individuals prevailing in that society. It is in this spirit that in the present book I attempt to tell the story of Iranian immigrants and the public or collective "issues" and challenges they have confronted in exile.

Acknowledgments

For critical review of various drafts of the manuscript I owe especial thanks to and am indebted to my colleagues and friends Greg Getz and Robin Davidson at the University of Houston–Downtown and Mahmoud Sadri at Texas Woman's University. They patiently read the entire manuscript, discussed the project with me, offered critical comments and insightful suggestions, and provided support and friendship. My long discussions with Sadri helped me to refine my ideas and articulate them in clearer ways. I would also like to thank Greg Getz for understanding the challenges of my research and giving me the most flexible teaching schedule, which provided me ample time to complete this project. I am also greatly indebted to Mehdi Bozorgmehr at City University of New York and Nestor Rodriguez at the University of Texas at Austin for reading the final draft of the manuscript and making remarkable suggestions for improving it. Undoubtedly, their insightful comments and remarks enriched the overall quality of the book.

Also to be thanked deeply are Nazbanou Sedghi and Jairan Sadeghi, my two outstanding, omnicompetent research assistants, who were always available to help. They never refused to help with data collection and data analysis and super-generously offered their time throughout the entire project.

I thank the University of Houston–Downtown and members of the Faculty Leave Award Committee for bestowing on me the Faculty Leave Award in spring 2006 to complete the first draft of the manuscript. I also thank my late chair, Bill Brigman, as well as Susan Ahern, the dean of the College of Humanities and Social Sciences, and Adolfo Santos, the chair of the Social Science Department, for supporting my research activities. I would like to thank our wonderful interlibrary loan staff members Alice Lewis and Anita Garza at the University of Houston–Downtown for requesting and obtaining hundreds of books and articles for this project.

At the University of Texas Press, I am deeply grateful to Jim Burr for his patience and support. I am also grateful to Lynne Chapman and Tana Silva for copyediting and preparing the final manuscript, to Karen Broyles for preparing the index, and to Nancy Bryan for marketing and promoting the book.

I would like to thank all Iranians who participated in this study and those who generously offered their time for long interviews and shared their views and feelings with me. This book would not exist were it not for their participation. Many individuals, associations, and business establishments in the Iranian community in Texas helped with data collection for this book, and I am grateful to all of them.

As always, I am indebted to my sister, Maryam, brother-in-law, Bijan, my nieces, Keyana and Donna, and my nephew, Kameron, for their unlimited support during the entire project. Last but not least, I wish to express my deepest gratitude and thanks to my dear friend and partner, Afsaneh Ilkhan, for her patience, encouragement, full support, and invaluable presence as I worked through the various obstacles in researching and writing. I owe her a great deal for deferring, suspending, and putting many of our plans on hold until this book's completion.

IRANIANS IN TEXAS

Introduction

Each immigrant group in America has its own story. Some of these stories are about the successful adaptations and significant accomplishments of immigrants in their new homeland. Other stories, however, are about immigrants' challenges of adjustment and difficulties of integration in their host society. Still others are descriptive community studies, and the story is about who they are, why they came to America, what they do, what problems they encountered, how they feel about being in America, what types of relationships they have with Americans and other ethnic groups, and how they maintain contact with the home society and preserve their culture, language, and ethnic identity. This book is about an immigrant group with a relatively short record in the history of American immigration: that of Iranians. Although this book highlights some of the common themes often told in stories of other immigrants, it mainly focuses on the impact of a series of indomitable political forces in Iran and the United States during the past half-century on migration experiences of Iranians and their integration in exile. I highlight the political forces in Iran and the United States in narrating the story of Iranian immigrants for five reasons.

First, as indicated by most migration scholars, to better narrate and understand the story of any immigrant group experience we need a dual perspective that examines both ends of the migration chain, attending to the sociological context of migrants' country of origin and host society. If this is true, then we cannot hope to understand the story of Iranian immigrants in isolation from social, cultural, political, and economic forces in the United States and Iran as well as the relations between the two countries. In other words, the story of Iranian immigrants in the United States has been as much a response to political, economic, and social developments in the United States as it has been to the consequences of the Iranian revolution and political conditions that have forced as many as two million Iranians to leave Iran.[1]

Second, I strongly believe that such distinctive political events as the 1953 CIA coup d'etat and the subsequent strong ties between Iran and the United States, the 1978–1979 Iranian revolution, the hostage crisis and the ensuing U.S.-Iranian hostility and diplomatic break, and the 9/11 attacks have had a powerful impact on the migration history of Iranians and the mode of their integration in the United States. Had there been no strong political and economic ties between Iran and the United States after the 1953 CIA coup and restoration of the shah's power and the subsequent American aid and push for modernization of Iranian society, the immigration of thousands of Iranians to the United States for education and training would not have occurred so rapidly before the revolution. Similarly, had there been no revolution in Iran in 1979, thousands of disenchanted and alienated intellectuals, political activists, professionals, industrialists, artists, journalists, and members of religious minorities would not have preferred exile to life in Iran. Also, had fifty-two Americans not been taken hostage in Iran in 1979, there would have been no nationwide demonstrations, hate crimes, immigration restrictions, and various forms of discrimination and prejudice against Iranian nationals in the United States. Finally, had the 9/11 attacks in 2001 not occurred, Iranian immigrants would not have been stigmatized as a suspicious group once again and would not have become exposed to fresh instances of prejudice and discrimination. Therefore, to have a better understanding of Iranians' story in the United States it is essential to address the political context within which their mass migration occurred.

Third, much as with other political immigrants such as Cubans, the story of Iranian immigrants in the United States, particularly in the past thirty years, has largely been a political saga permeated with themes of loss, forced displacement, political asylum, exile, political resistance and opposition, and political activism stemming from consequences of the Iranian revolution, as well as tenors of discrimination and prejudice, exclusion stemming from the U.S.-Iranian tensions after the revolution, and persistent media stereotypes of Iranians as religious zealots, terrorists, and hostage takers. The themes of loss, alienation, and exile among Iranians are best reflected in the poetry of the Iranian diaspora. As indicated by Persis Karim (2008), Iranian poetry in exile expresses the collective anguish, pain, and ambivalence that Iranians in the United States have experienced since the hostage crisis. It also addresses narratives of revolution, war, exile, becoming American, language, and self-identity, as well as gender and culture and critiques of both Iran's and the United States' governments.

Fourth, despite their overall high educational degree, completed mainly in American universities, and long residence in this country, the proportion of Iranians who have a favorable image of the United States and its people and who express high levels of satisfaction and fulfillment about living here is surprisingly low. As indicated in Chapter 3, except for a small number of optimists, a significant proportion of Iranian immigrants in the research sample remains ambivalent or conflicted about American society. They make a clear distinction between the U.S. government and the American people. What is more, they make a distinction between American people's benevolence and kindness and their lack of political knowledge and sophistication. Furthermore, these Iranian immigrants seem to have two distinct and conflicting images of the United States: a positive perception of a land of economic opportunity, democracy, pluralism, individual freedom, religious tolerance, and material comfort based on the rule of law and protection of civil rights coexists with a negative perception of political dynamics and cultural practices that generate hostile, duplicitous, arrogant, and malevolent behaviors around the world and with respect to their homeland of Iran. This latter perception includes images of a racist, imperialistic, ambitious superpower with a "young," "decadent" culture obsessed with materialism and individualism and devoid of humanitarian and family values. In addition to the optimists and the ambivalent Iranians, another small group is cynical about almost every aspect of life in the United States and categorically rejects the host culture and compounds rejectionism with conspiracy theories about the forces that run the American society. For the cynics, the government of the United States is no more democratic than that of any other country. To this group, Americans, despite their freedoms and myriad opportunities, appear no more open-minded and conscious of social and political events than illiterate people in third-world countries.

Finally, in my opinion, other than the relocation and internment of Japanese Americans after the attack on Pearl Harbor in 1941, and the post-9/11 treatment of Muslim Arabs from the Middle East, no other immigrant group in the most recent migration history of the United States from an "enemy state"—as proclaimed by mainstream media, public opinion polls, and government officials—has been so politicized, publicly despised, stigmatized, and traumatized by the U.S. government as have Iranians. Indeed, many Hispanic, Asian, black, and Middle Eastern immigrant groups in the United States have faced substantial and often similar prejudice and discrimination (Feagin and Feagin 1999). Nevertheless, no other immigrant group from a former ally country of the United States has lost its positive social image so quickly and has been so misrepresented, stereotyped, misunderstood, and made to feel unwelcome despite its overall high socioeconomic status and record of accomplishment in a short period as Iranians have. Unlike many other immigrant groups who suffered much discrimination and prejudice because of economic forces and labor-force competition, as aptly indicated by Bakalian and Bozorgmehr (2009), civil rights violations and the nativist backlash against Iranian immigrants in the United States were caused by a political and ideological conflict or followed a major national crisis. In less than fourteen months, between the time that President Carter visited Iran in 1978 and when the hostages were taken on November 4, 1979, the image of Iran changed from, in Carter's words (1995:445), an "island of stability in one of the more troubled areas of the world" to what another observer (Gerges 1997:70) terms an "extremist," "terrorist," and "fanatical" country dominated by a "crazy group" of mullahs. Shortly after the hostage crisis, Iranian diplomats and military trainees were expelled from the United States under instructions from Carter. A massive crackdown on Iranians began in the United States, and they were given one month to report their location and visa status to the closest U.S. Immigration and Naturalization Service (INS) office. Furthermore, all Iranian assets in the United States were frozen, tighter restrictions on visas for Iranians were implemented, all visas issued to Iranians in the United States were revoked, and as many as 6,906 students were subject to deportation.[2] Government abuses of civil rights of immigrants and ethnic populations who were victims of hostility between the United States and their countries of origin are not without historical precedent. As described by Bakalian and Bozorgmehr (2009), the Japanese internment during World War II, the mandatory registration and detention of German immigrants and citizens during World War I, the harassment and deportation of communist sympathizers after the Palmer raids (1919–1920), and the witch hunt against suspected Communist Party members during the era of McCarthyism are other examples of minority targeting by the U.S. government in times of war or political and ideological crisis.

Prior to the Iranian revolution and the hostage crisis, Iran and the United States had very strong economic, political, and cultural ties, and Iran was viewed as a close U.S. ally in the Middle East. Also, the U.S. government and informed American citizens considered Iran as an ancient civilization with a rich cultural heritage and viewed Iranian immigrants as professionals who made great educational and entrepreneurial contributions to the United States. The hostage crisis created an unprecedented, xenophobic, anti-Iranian, and anti-Islamic reaction with new images of Iran, Iranians, Islam, and other Muslim immigrants as barbaric, uncivilized, and terroristic. This perception has continued until today. In a Gallup poll conducted in June 1976, two years prior to the start of the Iranian revolution, only 37 percent of Americans gave Iran low ratings.[3] In a poll taken about one year after the Iranian revolution, 60 percent of Americans viewed Iran as an enemy of the United States, and another 34 percent as an unfriendly country. In a poll conducted in 1989, a decade after the Iranian revolution, the number of Americans who held an unfavorable opinion toward Iran had increased to 91 percent.[4] Seven years after the hostages were released a majority of Americans still believed that Iran was the only "enemy" country, compared to 39 percent who considered the Soviet Union as an enemy. In another poll, more than half of the respondents cited hostages, Khomeini, oil, the shah, anger, hatred, trouble, and troublesome country as coming to mind when Iran was mentioned. Moreover, close to half of the respondents described "all" or "most" Muslims as "warlike," "bloodthirsty," "treacherous," "cunning," "barbaric," and "cruel" (Gerges 1997). As Edward Said's (1997) critical evaluation of "the Iran story" indicates, after the hostage crisis, night after night programs such as *America Held Hostage* and *Nightline* represented the Iranian people, culture, and religion as "militant, dangerous, and anti-American."

The unfavorable attitudes of Americans were not limited to the Iranian government and people; they were applied as well to Iranian immigrants living in the United States. Between 1985 and 1993 the percentages of Americans who believed that the presence of Iranians in the United States created problems for the country increased from 40 to 60 percent. Only 20 percent of Americans interviewed in 1993 held a positive view of Iranians and perceived their presence to be beneficial to the country (Lapinski et al. 1997).

After 9/11, George W. Bush's declaration that Iran was a terrorist sponsor state and a link in the infamous "axis of evil" deepened and added fuel to the existing anti-Iranian attitudes of Americans. Immediately after 9/11, the U.S. government targeted persons of suspect nationalities and ordered males between the ages of sixteen and sixty-five from twenty-five Middle Eastern countries including Iran who entered the United States by September 10, 2002, to register with the INS, comply with the new federal alien registration program, and submit to being fingerprinted, photographed, and interrogated by federal agents or face deportation. The process was called the National Security Entry Exit Registration System (NSEERS). In southern California, after approximately one thousand Iranians voluntarily registered, U.S. immigration officials handcuffed, arrested, and detained between five hundred and seven hundred men; they were not allowed access to attorneys, their families, or doctors. Although the order was directed at immigrants on temporary visas, many Iranians who were arrested had green-card applications pending and assumed they were protected under the law while they waited for the INS to finish processing their paperwork.

Labeling Iran as a state sponsor of terrorism increased the number of Americans who view them unfavorably. Results of a public opinion poll taken after the 9/11 attack indicated that 27 percent of Americans considered Iran as the country that posed the greatest danger to the United States, and 47 percent thought Iran was a greater threat to the world than Iraq was before the removal of Saddam Hussein.[5] This poll puts Iran as a greater threat to the United States than China (20 percent), Iraq (17 percent), North Korea (11 percent), or even al Qaeda terrorists (4 percent). The number of Americans who consider Iran as the single biggest threat to the United States has quadrupled since 1993. The results of a Harris Interactive poll conducted in March 2006 indicate that an overwhelming majority (85 percent) of Americans believed that Iranian nuclear research is a cause for concern. In a Pew poll the month before, nearly 65 percent of Americans believed that Iran's nuclear program was a major threat to the United States, and another 82 percent believed that a nuclear-armed Iran would be likely to provide nuclear weapons to terrorists. In a poll taken by the *Washington Post* and the ABC television network, Americans were asked if they would support U.S. bombing of Iran's nuclear sites if diplomatic efforts and economic sanctions failed. While 42 percent of Americans were in favor of such a bombing, 54 percent opposed it.[6] Asked if it would be responsible or irresponsible for the United States to have war plans for Iran already prepared, 67 percent responded that it would be a responsible action. Another 47 percent thought the United States would eventually have to take military action against Iran.[7] In case of a military attack, 54 percent of Americans supported only air strikes, and another 42 percent supported using air strikes and ground troops.

As indicated before, Iranians are not the only immigrant group in the United States whose members have either suffered great oppression in U.S. history or have collectively been stereotyped and traumatized by the U.S. government because of political actions of their home countries' governments. There is a long list of immigrant groups that have been and remain stereotyped and discriminated against for economic and political reasons. Nevertheless, the case of Iranians is very similar to those of Japanese and Cubans in some respects. Nearly forty years before Iranians, more than seventy thousand American citizens of Japanese ancestry and another forty thousand legal permanent resident Japanese on the West Coast were evacuated, relocated to camps, and imprisoned without any charges, trials, or criminal convictions because of hostility between the United States and Japan (McLemore and Romo 2005). Just as Japanese immigrants who were never proven to have collaborated with the enemy during World War II, Iranian immigrants in the United States have never been proven to have been involved in 9/11 or any other terrorist act before or since. Although much less traumatic, the experience of Iranian immigrants after the hostage crisis and 9/11 terrorist attacks (to be discussed in Chapter 1) has been humiliating and dehumanizing with significant emotional costs. Despite their innocence, Iranian nationals experience discrimination, racial profiling, and prejudice at all levels. For example, immediately after the hostage crisis, the INS ordered all Iranian nationals residing in the United States to report to their local immigration offices for interviews.

The migration experience of Iranians in the United States also bears a strong resemblance to that of Cuban exiles. Both groups came to the United States because of revolutionary change and political turbulence in their home countries. Emigration of a large number of Iranians to the United States was the consequence of a revolutionary change in Iran that occurred after the overthrow of the shah and his monarchy in 1979. Just like the Iranian revolution, the Cuban revolution threatened the economic and political interests of the U.S. government and led to open hostility between the two governments that has continued until now. Nevertheless, unlike Cuban exiles who benefited from the approximately one-billion-dollar federally funded Cuban Refugee Program for resettlement, employment, health services, food, and educational training programs (Feagin and Feagin 1999), Iranians were subject to various forms of individual and collective prejudice and discrimination. In the face of overall similarities in the situations of Iranian immigrants with Japanese regarding host discrimination on the one hand and Cubans with respect to political forces of immigration on the other, there is a fundamental difference that makes the case of Iranians more complex and sets it apart from these two and other immigrant groups. Although Japanese nationals in the United States could and often did turn to their government for assistance when they experienced discrimination before the aerial attack on Pearl Harbor (McLemore and Romo 2005), Iranian immigrants have been deprived of any support from their new government and have had nowhere to turn for legal support since massive discrimination against Iranians began in 1979. Moreover, while the financial aid provided by the Eisenhower and Kennedy administrations was a major asset in helping Cuban exiles to build and sustain their community and economic infrastructure, canceling visas issued to Iranians and freezing their assets by President Carter decimated Iranian communities and punished many immigrants who had fled the same "enemy" a few years earlier.

In sum, it can be argued that no other recent refugee or exile group in the United States has experienced the same intense, sudden sense of double loss or double exile and trauma that Iranians have. On one hand, the disastrous consequences of the revolution—including social disorganization, war, cultural breakdown, economic chaos, population explosion, and deterioration of social life and standards of living—forced thousands of Iranians into exile and detached them from the pre-revolution familiar home culture. The Iranian revolution not only reversed the foundation of the earlier system and touched every aspect of Iranian culture but also affected the collective identity of Iranians in exile and deterred many from returning to Iran. On the other hand, the anti-Iranian attitudes of many Americans since the hostage crisis in 1979, the end of political and diplomatic relations between Iran and the United States, and sanctions against Iran in response to the Iranian government's continued support for international terrorism (as claimed by the U.S. government) stigmatized and humiliated Iranians, resulted in loss of cultural and ethnic pride, and pushed many Iranians to conceal their religious, national, and ethnic identities. These events separated most Iranians from mainstream American social, economic, and political life and hampered their integration into American society. In short, unlike most other immigrant groups, Iranians as a whole have confronted simultaneous loss of home and perceived repulsion by the host society. This double loss and double social trauma left an indelible mark upon Iranian immigrants' collective consciousness and affected their ethnic identity fundamentally. It imposed upon them a social life full of dilemma, cultural inconsistency, religious and political ambivalence, ambiguity, and paradox personally and collectively. This situation encouraged the employment of a variety of new adaptive strategies to cope with the following dilemmas: the choice between revealing one's Iranian national identity versus avoiding the stigma attached to being Iranian; practicing Islamic faith versus giving in to the fear of being viewed as a fundamentalist Muslim or a terrorist; defending Iran's right to pursue its economic and technological goals versus remaining adversarial to its government; desiring to return home versus abhorring the social conditions of life in Iran; and last but not least, maintaining ethnic attachment and preserving the Iranian cultural heritage versus acculturating into American society and being accepted as an Iranian.

Inability to find effective coping mechanisms for these sustained dilemmas has culminated in a considerable number of institutional crises within the Iranian community in exile. In spite of nearly three decades of diasporic history and remarkable intellectual, entrepreneurial, and educational accomplishment, as will be discussed in the chapters that follow, the Iranian community in exile is plagued with a number of cultural, political, religious, familial, and other social problems causally contextualized by the aforementioned, more macroscopic issues. For instance, religious values and rituals have lost their moral and symbolic significance and are no longer a major basis of family and social conduct for most Iranians. Moreover, there has been a sharp increase in the number of Iranian-born Muslims who either have converted to Christianity or advocate return to the pre-Islamic faith. At the same time, many Iranians have become resentful of Islamic teachings and faith and publicly express their anti-Islamic sentiments.[8] The number of Iranians who celebrate or observe religious events has declined sharply. Practicing Iranian Muslims, particularly women, who aspire to maintain their religious identity have become detached from the ethnic community and have created their own sub-ethnoreligious community within the larger Iranian community. Iranian identity has become a contested and problematic issue for many Iranian immigrants. The Iranian community in exile suffers from an identity crisis. It lacks a unified sense of national identity strong enough to bind Iranians together. While weak collective consciousness is characteristic of all urban industrial and post-industrial societies, Iranian American subculture is especially fractured in this respect. Some members of the community identify themselves as Iranian, while others call themselves Persians. Many others vary their self-descriptions among several possibilities—Iranian, Persian, Persian American, Iranian American, and American Iranian—depending on the situation and the audience. Similarly, members of Iranian religious minorities (Jews, Christians, Armenians, Assyrians, and Baha'is) often identify with their ethnoreligious backgrounds rather than with their Iranian nationality. Rivalry and competition caused by different political and religious ideologies and factions have divided the Iranian community. As a result, political organizations and activists have lost their reputation for working together for a free Iran. Professional associations are weak and unable to attract enough members. And participation of Iranians in intellectual activities is lower than ever before. In addition, most are disenchanted about social relations among Iranians and complain about dishonesty, rivalry, backstabbing, gossip, distrust, disorder, disorganization, chaos, and disarray within the community. As such, many Iranians have lost pride in their culture and community and have become detached and dispassionate about community affairs. The lack of community support and low turnout in community events, in turn, has driven many ethnic establishments and ethnic associations out of existence, causing concern for community leaders and organizers.

In the past twenty-five years a considerable amount of research and theoretical effort has focused on understanding the root causes of these problems and examining patterns of acculturation and integration of Iranians in the United States. Most of this research, however, has been primarily based on the assumptions of the assimilation theory developed by Robert Park, a sociologist, and his students at the University of Chicago in the 1920s and 1930s. Park's pioneering work on race-relations cycles and the marginal status of immigrants guided the scholarly research for several decades on immigrants' assimilation into their new society. According to Park and his colleagues and students at the University of Chicago, new immigrants would eventually lose their cultural distinctiveness and gradually adopt the customs and attitudes of the prevailing culture and "assimilate" into the host society. Park asserted (1939) that assimilation is a "progressive" and "irreversible" process that would remove "the external signs" such as patterns of speech, dress, manners, and food preferences that would distinguish immigrants from native-born Americans. The first-generation immigrants probably would not be able to make a complete transition to the new way of life, but their grandchildren, the third generation, eventually would make "progress" and become full members of the host society. Social problems of immigrants such as finding jobs, family and community disorganization, and conflict with members of the host culture, the Chicago social scientists argued, were inevitable, temporary conditions on the path toward complete assimilation and would ultimately disappear.

Since Park's pioneering work in the 1920s, many race/ethnic relations scholars in the United States have adopted and made new and significant contributions to the assimilationist perspective. One of the most valuable contributions to Park's framework is the influential work of Milton Gordon, author of *Assimilation in American Life* (1964), in which he distinguishes an array of possible assimilation outcomes. Unlike Robert Park, who contended that a group might assimilate culturally without necessarily going to the remaining stages, Gordon identified seven subprocesses of assimilation, each of which may occur simultaneously and in varying degrees. According to Gordon, the complete merging of one group into another requires more than accepting and practicing the culture of the host society or the majority. It also requires structural assimilation or primary relationships. By primary relationships Gordon means intimate, enduring interaction of a large number of a minority or immigrant group with members of the host society as close friends, neighbors, and social club members and in other private spheres of social life. Relationships between members of minority and majority groups that take place in such public spheres as work, school, and public recreation, although important, result in secondary structural assimilation. The next phase of assimilation involves gradual merging of minority or immigrant groups through intermarriage or marital assimilation. Identification assimilation or identifying with the host society does not happen until the members of both the immigrant minority group and the host society share the view that they are part of the same group subordinate to their original ethnic subcultures. This stage of assimilation is a two-way process and involves recognition of minority group members by members of the host or majority society.

When immigrant minority groups no longer have mental ties with or identify with their countries of origin or ethnic communities and are no longer perceived by members of the host society as foreigners, prejudice and discrimination against the minority groups disappear. Gordon refers to the disappearance of prejudice as attitude receptional assimilation and to the disappearance of discrimination as behavioral receptional assimilation. Finally, in Gordon's terms, when the remnants of group differences are eliminated and the conflicts between groups over values and power subside, separate groups become one and civic assimilation occurs. The crucial stage in the assimilation process for Gordon is the formation of primary group relations, or entry "into the social cliques, clubs, and institutions of the core society at the primary group level" (Gordon 1964:80).

Once immigrant minority group members develop intimate relations with members of the host culture in the private sphere, marital assimilation will follow. As intermarriage advances and more members of a minority group marry partners from the host society, intergroup prejudice, discrimination, and conflict will decline.

During the past few decades scholars have raised serious questions about major assumptions of the assimilation theory and have criticized it for being ethnocentric, linear, and based on experiences of white Europeans who migrated more or less voluntarily to the United States; they have developed new, broad theories of racial and ethnic relations. Unlike the assimilation theories that emphasize the orderly adaptation of immigrants to the culture and institutions of their host society, the new theories place much greater emphasis on institutionalized discrimination, social inequality, power relations, interrelationships of racial inequalities, the role of government, cultural stereotyping and racist ideologies, and the importance of oppositional cultures in resisting racial oppression (Feagin and Feagin 1999).

In recent years two new perspectives on the integration of immigrants into their newly adopted societies, called "segmented assimilation" and "transnationalism," have emerged. Like traditional assimilation theory, segmented assimilation theory emphasizes integration of new immigrants into the new society. Unlike the traditional assimilation theorists, however, the segmented assimilation theorists assert that the process of assimilation and adaptation among new immigrants may be different from those experienced by earlier European immigrants. Moreover, in contrast to the classical assimilation theories that linked assimilation and upward mobility and expected higher social and economic status for each subsequent generation of immigrant descent, the segmented assimilation scholars assert that the United States is a stratified society with different "segments" to which immigrants and their children may assimilate (Portes and Zhou 1993, Portes and Rumbaut 2006). Therefore, instead of assimilating to the American mainstream, immigrants may assimilate into three distinct segments of American society, each with a different outcome. The first path is to assimilate into the American middle class, leading to upward mobility as predicted by classic assimilation theory. The second is acculturation and assimilation into the urban working class, which leads to poverty and downward mobility. The third route is "selective acculturation" and leads to deliberate preservation of immigrant cultural values and practices along with economic integration. Various social settings have an impact on assimilation of different immigrant subgroups in different ways. Moving into the mainstream and adapting to their new society, the segmented assimilation theorists maintain, are swifter and easier to reach for educated, affluent, and skilled members of immigrant groups than for lower-class individuals with little education and fewer occupational skills (McLemore and Romo 2005).

While assimilation and to some extent segmented assimilation theorists have argued that immigrants would eventually abandon their unique cultural practices and homeland ties, scholars of a transnational perspective contend that immigrants and their descendents remain strongly influenced by their continuing ties to their home societies. Rooted in a global perspective, the central element of this conceptual framework is that immigrants establish and maintain cultural, social, economic, and political relations in both the home and host societies. Through these relations, immigrants link their country of origin and their country of settlement. In contrast to static theoretical models that viewed immigrants and their experiences in each society as a discrete phenomenon and "bounded" by separate culture, economy, and political systems, a transnational perspective views immigration as a dynamic process bound together by a global capitalist system and affected by the interplay of historical experience, structural conditions, and the ideologies of home and host societies (Schiller, Basch, and Blanc-Szanton 1992). Although they acknowledge that many earlier immigrants were in some sense transmigrants who maintained economic and political ties to their home societies, transnational analysts argue that "the current transnationalism is a new type of migrant experience" (ibid., 9).

One important point that transnational analysts make is that by drawing upon their multiple identities grounded in their home and host societies, transmigrants create and maintain linkages between different societies in the context of families, institutions, economic investments, business, and financial and political organizations. Given their simultaneous participation in multiple transnational settings or social fields, transmigrants continuously convert the economic and social status gained in one society into political, social, and economic gains in another. Moreover, they can contribute both positively and negatively to global political and economic transformations, fortify or impede global religious movements, fuel social movements, and influence the internal functions of states (Levit and Schiller 2004). Therefore, to have a better understanding of immigrants we need to adopt a transnational approach that adequately captures the complex interconnectedness of immigrants to multiple nation-states as well as to multiple legal, political, and economic institutions.

14

Despite the increasing number of publications on Iranian immigrants in exile and the considerable contributions and insights regarding the experience of Iranians in the United States, the theoretical focus of the emerging field of Iranian American studies has been for the most part consistent with theoretical assumptions of the assimilationists.[9] These studies, in various contexts, stress either the impact of socioeconomic status (education, class resources, and so forth) of Iranian immigrants or the cultural practices and transformation of Iranian institutions—mainly the family—after they immigrated to the United States, and they view loss of ethnic heritage, religious beliefs, and family values as inevitable evolutionary outcomes of assimilation. Considering the theoretical significance of discrimination, host hostility, prejudice, and stereotyping in migration literature and their powerful impact on the integration of immigrants into the mainstream society, with the exception of one particular article by Bozorgmehr (2000) and a few brief references in some other publications, the published work on Iranian immigrants has generally ignored exploration of the link between the impact of these forces on assimilation and the integration of Iranians in any great detail in a book-length manuscript.

As I indicated earlier, this book takes as axiomatic the proposition that political forces in Iran and the United States as well as the hostile relations between the two countries constitute macroscopic conditions contextualizing the integration of Iranians in exile into American society. Understanding the impact of these political forces not only sheds light on the intricate integration of Iranian immigrants but also provides a more nuanced framework for explaining the loss of family values, changes in gender roles, rising divorce rate, rise of anti-Islamic religious sentiments, masking of Islamic identity, political apathy, loss of cultural pride, lack of community support, veiling of national or ethnic identity, and community disorder among Iranians. Therefore, unlike the proponents of the assimilationist perspective, I believe that these are some of the most critical forces best employed as starting points for understanding the experiences of Iranians in the United States. The Iranian revolution and the ensuing social, political, and cultural consequences were at least as powerful as host discrimination in shaping migration experiences of Iranians in the United States. In fact, one could argue that the enormous level of hostility, prejudice, and discrimination targeted at Iranians in exile was a reaction to the foreign policies of the Iranian government, instigated by the hostage crisis in 1979. We cannot fully understand the story of Iranian immigrants and their patterns of integration and address their institutional crisis in exile in isolation from all social, cultural, political, and economic forces in the United States and Iran as well as the relations between the two countries.

In emphasizing the powerful impact of the anti-Iranian media stereo-typing, prejudice and discrimination against Iranians, and the Iranian-U.S. conflict on the lives of Iranian immigrants in exile, we should not ignore or deny the role of cultural beliefs in contributing to their detachment from American society, disassociation from American people, and ambivalence about living in the United States. Indeed, as spelled out in chapters 3 and 4, some Iranian beliefs regarding American people, American family, and the U.S. government and its powerful role in shaping public opinion represent cultural responses that often lead to marginalization of Iranian immigrants in the political scene and their detachment from the American society and its people. "Culture" refers to the totality of socially learned patterns of acting, thinking, and feeling (Harris 1995), and it includes language, beliefs, tools, symbols, norms, and values. As a dynamic phenomenon, culture is subject to change, transition, evolution, and transformation. As a depository of continuity, heritage, tradition, and identity of a group, however, culture is most sensitive to traumatogenic changes, that is, changes that are sudden, comprehensive, and unexpected that touch the core aspects of one's personal life or the social life of a group. Traumatogenic changes may harm the cultural tissue of a group and bring shock, wound, normative chaos, anomie, and ambivalence and disturb the cultural equilibrium (Sztompka 2004). The Iranian revolution exemplifies this notion of traumatogenic change. The wounds inflicted upon the Iranian culture made many Iranians ambivalent about returning to their homeland and contributed to the emergence of various institutional crises and paradoxes that Iranians in exile have experienced.

Research Methodology

This book draws upon personal narratives of real persons, including myself, and empirical data collected from government sources, surveys, interviews, and participant observation. Most of the following chapters rely heavily on data collected during the course of two research projects in Texas. The first project was conducted between 1993 and 1995 in Dallas, and the second project was completed over a two-year period from 2003 to 2005 in Dallas, Houston, and Austin. Participant observation was the primary method employed for both projects. This approach helped me to acquire a broader—more "holistic"—view of the Iranian community and to understand the relationships among its various institutions. Government data sources including the U.S. Census Bureau's 2006–2008 American Community Survey 3-Year Estimates and the statistical yearbooks of the

INS and the Department of Homeland Security (DHS) from 1955 to 2005, although not completely accurate, made it possible to reconstruct the migration history of Iranians for the past fifty years and provided valuable information about the size and demographic characteristics of the Iranian population in the United States. To gain a better understanding about Iranian immigrants, the census, INS, and DHS data were augmented by three nonrandom surveys of first- and second-generation Iranians in Texas. Unlike the census data that provide information about demographic characteristics of Iranians, the survey data provide rich information about Iranians' patterns of behavior, political participation, religiosity, interethnic relations, beliefs about American people and society, social mobility, reasons for migration, concerns about their children, and views about the Iranian community and immigrants. The first survey was carried out in 1994 during my fieldwork in Dallas and included 485 first-generation Iranian men and women. The remaining two more recent surveys were conducted between September 2003 and May 2004 primarily in cities with the largest Iranian populations in Texas (Houston, Dallas, and Austin). The first of the two more recent surveys included a nonrandom sample of 105 young Iranians who were either born and raised in the United States or were born in Iran and migrated here when they were very young. The respondents from the second survey, however, included 507 adult Iranians, most of whom left Iran during or after the Iranian revolution. (Details of my fieldwork and the design, distribution, and collections of questionnaires are provided in the appendix.)

To develop the historical aspect of Iranian migration to the United States, reconstruct the impact of political and social events on their lives, and obtain a broader view of the nature and roots of interethnic relations between Americans and Iranians in exile, I reviewed and analyzed about two hundred articles in major local and national magazines and newspapers, including *Time, Newsweek,* the *Dallas Morning News,* and the *Houston Post,* published in 1977 through 1980. To get a better perspective on Americans' perception of Iran and Iranians before and after the revolution I reviewed more than fifty public opinion surveys by the Gallup poll and other public opinion polling agencies.

In addition to the questionnaire, fieldwork, and content analysis of magazines and newspapers I also turned to the Internet for supplementary information on organizations and associations that coordinate or sponsor activities and undertakings of Iranian immigrants. I was specifically interested in identifying organizations that made overt mention of second-generation Iranians as their core participants. In so doing, I sought to generate a reliable panorama highlighting the types of activities behind which Iranian immigrants are most likely to organize, to explore how Iranians choose to verbally identify themselves as part of their descriptions and mission statements for these organizations and activities, and finally, to detect the connection, if any, between the type of organization or activity and the lexical construction ("Iranian" versus "Persian" versus "Iranian American," and so on) that Iranians choose as ethnic demarcations to describe their members and participants.

Government documents, magazines and newspapers, surveys, and Internet sites, however, do not allow researchers to capture and understand immigrants' rich personal experiences and the feelings associated with them. To uncover and piece together the unobservable subjective experiences and emotions of Iranian immigrants, I conducted face-to-face and telephone interviews with close to one hundred first- and second-generation Iranian men and women and crafted numerous life histories, including my own.

By sharing my own life history and personal narratives of other Iranians I aim to expose the reader, especially American college students with no background in migration studies, to the challenges of migration in general and the politics of being Iranian in particular, which are very hard to capture and appreciate through mainstream media and accounts of uninformed, biased individuals. I would hope that students would gain a better understanding of the politics of migration and the impact of social, cultural, economic, and political forces on the integration of immigrants into American society.

Since I am an Iranian and have been a member of the Iranian immigrant community, this may seem to be a biased endeavor of an insider. In some respects, however, it may actually be a more reliable attempt to understand what forces have shaped the migration experiences of Iranians and why Iranian immigrants have so many problems. I have been studying Iranian communities in Texas since I conducted my first fieldwork in Dallas toward completion of my doctoral degree at Southern Methodist University in 1993. My long-term relationship with the community as an anthropologist provides a great opportunity for a longitudinal assessment of change and stability within the Iranian community. Also, I do not have to spend years acquiring the Persian language or understanding the beliefs, values, and norms of Iranian culture. Being an Iranian native, having lived in exile for almost three decades, and having visited Iran many times since I left the country, I have seen the changes in Iran and the United States and have acquired a broader view of both ends of Iranian immigration. I have also been an active member of the Iranian community and have met and been in close contact with hundreds of Iranians from various religious, ethnic, class, and political backgrounds since I immigrated to the United States in 1978. During this time, I have witnessed numerous political rallies and demonstrations for different causes, fund-raising events for humanitarian projects, the breakup of old ethnic and professional associations due to ideological differences, the formation of various cultural centers, business rivalries and competitions between Iranian entrepreneurs, and many other similar community events and developments.

I have attended hundreds of small and large community gatherings, cultural celebrations, film festivals, professional and scholarly seminars, and concerts. My close association and interaction with hundreds of diverse men and women from all over Iran both as a participant and an observer since 1978 have provided me with a great opportunity (for which any anthropologist wishes) for listening to stories told by elites of the former government, professionals, political activists and leaders, intellectuals, religious fundamentalists, other religious minorities, poets, artists, entertainers, refugees, entrepreneurs, housewives, students, homeless, homosexuals, punks, strip dancers, teenagers, drug addicts, and many of other social types in the Iranian community. I have listened to heart-breaking accounts of newly arrived Iranian brides who suffered from loneliness, homesickness, and lack of family support; husbands who complained about their empowered wives and the loss of the traditional Iranian family; Iranian parents who grumbled about the behaviors of their Americanized teenagers; second-generation Iranian American teenagers who expressed their frustration and disappointment with both the Iranian community and American society; Iranian elderly men and women who bore the pain of imposed loneliness and isolation of exile; and unhappy Iranian grandparents who complained about disrespectful grandchildren who had lost their native language and had become alienated from Iranian culture.

I have met and interviewed prerevolutionary Iranian elites who suffered from depression because of a loss of social status and displacement in the United States, political activists and prisoners before and after the revolution who dreamed about returning to a free and democratic Iran, unaccredited Iranian doctors and nurses who worked as cashiers and clerks, and Iranian refugees who were disillusioned about America as a great "land of opportunity" and disputed constantly with case workers and managers at local refugee centers about the lack of services and resources. I have interviewed Iranian employees in Iranian-owned businesses, small and large, who accused the owners of unfair treatment and exploitation and Iranian business owners who complained about the lack of support from community members. Finally, often, the subjective experiences of migration and its emotional, cognitive, and behavioral transformations may not be perceived by scholars who have not personally experienced the process firsthand. Because I have experienced the same hopes, challenges, successes, ambitions, despairs, prejudices, frustrations, disappointments, and disillusionments that many other Iranians in the United States have encountered, I have a deep and intimate understanding of what Max Weber (1949) calls the "sympathetic understanding" (*verstehen*) in telling the story of Iranian immigrants. Thus, this story is my personal story as much as it is the social story of thousands of Iranian men and women in exile.

As indicated by Fischer and Abedi (1990), storytelling comes in various genres, depending upon audiences. Despite its different forms, storytelling, Fischer and Abedi maintain, has "reinvigorated recent thinking about ethnography . . . and . . . use of cultural idioms, concepts, tropes, and discourse styles as epistemological guides" (1990:xix). My own personal account or "autoethnography" serves as a starting point from which the history of Iranian immigration to the United States is told, and it is a detailed account of major social, cultural, and political events since my teenage years. Through my autoethnography or life history I have tried to contextualize my life in modern Iranian history and explain how complexities of culture, politics, revolution, exile, family, and social events profoundly shaped my social biography and those of thousands of other first-generation Iranians in exile. Following Roy Mottahedeh's creative and innovative style in his pathbreaking work *The Mantle of the Prophet* (1985), I have incorporated extended historical information and political facts from multiple authoritative primary sources between the accounts of the lived experience of migration from Iran and the experiences of Iranian immigrants in the United States. I have included census and immigration data about the migration and settlement patterns of Iranians in the United States for the past fifty years.

My goal in including these facts is twofold: first, to give the reader a better understanding about the major transformative events in Iran before and after the revolution and their consequences on Iranian immigration trends to the United States; and second, to offer a different and richer perspective than hitherto suggested that takes into account the impact of intergovernmental political relations and the politics of migration on the integration of Iranian immigrants into American society.

Scope and Organization of the Book

20   This book is organized into five chapters. Following this introduction, Chapter 1 narrates my personal life history and tells in detail what social, cultural, economic, and political forces in Iran and the United States contributed to my journey from Tehran to Texas in 1978 and shaped my life chances since then. Chapter 2 examines the links between the hostage crisis and American media and anti-Iranian stereotypes and narratives. This chapter demonstrates how unfavorable depictions of Iranians as terrorists, fundamentalist Muslims, and fanatics illogically stigmatized and devalued Iranians and pushed them to conceal their national identity and to develop a new, less threatening "Persian" identity. After a concise presentation of Jeffery Alexander and coauthors' cultural trauma theory (2004), the second part of this chapter examines the role of political opponents of the Islamic Republic of Iran as a "carrier group" in construction of an anti-Islamic master narrative and promotion of a non-Islamic Persian identity.

Chapter 3 examines the impact of the discriminatory immigration policies against Iranians and anti-Iranian stereotypes in mainstream media on Iranians' perceptions of the United States and its people. Based on interviews with Iranians, this chapter presents and describes three distinct images of the United States and American people that exist in the minds of Iranian immigrants. The second section of this chapter looks at Iranians' perceptions of their co-ethnics and ethnic community in the United States. This chapter ends with a review of sociological theories of "marginal man" and "sociological ambivalence" and offers an explanation for Iranians' feeling of double ambivalence and double detachment. Contrary to fundamental premises of the assimilation theory, in this chapter I argue that Iranians' double ambivalence and marginality appears to be linked neither to a collision between the Iranian and American cultures and cultural transition nor to a simultaneous orientation to different sets of cultural values and normative expectations. Rather, the real source of Iranians' double marginality seems to be related to simultaneous rejection by both Iran and the United States.

In Chapter 4 I discuss the experiences of second-generation Iranians in the United States and discuss some of the major challenges they face in their interactions with their parents. In the second part of this chapter, I present a typology of second-generation Iranians and outline how members of each type define themselves and view the Iranian community and American society. The closing part of Chapter 4 examines the link between second-generation members' ethnic identity dilemma and Iranian parents' rejection of American family values as a form of cultural resistance.

Finally, the last chapter of the book focuses on the Iranian immigrant family and gender relations and discusses various cultural, economic, and political forces as well as conditions of exile that have transformed the idealized imagery of the Iranian family fundamentally and have created new challenges, tensions, and conflict within families for Iranian parents and their U.S.-born children. The first part of Chapter 5 is based on a discussion of socioeconomic and demographic characteristics of Iranian immigrant families. After a brief review of the literature, the second part of the chapter offers a new perspective in understanding the challenges of Iranian immigrant families that extends beyond the simplistic assimilationist model and takes political forces of home and host societies into consideration. In line with my discussion in other chapters and consistent with the central theme of the book, I argue that postrevolutionary political forces in Iran and the sociopolitical conditions and discriminatory immigration laws after the hostage crisis not only created a set of unforeseen problems for Iranian immigrant families but also played crucial roles in slowing the family's reconstruction, transforming its structure, and disintegrating it in exile.

1 The Paradox of Migration
Neither Happy in Exile nor Looking Forward to Returning Home

I was born in a relatively small lower-middle-class family in one of the oldest and most traditional neighborhoods of south Tehran in 1962. I was named by my paternal grandfather, who was a very religious, pious, and respectable man. Aside from the two brothers who had died a few months after birth, I was the youngest of the three sons in the family, followed by my only sister, born fourteen months after my birth. My mother never worked outside the home and has been a housewife all her adult life; my father was a real estate developer and an entrepreneur until his death twenty-five years ago. When I was six years old my family moved into another religiously conservative middle-class neighborhood closer to the city center, where I completed elementary school. In the early 1970s, economic expansion in Iran had a thriving impact on my father's real estate business investments and pushed my family one stratum up on the Iranian class rung. Despite my mother's reluctance and her desire to stay near her family, my father purchased a large modern house in a newly developed upper-middle-class suburb in Tehran where my family has remained.

I spent most of my adolescent years in this newly developed neighborhood composed of large European-style houses with swimming pools, modern buildings, new roads and wide streets, medical clinics, coed elementary and middle schools, sport centers, boutiques, music stores, popular fast-food hamburger and pizza restaurants, trendy cafés, and nice shops and supermarkets. It was in this suburb that I completed middle school and two years of high school before I left Iran indeterminately in

August 1978, a few months before the revolutionary uprisings. It was also in this new suburbia that I experienced my first culture shock and felt like an outsider for the first time in my life. It took a few years before my entire family acculturated to the radically different way of life in our new neighborhood and coped with the considerable subcultural differences between the two neighborhoods.

Everything in our new community, from architecture and house design to social discourse, public attire, community norms and beliefs, neighborhood resources, and gender relations, were fundamentally different from the neighborhood where I had spent my early childhood. Unlike my old neighborhood, where most of the families owned small retail shops or manufacturing firms of traditional goods or carried out export trade in the bazaar,[1] a majority of families in our new neighborhood were government employees, medical professionals, schoolteachers, university professors, engineers, high-ranking military officers, managers and administrators of private business firms, and employees of foreign companies. Moreover, in our old neighborhood most women had less than a high school education, were predominantly housewives, and practiced the "traditional" Islamic veiling norms or wore chadors,[2] while most women in my new neighborhood were more educated, had professional jobs, and often wore miniskirts and "modern" dress, and many drove fancy European cars. And while teenage boys in our old neighborhood amused themselves either by attending *heyat* (religious gatherings) or playing soccer in dirt fields all day long, teenagers in our new neighborhood entertained themselves by listening to the latest Western pop music, mingling in mixed parties, swimming at modern coed private or community pools, watching the latest Western movies in chic and expensive theaters, and frequenting fancy upscale cafés and fast-food restaurants.

The most striking difference between our new and old neighborhoods, however, was the prevalence of migration to the West, particularly to the United States. In contrast to our previous "conservative" and "traditional" neighborhood, where migration to the West was either distasteful culturally or precluded for economic reasons, much like in many other upper-middle- and upper-class neighborhoods in Tehran in the early 1970s, long-term or even permanent residence in Europe or the United States for education, business, professional training, and pleasure had become fashionable and a common practice for many families in our new "modern," "Westernized" neighborhood. Unlike men and women in my old neighborhood who would find pilgrimages to Mecca and other holy Muslim shrines religiously gratifying and fulfilling, men and women in my new neighborhood would find visits to Paris, London, Frankfurt, New York, and other major European and American cities socially aggrandizing and immersion into the prevailing Western way of life culturally chic and elegant.

The vast disparity in the scale and perception of migration between the two neighborhoods in Tehran was mainly the outcome of a series of cultural, economic, and social reforms that had swept the country in the late 1960s and early 1970s. In addition to these extensive reforms, Iran's rapid modernization process and economic development—assisted and financed primarily by the United States in that period—created a big demand for skilled workers and provided a training and educational opportunity in the West for thousands of Iranian men and women from the growing middle class in Iran. Iran's political instability and its foreign occupation during World War II had severely damaged the Iranian economy. Moreover, the reduction of oil revenues, precipitated by the Western boycott of Iranian oil imposed in response to the oil nationalization movement of 1951–1953 under the leadership of Prime Minister Mosadegh, led to further deterioration of Iran's economic conditions (Katouzian 1981). The 1953 military coup d'etat financed by the CIA and British intelligence and the overthrow of the nationalist government of Dr. Mosadegh changed the postwar cultural, economic, social, political, and class structure in Iran and affected, in several ways, the migration of thousands of middle- and upper-class Iranians to the West, particularly to the United States.[3] Prior to the 1953 coup, the United States dominated Iran's military. Despite the strong presence of the United States in the Iranian military during World War II and diplomatic relations between the two countries, there are no reliable data on the total number of Iranians in the United States.[4] It is believed that between 1842 and 1903 as many as 130 Iranian nationals entered the United States. This number increased to 780 between 1925 and 1932. Data for 1933–1944 are not available, but 82 Iranians immigrated to the United States in 1945 (Lorentz and Wertime 1980).

After the coup and restoration of the shah's power, however, the United States became a dominant foreign power in Iran politically, economically, and culturally. The 1953 coup and the shah's determination to ally with the West was a turning point in the migration of Iranians to the United States. After the coup the United States established strong economic, political, and cultural ties with Iran. As a result of this extensive partnership, which lasted until the overthrow of the shah in 1978, the number of Iranians who moved permanently to or visited the United States for pleasure, educational training, and business increased substantially. Development of the Iranian economy, modernization of Iran along Western lines, and Iran's dependence on millions of dollars in loans and direct financial aid from the United States facilitated the continuous migration of thousands of Iranians to the United States for nearly three decades. In addition to substantial U.S. loans, Iran's huge oil revenues between 1963 and 1977 moved the Iranian economy toward modernization too extensively and rapidly. For example, between 1963 and 1969 the Iranian oil income increased from $555 million to $958 million per year. The oil income continued to climb, reaching $1.2 billion in 1970–1971 and $5 billion in 1973–1974. With the increase in world oil prices, Iranian oil revenues reached $20 billion in 1975–1976 (Abrahamian 1982).

To construct his version of the new Persian empire and gain hegemony in the Persian Gulf region, the shah invested billions of dollars of Iran's oil revenues in military hardware. In 1973 alone, the shah spent $3 billion on arsenal. By 1975 the shah's spending on arms increased to $5 billion a year.[5] Although a substantial amount of Iran's oil revenues were squandered on a military buildup, much greater sums were productively spent on the country's infrastructure through various economic development plans. Transportation, notably the railway and roadway systems, were improved; dams were built; agricultural production was modernized through land reform, the use of tractors, fertilizers, and pesticides, and irrigation projects; new and large manufacturing plants were built to produce automobiles, textiles, food, and consumer goods; production in some leading industries such as coal, iron, and steel was revolutionized with rising output; hospitals, health clinics, and medical technology were improved; and universities as well as technical, vocational, and teacher training schools were established.

In addition to this economic expansion and modernization project, the shah persisted in the cultural reforms launched by his father, Reza Shah Pahlavi, decades earlier for transforming Iran into a modern secular society.[6] After his return in 1953 the shah Mohammad Reza followed in his father's footsteps and continued the glorification of Iran's pre-Islamic culture and modernization of the country on the model of the West during his thirty-eight years of reign. He introduced a number of reforms including family and election laws that were denounced by the clergy. The shah's modernization also brought a massive infusion of Western culture to Iran. He abandoned the Islamic calendar altogether and adopted a new calendar that began with the rule of Cyrus; adopted "Aryamehr" (light of Aryans) as a prefix to his title, in clear reference to pre-Islamic Iran; and commemorated the 2,500-year anniversary of the Persian Empire founded by Cyrus the Great in Persepolis (Farr 1999, Keddie 2006, Mackey 1996). These cultural reforms, combined with the rapid economic expansion and investment in industrialization, modern technology, and military buildup in the 1960s and 1970s, attracted thousands of European and American military technicians, advisers, teachers, and entrepreneurs to Iran and poured Western products and pop culture into Iranian society.[7] Concurrently, a lack of skilled workers and higher educational institutions for training in Iran pushed thousands of Iranians to emigrate to Western countries in an unprecedented manner, mainly the United States, for the purpose of acquiring technical skills and advanced educational training.

Iran's march toward modernization kicked off by the shah's economic plans and the strengthening of political, economic, and cultural ties between Iran and the United States facilitated an exchange of government officials and inspired thousands of Iranian nationals to visit the United States temporarily for business, pleasure, or both. The number of Iranian nationals who arrived in the United States between 1960 and 1970 was 11,410 government officials and 28,489 visitors for pleasure or business. The comparable numbers for 1971 through 1977 were 25,984 and 140,539, indicating an annual average of 3,712 government officials and 20,219 visitors. Most of the nonimmigrant Iranians who entered the United States between 1960 and 1970 belonged to the elite and the professional middle-class groups in Iran and had an understanding of Western culture. Besides the nonimmigrant Iranians who visited the United States temporarily each year for business and pleasure, many other Iranians entered permanently as spouses, children, and parents of Iranians who were U.S. citizens. Between 1970 and 1976, a little more than one-third (6,240) of all immigrants (19,664) admitted to the United States from Iran were spouses, children, and parents of U.S. citizens.[8]

The most notable nonimmigrant group that played a big part in the admission of Iranians to the United States in the 1960s and 1970s was students. Between 1960 and 1977 around 82,288 students came to the United States to study.[9] A salient characteristic of Iranian students in the United States and other Western countries in that period was their political activism against the shah's government. After the overthrow of the secular nationalistic government of Mosadegh and the return of the shah to power and subsequent establishment of his repressive dictatorship, all forms of open political activities, opposition, and political parties in Iran were destroyed, crushed, or paralyzed (Keddie 2006). Consequently, the only large, open, organized opposition movement that survived the political repression of the shah existed outside of Iran among a growing number of Iranian students led by the Confederation of Iranian Students, National

Union (CISNU).[10] The confederation was primarily a political organization composed of a variety of groups from Muslim activists to secular nationalists and leftists aiming to represent all Iranian students within and outside of Iran. CISNU's opposition abroad posed a threat to the political stability of the shah's government and contributed to the political movement in Iran that led to the Iranian revolution in 1978.

Throughout the 1960s and 1970s, CISNU organized demonstrations across Europe and the United States on occasions of visits by the shah, members of the royal family, or high-ranking government officials and publicized the political repression of the shah's regime internationally.[11] One of the most violent protests organized by student activists in exile brought humiliation for the Iranian government internationally during the shah's trip to the United States and his visit with Carter in November 1977. While the shah was being welcomed, anti-shah Iranian students were demonstrating near the White House. They carried signs reading: "Down with the shah," and "U.S., keep bloody hands off Iran," and "Death, death, death to the shah."[12] Another means the confederation employed to support the students' struggle against the shah's dictatorship was to send, with the help of international organizations such as Amnesty International and world-famous intellectuals including Bertrand Russell and Jean-Paul Sartre, an official delegation to Iran to investigate the conditions of political prisoners and university students.[13]

From Tehran to Texas

I was among the 130,545 temporary or nonimmigrant Iranians, mostly students, who entered the United States in 1978. I left Iran with two of my best friends a few months before the uprisings and massive demonstrations in Tehran and other big cities that led to the Islamic revolution. Given the rapid transformation of Iranian society and its march toward modernization during such a short period in the 1960s and 1970s, like most middle-class parents, my parents believed that my only ticket for success in the new modern Iran was a degree, preferably in medicine or engineering, from an American university. Despite the pain of separation at age sixteen and emotional distress that tormented me and my family for years, my parents perceived this opportunity as being too crucial for my future to ignore. Because I was a minor with no legal guardian in the United States and I lacked proficiency in English, my parents decided to send me to a Reserve Officer Training Corps (ROTC) military boarding school in

Harlingen, Texas, where I would be safe and legally protected.[14] The academy in Harlingen was recommended to my father by one of his long-term best friends in our neighborhood who had sent his oldest son to the same academy a year earlier. Our neighbor's choice of the academy for his oldest and then the youngest, who accompanied me, was also supported by the recommendation of another neighbor who had learned about the military academy through his personal trips to the United States and through the suggestion of his American coworkers in Iran at Bell Helicopter, where he worked in the 1970s.

A few months after I left, Iran went through widespread strikes and unrest and calls for the overthrow of the shah and his dynasty that had ruled Iran for nearly fifty years. In Tehran and other big cities mass protests were organized by religiously led opposition and secular liberal forces. Anti-shah demonstrations and riots continued for several months, leading to the shutdown of schools and universities. Banks, movie theaters, and many government offices were attacked by street protestors and burned. For months, thousands of young and old men and women rallied on the streets of Tehran and other big cities and shouted "Death to the shah." The government implemented martial law, and hundreds of people died in scattered clashes between troops and demonstrators. The shah's government was getting weaker every day, and his army was unable to control the fierce political and religious forces that were sweeping the country. As riots and demonstrations escalated, the shah was finally swept out of power by the forces of the Islamic revolution led by Ayatollah Khomeini. The shah left Iran in January 1979.

The revolution had a significant impact upon the international emigration of Iranians. It drastically changed the pattern, the volume, and the nature of Iranian migration to the United States. With the exception of a relatively massive migration of Iranians to India in the seventh century, the Iranian revolution of 1978-1979 was the only time throughout Iranian history that an enormous number was uprooted and forced to live in exile indeterminately.[15] Between the outbreak of public discontent and opposition to the shah in 1978 and when he left the country in January 1979, thousands of Iranians entered the United States. Never before were so many young Iranians admitted as immigrants and nonimmigrants in such a short period. Much the same as in the prerevolutionary period, a significant number admitted to the United States were students. In the 1977–1978 academic year as many as 36,220 Iranian students were enrolled in American universities and colleges. The number in the 1978–1979 academic year increased to 45,340 (Hakimzadeh 2006).

After students, a great majority of Iranians who entered the United States during this time were elites and members of the former ruling class, high-ranking officials, bankers, investors, members of the parliament, ministers and members of the former political classes holding managerial positions, and members of religious minorities, particularly Jews and Baha'is.[16] Some left the country legally and went to the United States after they obtained visas in a third country where there was an American embassy, while others first sneaked into neighboring countries illegally and then went to the United States as refugees after a few years of residence in another country. Most of the individuals who left Iran for various political and social reasons during the revolutionary period expected to return home soon. However, as the revolutionary forces gained momentum and the new political, economic, and cultural forces unfolded, the hope for return gave way to indefinite exile. Therefore, many of them changed their visa status and obtained permanent residency or green cards through kinship ties, marriage with U.S. citizens, or occupational preferences after their arrival.

The 1978–1979 Iranian Revolution

Regardless of its roots, a distinctive character of the Iranian revolution of 1978–1979 was the prominent role of clerics and their monopoly of power after the downfall of the shah.[17] Unlike the shah and his father, Reza Shah, who emphasized and reestablished the Persian national identity throughout their reign, the new government promoted the religious ideology and Islamic identity of Iranian society. To the new revolutionary religious leaders, the prerevolutionary social and political reforms of the shah and his father and the promotion of the Western culture with its values of individualism, sexual freedom, and secularism were against the fundamentals of Iranian culture and the Islamic faith. To save Iran from corruption and to regain its Islamic heritage, the first task of the postrevolutionary government was to revive and promote Islamic cultural practices by creating a new government based on the principles of Islam. To assure that the government adhered to Islamic principles, a Council of Guardians composed of Islamic clergy was established to oversee and make sure that all laws were in accordance with the tenets of Islam (Farr 1999). Contrary to his earlier public statements against direct clerical rule, Ayatollah Ruhollah Khomeini and his followers ruled the country through powerful clerical institutions such as the Council of the Islamic Revolution and political parties such as the Islamic Republic Party (IRP). Furthermore, to purge the universities from "subversive" professors, students, and leftist political activists, the new government started a *paksazi*, or cleansing process, and established a council to instigate a "cultural revolution." The paksazi not only had disastrous consequences for Iranian educational and intellectual life but also encouraged emigration of many students, professors, professionals, doctors, and intellectuals from Iran.

Besides the disenchanted and alienated intellectuals, political activists, and scholars and scientists with various specializations, a large number of entrepreneurs, industrialists, artists, musicians, entertainers, journalists, and self-employed professionals left the country. These educated middle-class and upper-middle-class professionals preferred exile to socially and politically deteriorated life in postrevolutionary Iran. Soon after the cultural revolution a new wave of young emigrants and exiles left Iran to escape conscription for the bloody war between Iran and Iraq that lasted for eight years.

For most Iranians in exile the 1979 revolution was a traumatic event with catastrophic consequences that has been marked as a defining moment in their lifetime and migration history. Like millions of other Iranians who left their country for economic, political, social, and educational reasons, some members of my extended family departed. Some went to Europe for business investments. A larger number went to Japan as labor migrants in search of jobs and higher wages. Others immigrated to the United States to pursue educational opportunities. A few of my young first cousins fled to neighboring countries to escape the military draft for the Iran-Iraq war. Still others settled in Europe as "social migrants" for better social life and political freedom. Finally, a few, including my mother, left Iran to reunite with their family members and have become "astronaut migrants," traveling back and forth between Iran and America.

The emigration of individuals and families in my middle-class neighborhood was even more dramatic. In less than two years, from the downfall of the shah's government in 1979 to the outset of the Iran-Iraq war in 1980, as many as twenty-eight young men and women between the ages of fifteen and twenty-five from nineteen families in my neighborhood settled in Canada, Italy, Great Britain, Germany, and the United States. Some left alone illegally for neighboring countries to escape military conscription. Others fled with their entire families as emigrants to escape the uncertain postrevolutionary social conditions in Iran. In response to illegal emigration, the new government secured the Iranian borders. The tightening of control by the new regime coupled with closing of the American embassy in Iran contributed to a significant reduction in the volume of emigration and led to a drastic decline in immigration to the United States during the first few years following the revolution.[18] Despite the sharp downward trend in the immigration of Iranians to the United States during the initial phases of the postrevolutionary era, the Islamization of Iran initiated by the new government, coupled with the enormous social, cultural, political, and economic problems following the revolution, pushed many more Iranian individuals and families to leave the country.

Unlike the steady emigration of students before the revolution and the swift flight of elites, high-ranking members of the former government, and investors during it, the postrevolutionary period consisted of several phases of exodus. These included multiple waves of immigrants with more diverse economic, religious, political, social, and professional backgrounds that have continued to the present day. The first wave began soon after the establishment of the new government and included a large number of members of religious minorities and of political dissidents. The flight among religious minorities and opponents of the Islamic government continued for several years after the revolution. However, Iraq's invasion of Iran on September 22, 1980, marked the beginning of the second wave of postrevolutionary exodus for thousands of Iranians. Soon after the war began, many middle-class and upper-middle-class professionals left Iran for better social conditions, economic opportunities, and a more promising future for their children. Young men in particular left the country to escape the military draft. Others left in search of educational opportunities after the closing down of universities.

Overall, compared to those who left the country before and during the revolution, the postrevolutionary Iranians who have continued to emigrate have been a more heterogeneous group with regard to sociocultural background, religious affiliation, political orientation, family situation, and age distribution. The most distinctive contrast between Iranians who entered the United States before the revolution and those who came during the first decade after the revolution was a sharp increase in the number who were granted refugee or asylum status.[19]

In April 1979, several months after the victory of the revolution and establishment of the provisional government, I joined the other 3,500 Iranians who had come from all over Texas and Louisiana to the Iranian consulate in Houston to cast our ballots as part of a referendum for or against the Islamic Republic. The Iranian consulate in Houston, which primarily served Iranians in Texas, New Mexico, Oklahoma, Arkansas, Tennessee, Mississippi, Louisiana, Alabama, Georgia, and Florida before the revolution, was one of the four Iranian consular offices in the United States.[20] During my visit to Houston, I bumped into Reza, a close friend of my older brother who was attending the University of North Texas in Denton. He and his younger brother had joined their older brother in Texas a few months before I left Iran. Reza's older brother was an anti-shah political activist who returned to Iran with thousands of other supporters of the revolution for political participation in and reconstruction of postrevolutionary Iranian society in 1979. Upon returning from my first visit to Iran in the summer of 1979, Reza kindly agreed to be my legal guardian and to transfer my friends and me from the military school to a predominantly white upper-middle-class private religious school in the Dallas area that his teenage brother was attending. He leased an apartment for us near our high school, while he and his three other roommates were attending a university thirty miles away. We saw Reza at times when we needed him for advice or legal issues regarding school or our landlord. When I moved to Dallas in the summer of 1979, Iranian students were visible in every major university and college campus in the region. In the late 1970s and early 1980s Iranians comprised one of the largest foreign student populations on most college campuses across the country.[21] As many as 4,000 Iranian students were studying in junior and senior colleges in Texas alone.[22] The University of North Texas in Denton, which I attended after graduating from high school, had as many as 750 Iranian students in 1980. The influx of Iranian students to universities in Houston in the 1970s was even greater.[23]

The Iranian students in Dallas were predominantly young middle-class or upper-middle-class men and women who had come directly from large Iranian cities between 1977 and the revolutionary upheavals. While some were already pursuing a degree at a major university, an overwhelming number of them were enrolled in expensive intensive English programs at local language institutes. In addition to the student population, a small minority of affluent professionals who had left Iran in the early 1970s for educational and economic opportunities and had already finished their degrees were among the immigrants in Dallas. Except for a small minority of the affluent professional entrepreneurs who were homeowners, the majority of Iranian students lived in rental apartments near college campuses. Despite short intervals in their arrival time, most of them belonged to the first major wave of Iranian students who came to Texas several years before and during the revolution.[24] Most of them intended to return to Iran after completing their studies. Due to the economic and political situation after the revolution, however, a sizable portion of them faced indefinite exile and adjusted their immigration status to permanent residency and eventually became U.S. citizens.[25]

The most striking aspect of life in exile for the majority of Iranians, particularly Iranian students, in Dallas and other U.S. cities with large Iranian populations was political activism. Universities were the battleground for political debates between Iranian students with different ideological orientations, from far-left Marxists and moderate nationalists to ultra-right religious conservatives. In college towns and universities with sizable Iranian student populations, participation in political speeches, demonstrations, festivities, book-reading gatherings, and debates were the only pastime for most during the first years following the revolution. Almost everyone sympathized and supported, or was actively involved with, an Iranian student political organization. To be a political activist was synonymous with intellectualism, nationalism, and the revolutionary avant-garde. Revolutionary fervor and concerns about its outcomes overshadowed challenges of exile and integration for Iranians. The strong postrevolutionary political culture of Iranian students was the legacy of thirty years of opposition to the shah's regime in exile that had begun in the 1960s among the growing number of anti-shah students. Sympathizers and active members of the CIS (Confederation of Iranian Students), Muslim student associations, the Islamic leftist Mojahedin-e Khalq, and supporters of the guerrilla Marxist Fedayian-e Khalq were very visible and active on large university campuses in Texas. The only other major political group that was active outside of the college campus was that of the royalists who supported the Pahlavi monarchy.

Despite their relatively large size, strong political visibility, and heavy concentration in several clusters near the major colleges and universities, Iranians in Dallas lacked any "Iranian enclave" or "Iranian neighborhood" similar to the ones established by European immigrants who entered the United States in the early part of the twentieth century. Iranian ethnic food stores, restaurants, cultural centers, religious organizations, or professional associations were practically nonexistent.[26] During the first stages of development of the Iranian community, when prominent ethnic institutions and community centers were either nonexistent or underdeveloped, Iranian ethnic grocery stores in Dallas provided a multitude of social and economic services and functioned as information centers in the community, providing names and telephone numbers of immigration attorneys, government institutions, and community specialists such as entertainers, religious leaders, and advisers. Ethnic grocery stores helped many newly arrived immigrants find housing and employment.

The Trauma of the Hostage Crisis

On the morning of November 4, 1979, as my two Iranian roommates and I were approaching our school lockers to grab our books before our first class, a screaming group of American students surrounded us asking furiously why the American embassy in Tehran was seized and the embassy personnel were taken as hostages. Ignorant about the English meaning of hostage and uninformed about political events in Iran, we were confused, perplexed, dumbfounded. With help from our English teacher we soon realized that a group of militant students in Iran had taken American personnel at the embassy in Iran and were demanding that the deposed shah, who was in a hospital in New York for cancer treatment, be returned to Iran for trial.

The American embassy occupation by pro-Khomeini militant students spread rage across the United States. Fear of retaliation or physical attack forced many Iranians in the United States into hiding in their own homes. During the first several days of the crisis my roommates and I retreated from social life completely and took refuge in our apartment as if a war had been declared. We were glued to the TV, following the news minute by minute hoping that the conflict would come to an end soon. My life had never been so threatened and my social existence never so denied.

The hostage crisis created a wave of American backlash protests against Iranians in U.S. cities from coast to coast. Hundreds of American demonstrators burned a replica of an Iranian flag and carried placards reading "Have a Happy Thanksgiving—hold an Iranian hostage," "Roast an Iranian for Thanksgiving," "Deport Iranians," "Send in Marines," "Death to Khomeini," "Eat your oil," "Bomb Iran," "Nuke Iran," "War with Iran," "We won't take this anymore," "Support Iran's revolution, send an Iranian home," "Deport Iranians," and "Go home dumb Iranians." In Texas, for two days a thousand vocal anti-Iranian demonstrators gathered at the Dresser Tower in downtown Houston, the site of the Iranian consulate, carrying placards saying "Give Americans liberty or give Iranians death," "Kill Khomeini," and "10 Iranians equal a worm." Other posters read "60 Americans for 10,000 Iranians," suggesting that the United States should trade the Iranians living in the United States for the hostages being held in Iran. In another demonstration in Houston a crowd of one hundred anti-Iranian demonstrators appeared outside the Grand Hotel and protested the hiring of Iranian students.[27] On another occasion, a biplane dropped leaflets signed by the John Wayne Society urging Americans to boycott stores where Iranians work, fire Iranian employees, deny housing to Iranians, and take other actions against citizens of that country.[28]

The demonstrations in Texas were just part of the furious backlash protests against Iranians in the United States. Some protestors burned the Iranian flag and effigies of the ayatollah. In almost every major university across the country, American students organized protests to vent rage against Iran and Iranians in the United States.[29] Increased security was needed at several universities to protect Iranian students from angry demonstrators. Hate crimes directed against Iranians increased on some college campuses, and campus police were called to protect Iranian students. At the Reno campus of the University of Nevada, a group of about eighty Americans—some waving flags, others brandishing beer bottles and golf clubs—confronted about thirty Iranian students.[30] A St. Louis man was arrested after police said he pointed a loaded shotgun at a telephone operator at St. Louis University and demanded the names of Iranian students.[31] Campus police at the University of Wyoming protected Iranian students who received death threats.[32] To protect their lives and defend themselves against angry American attackers, friends and relatives lived together. Others attempted to acquire weapons. In Huntsville, Alabama, more than twenty Iranian students at Alabama A&M University applied for pistol permits after rumors that the Ku Klux Klan planned to confront the two hundred Iranian students at the school. None of the permits were granted because the Iranians were not U.S. citizens.[33]

In addition to students, some teachers, administrators, and university boards acted prejudicially and implemented discriminatory policies against Iranian students. A Houston Independent School District board of trustees refused admittance of Iranian youngsters to school.[34] The board of Greenville, a two-year college in South Carolina, voted to bar Iranian students from classes during the quarter after the hostage crisis if the American hostages were not released. State universities in Louisiana and New Mexico stopped enrolling Iranian students. The Mississippi legislature passed a bill doubling the tuition for Iranian students attending public universities in that state. Local radio and television programs expressed and incited anger and hostility by encouraging callers to boycott Iranian-owned businesses and to put anti-Iranian bumper stickers on their cars.

Elsewhere in public places, Iranians in the United States felt the ire and frustration of their host society and in some cases blatant discrimination and prejudice against them. Occasionally Iranians were refused service at restaurants and retail stores. A bar near the University of North Texas in Denton, where I attended college, posted a sign reading "No dogs or Iranians allowed." Besides civilians and employees in public and private institutions, labor organizations reacted to the hostage crisis. The Transport Workers Union in New York and the International Longshoremen's

Association, among others, boycotted Iranian goods and ship handling. They also refused to load or unload any Iranian planes and cargo.[35]

Various petitions calling for the United States to strike back by taking political and economic action against Iran were circulated by individuals, politicians, and organizations. An independent businessman in Houston circulated a petition titled "Iranian Eviction Notice," which called for deportation of Iranian students with expired visas, deportation of Iranian military personnel, an end to welfare aid for Iranian students, and confiscation of all Iranian assets in U.S. banks. Between twenty thousand and thirty thousand people signed the Iranian Eviction Petition.[36] Ultraconservative groups like Texas Young Americans for Freedom urged President Carter to order a naval blockade of Iran and distributed petitions around Texas asking Carter to take stronger action against Iran.[37] Texas citizens urged Senator Lloyd Bentsen to ask the administration to discontinue the training of 193 Iranian military pilots and 24 navigators in America as quickly as possible and to send the trainees and their dependents back to Iran.[38]

Some members of the Texas congressional delegation issued severe reactions against Iran and Iranians in the United States. Some proposed military action against Iran, while others suggested a diplomatic break, economic embargo, and deportation of Iranian students. One member said the United States should use military force to destroy weapons Americans sold to Iran. A congressman from Texas who spoke out on the problem in Iran said, "The United States should bomb sites in Iran to destroy the weapons."[39] A senator from Texas argued that the United States should not continue to train fighter pilots for a "renegade government" that was holding American hostages in Tehran.[40] Other congressmen and senators called for the deportation of lawbreaking Iranian students in the United States. Still others went a step further and introduced legislation mandating the roundup and deportation of all protesting Iranians, even those acting legally. A Republican senator from California said the Senate should pass a bill that would allow President Carter to round up Iranian nationals in America and hold or deport them.[41] Legislation was introduced calling for Iranian nationals to be expelled from all tax-supported colleges and universities in the United States. On many occasions fighting broke out between Iranians and Americans, and many Iranians were arrested. In some cases persons of Middle Eastern descent with features similar to Iranians were either harassed and beaten by angry protestors or subjected to prejudice and discrimination. To make clear that they were not Iranians, many Middle Easterners printed their nationalities on their T-shirts.

A company in Houston ordered its non-Iranian employees who looked like Iranians to wear name tags showing their nationalities.

In the mid-1970s many Americans already resented Iranian students who frequently demonstrated to protest U.S. support of the shah who then ruled the country. The resentment turned to hatred after the Iranian revolution and peaked during the hostage crisis and pro-Khomeini demonstrations in the United States. Demonstrations of pro-Khomeini Iranians in support of the revolution and return of the shah to Iran were viewed by government authorities as disruptive and threatening to the lives of American hostages. State officials including the Houston police chief and the mayor said Iranian students involved in disruptive activities in Houston should be deported immediately.[42]

In response to the Iranian seizure of American hostages in Tehran and to discourage further potentially violent anti-shah demonstrations by pro-Khomeini students in the United States that might endanger U.S. hostages held, President Carter ordered an investigation of the visa status of Iranian students in the United States. On November 13, 1979, on Carter's order, Benjamin Civiletti, who was then attorney general, published regulations giving Iranians one month to report their locations and visa status to the closest INS office. Students were interviewed by immigration authorities and were asked to provide their school locations and documents showing they were full-time and their tuition had been paid. After the initial interview stage of the examination by INS officers and determination of the students' status, violators were scheduled for hearings before immigration judges for deportation. Students with visa violations were accorded due process of law with the opportunity to take their cases to the Board of Immigration Appeals and on up the ladder through federal district and appeals courts.

To comply with President Carter's crackdown on Iranians, universities and colleges were asked to report the status of Iranian students to the local INS offices. Some colleges with large Iranian enrollments, such as San Jacinto Junior College in Houston with 262 Iranians, considered busing students to the immigration office for interviews.[43] Within a week after Carter ordered the INS to check the status of Iranian students in the United States, an estimated 4,000 students were interviewed.[44] Two weeks later the number of Iranian students who reported to the INS reached 35,584. Of this number 4,592 were found to be deportable, 536 of whom agreed to leave voluntarily and another 326 of whom applied for political asylum. Several months after Carter's order, about 56,694 students had reported to immigration officials, and 6,906 had been found not in compliance with immigration regulations and deportable.[45] Another 3,000 students were under examination, and 9,000 others who refused to report to immigration authorities were hunted.[46] Of the 6,906 Iranian students found to be out of legal status and in violation of their visas, some had overstayed in the country without applying for extensions.[47] Other violators had either transferred between schools without INS permission or had course loads of less than the required twelve-hour minimum. Iranian students who were working off-campus without permission from the INS were also found subject to deportation.

Some of the deportees agreed to return to Iran voluntarily. Others applied for political asylum on grounds that they might be persecuted and their lives might be in danger if they were forced to go back to Iran. Of the 6,906 students subject to deportation, the INS deported 19 and ordered 43 more to leave. Another 321 had completed hearings, and 5,019 cases waited for completion of their hearing process.[48] The INS received 514 requests for political asylum from Iranian students. Overall, between the time the hostages were taken in November 1979 and April 1980, when immigration officials completed reviewing the legal status of Iranian students, 14,768 Iranians, including 2,204 students, left the United States.[49]

Eric Lieberman, an American attorney for the National Emergency Civil Liberties Committee and the Confederation of Iranian Students, with support from the American Civil Liberties Union, filed two class action lawsuits on behalf of Iranian students and challenged President Carter's order that the visas of Iranian students be reviewed by Immigration and Naturalization Services.[50] They argued that the president and attorney general did not have the authority to change immigration policy and conduct more forceful regulation against a particular nationality. A federal judge overturned President Carter's order and ruled that the roundup and crackdown on Iranian students in the United States illegally were unconstitutional and had to be halted.[51] According to U.S. District Judge Joyce Green, singling out Iranians for possible deportation was unfair and violated the equal protection guarantee of the Fifth Amendment. In her view checking the visas of Iranian students as ordered by the president created two classes of nonimmigrant students, Iranians and non-Iranians, each subjected to a different type of executive action. The judge said the classification was based on national origin and noted that it violated the equal protection clause of the Constitution because it singled out Iranians for investigation. Some human rights professors and organizations praised the U.S. court ruling and argued that President Carter's order violated human rights and international laws because it discriminated based on national origin, was motivated by reactionary purposes, and punished Iranian students for the conduct of others in their country.[52] At the time of the judge's ruling, federal officials already had interviewed more than 50,000 Iranian students and found that about 6,042 were subject to deportation. Moreover, they had asked more than 3,000 of the students for additional information to determine their status.[53] The judge's order not only stopped deportations but relieved the students from the responsibility of reporting to immigration offices for interviews.

Following the federal court ruling that Iranian roundups by the INS violated the Constitution, immigration officers halted the processing of students. To stay the judge's ban, however, the Justice Department filed a motion with the U.S. Circuit Court of Appeals for the District of Columbia. Government lawyers argued that the judge's ruling was a serious and unwarranted intrusion by the judiciary and asked the appeals court for a full appeal of her decision.[54] In their view the federal trial judge was wrong to hold the deportation program unconstitutional. They urged the three-judge panel of the U.S. Circuit Court of Appeals to rule that in this "time of international crisis" the government had the right to single out Iranian students and deport those who were in the United States illegally.[55] Several days later, the U.S. Court of Appeals ruled that the president had the right to order the special program under the Immigration and Nationality Act and that the government could continue to investigate Iranian students but could not take any deportation action until the issue was settled. Just days after the ruling, the INS resumed reviewing visas of students and holding deportation hearings but did not enforce any deportation orders. The lawyers representing the Confederation of Iranian Students filed an appeal asking all nine judges on the court to rehear the case.[56]

In December 1979, about a month after the hostage crisis began, Carter ordered Iran to reduce the size of its diplomatic staff in the Iranian embassy in the United States from 150 to 35 people. Four months later, on Monday, April 7, 1980, President Carter gave a thirty-six-hour expulsion notice for all Iranian diplomats.[57] As instructed by the president, agents of the FBI and the U.S. Marshal's Office closed the Iranian consulate general offices in the United States.[58] In addition to the deportation of Iranian diplomats, all the 203 Iranians undergoing pilot, navigation, and other technical military training at seven U.S. Air Force bases in Texas, Mississippi, California, and Colorado were first restricted to the classroom and the flight simulator and then ordered to leave the country.[59] Another 14 students at Texas A&M who were attending the university on military visas were ordered to return to Iran. The military visas are the equivalent of diplomatic visas, which were revoked by the president.[60]

The expulsion of Iranian diplomats and military trainees from the United States was one element of the four-part program announced by Carter for applying pressure on Iran. The other parts of the program included new trade sanctions against Iran, a freeze of all Iranian government assets in the United States, tighter restrictions on visas for Iranians desiring to come to the United States, and revocation of visas for Iranians who had already entered the country.[61] The asset freeze was imposed by Carter after Iran threatened to pull an estimated $8 billion in funds from the United States. Due to the asset freeze, banks refused to cash checks written by Iranian students. At some universities, the business school office only cashed certified checks or checks written on a bank in the United States. After so many complaints, the U.S. Treasury Department issued special licenses allowing two Iranian banks, Bank Sepah in New York and Bank Melli in San Francisco, to bring in a total of $30 million for use by Iranian students in the United States. It also unblocked four Iranian embassy bank accounts with some $7 million in embassy funds, some of which went to students.[62]

Under Carter's new visa program, no Iranian was allowed to enter the United States except in the cases of major medical emergencies or political asylum. Because of Carter's order, U.S. airlines in London began refusing to allow Iranians to board planes bound for the United States.[63] The new visa program was partly a response to alleged fear of Iranian terrorists entering the United States.[64] Therefore, immigration officers at U.S. ports of entry were instructed to send Iranians entering the United States to a second checkpoint for further questioning and another look at their luggage.

To show Americans' support for the hostages, President Carter called for a National Unity Day. In a strong show of patriotism and support for the hostages and Carter's call, millions of Americans flew American flags at their homes and businesses as well as at government facilities, and some schools conducted flag-raising ceremonies and played the national anthem.[65] Also in support of the U.S. hostages in Iran and in response to Carter's call for the National Unity Day, on December 18, 1979, in some cities traffic signs urged motorists to drive with their headlights on. In some cities, including Huntington, West Virginia, at the stroke of noon, church bells rang and traffic lights turned red. For fifty seconds, motorists waited beside their cars, and city employees, shoppers, and schoolchildren stepped outside and stood quietly.[66] In hundreds of communities across

the country Americans held vigils and prayer services. After a series of negotiations mediated through the Algerian government, Iran and the United States reached an accord to release the hostages. Finally, on January 20,
1981, just after Carter left office, the American hostages were released. In
return, the U.S. government agreed to release Iran's frozen assets, pledged
not to intervene in Iran's political affairs, and promised to return the
shah's family wealth to Iran.

Although the crisis ended and the United States met some of Iran's
original demands, the hostage affair ruined more than thirty years of
strong cultural, political, and economic ties between the two countries.
The hostage crisis and the subsequent difficulty Iranians had in obtaining
any type of U.S. visas, as well as the cancellation of all visas issued to Iranians as announced by President Carter, reduced the immigration of Iranians to the United States drastically and created major barriers for Iranians who intended to visit Iran and return to the United States.[67] Therefore,
cancellation of my multiple student visa (which would have allowed me
to go home and return to the United States without requesting an entry
visa from an American consulate) turned me into a hostage in the United
States and prohibited me from traveling to Iran and visiting my family for
almost a decade. Ever since the closure of the U.S. embassy, Iranians who
wish to come to the United States must go to a third country where there is
an American embassy to obtain visas. Given the political tension between
Iran and the United States, I was afraid to be denied return to complete
my studies. Alternatively, my parents attempted to obtain visas and come
to the United States to see me. After two denials in two consecutive years
from the American embassy in Germany, we were eventually reunited
after seven long years of involuntary, traumatic separation. After a four-
month stay in the United States my parents returned to Iran, and I never
saw my father again. He passed away unexpectedly a few months after his
return. Apart from the return visa barrier, the devastating war between
Iran and Iraq and the Iranian drafting policy prevented me from attending
his funeral in Iran.

Becoming a Permanent Resident and Visiting Iran

My visa dilemma finally came to an end with the Immigration Reform and
Control Act (IRCA) of 1986. IRCA enabled me to change my status from
student to permanent resident and eventually to U.S. citizen. It offered
amnesty to foreigners who had lived in the United States illegally since be-

fore January 1, 1982. Three types of illegal aliens were qualified for amnesty—those who came into America illegally without visas, those who entered the country with legitimate visas but stayed on after their visas were expired, and those who entered the United States legally but violated the terms of their visas, usually by working without permission from the INS. I had entered the country legally in August 1978 on an F-1 visa, the type normally issued to foreign students, but I violated the terms of my student visa when I took my first part-time job as a cook at a restaurant in Denton, Texas, near the university I was attending. This violation counted in my favor, miraculously, and provided permanent residency and eventually U.S. citizenship for me and many other Iranians in America.

The first and most immediate consequence of IRCA and adjustment to permanent residency was a significant increase in the temporary return migration and short-term visits for many Iranians. In addition to the Immigration Reform and Control Act of 1986, the temporary return of thousands of Iranian expatriates to Iran was the outcome of a series of major economic and political reforms initiated by the pragmatist leaders of the Iranian government after Khomeini's death in June 1989. Unlike the first decade of the postrevolutionary era (1979–1989), during which the Iranian government controlled the economy, the new pragmatist government stressed privatization and liberal trade policies. Moreover, the leaders advocated a less confrontational foreign policy and more cordial diplomatic and economic relations with the West. Therefore, the new pragmatist government sponsored various plans aiming to repair economic and social damage caused by the Iran-Iraq war, improve the infrastructure, increase economic production through private and foreign investment, lower barriers for foreign investment in Iran, promote export, and privatize national industries (Keddie 2006). The end of the Iran-Iraq war after eight years, coupled with political and economic changes initiated by the pragmatists during the post-Khomeini period, encouraged many expatriates to visit Iran.

One specific initiative that directly affected young Iranian men and facilitated their return to Iran was a change in military draft policies of the Iranian government after the Iran-Iraq war ended. Regardless of their immigration status in the United States, for many Iranians the eight-year war between Iran and Iraq halted return migration. This was especially the case for young Iranian men of draft age. After the peace agreement between the two governments, however, the Iranian government passed an amendment that entitled Iranian immigrant men without the mandatory military service completion to obtain temporary exemption for a fee based on the highest level of education attained, payable to the Iranian government. The attainment of permanent U.S. residency through IRCA and the removal of such barriers as Iranian military conscription not only made it possible for young Iranian men to go home more often but also facilitated the migration flow of more Iranians, particularly women, to the United States and significantly altered the demographic structure of Iranian communities in two sequential ways. First, legalization of thousands of Iranians after IRCA subsequently increased the number who became naturalized citizens of the United States.[68] Second, an increase in the naturalization trend in turn increased the number of new immigrants who entered the United States for family reunification purposes. This has been especially the case for many women who entered the United States as wives of naturalized Iranians. Due to the migration of Iranian women as wives of naturalized Iranians, a new trend in the entire migration history of Iranians to the United States emerged, and for the first time in 1992, more than 50 percent of all Iranian immigrants who came to this country were women.[69] This trend has continued until today. Each year close to 55 percent of Iranians admitted to the United States are women.

Following the end of the war between Iran and Iraq in 1988, I returned to Tehran, the city where I had lived for sixteen years. I had never been so emotionally and mentally overwhelmed by such a deplorable experience in my life. My enthusiasm and nostalgia for returning to Iran and visiting my family was soon replaced with a bittersweet experience of disappointment that has fragmented my life since then. Upon my return from Iran, I came to the sad but undeniable realization that I no longer belonged to either Iran or the United States. My national identity and connection to Iran appeared to be based more on my birthplace as indicated on my birth certificate, familiarity with the Persian language, and emotional ties to my family than on sharing the same cultural worldview with most other Iranians and having any social status in the postrevolutionary Islamic culture of Iran.

After the first few days of constant emotional excitement triggered by every familiar voice, smell, and visual image from the past and the reawakening of and reflection upon memories from my childhood and teenage years, my blissful harmony ended. I felt out of place in my own native country, an exile in my own society. I was a familiar stranger in a strangely familiar place with mixed feelings of being at home and out of place, rooted and uprooted, attached and detached, and included and excluded. I had never felt so foreign in my own hometown. I felt as if I knew everyone and everything yet was distanced from them. Ten years of hiatus had engendered a huge gulf between my family and me. I had never witnessed such extreme change in my lifetime. Almost every aspect of Iranian society and culture, from people's attire to streets' names, had been affected by the revolution and had a distinctive Islamic identity. All prerevolutionary institutions were either abolished or restructured, and new foundations and agencies were created. A new collective or social memory based on the stories of the revolution, the Iran-Iraq war, and the subsequent economic difficulties and political struggles had emerged.

To reconfirm my membership as part of Iran and to restore and reconstruct the continuity in my linear social history, I visited the house where I was born, the elementary and middle schools that I attended, and the neighborhoods where I had grown up. I also desperately searched for my childhood playmates, high school classmates, and friends of my teenage years. Furthermore, to express and reclaim my Persian identity and regain my contested cultural identity, I collected every remaining object from my childhood period, spent hours talking with the elders in my family to reconstruct my genealogy, and collected hundreds of old pictures of my parents and siblings. The more I engaged in these efforts, the more I realized that I had lost something valuable that could never be restored or reconnected. My identity had been decentered. What I had lost was the continuity and harmony in my life history. I no longer could partake in the collective social memory of my family nor share the same social memory of Iranian society with my family, friends, and acquaintances. All of these had suddenly been ruptured, breached by the revolution and my prolonged separation from my country and home. In every gathering, everyone had a story to tell about the revolution and war except me. I no longer had shared memories with my family and friends, and my collective social memory had been suspended since I had left Iran in 1978. Memories of my family and Iran had become an idealized past and part of Iranian history. I had left as a teenager and returned during my early adulthood.

Throughout the 1990s the pragmatist government in Iran continued its economic reconstruction programs, paying noticeable attention to matters related to Iranians abroad and extending its return immigration policies to attract more Iranian expatriates to visit the country after years of exile. During the 1990s, obtaining necessary paperwork from Iranian embassies throughout the world became much easier. Moreover, the Iranian government accepted dual nationality for Iranians who had obtained American citizenship and carried two passports; provided a temporary exemption from the national military service for Iranian men abroad; and granted them a once-a-year trip to Iran for up to three months without being subject to the draft laws. Furthermore, the fee for obtaining or renewing an Iranian passport and other passport-related affairs was reduced significantly.

These changes encouraged many Iranians to visit Iran more frequently and retain contact with relatives and friends in Iran. The reestablishment of these contacts has had varying repercussions for first- and second-generation Iranian immigrants and their communities in exile. For one thing, since second-generation Iranians arrived at a very young age or were born, reared, and schooled in the United States, their knowledge of Iranian culture is very limited. Thus, the increased contact between Iran and Iranian immigrants has promoted the maintenance of Iranian culture and reinforced the attachment to Iran and Iranian culture in the second generation. It has also made many first-generation Iranian immigrants realize how culturally detached they had become from those who remained in Iran and how much social circumstances have changed since the revolution.

After the landslide election of President Khatami in 1997, Iran entered a period of a reformist movement comprised of a coalition of the pragmatists, Islamic liberals, and secularists aimed at promoting the rule of law, freedom, strengthening of civil society, and improved relations with the West. Khatami was the first Iranian president who attempted to improve U.S.-Iranian relations since the hostage crisis. During his term of office President Khatami granted an interview to CNN in which he called for a "dialogue of civilizations." As a result of Khatami's initiatives, Iran and the United States organized mutual wrestling matches, the economic embargo on two culturally renowned Iranian products—rugs and pistachio nuts—was lifted, and travel to and from the United States became much easier. With 9/11, however, all the diplomatic improvements in Iranian-U.S. relations came to a standstill. The Iranian and American governments denounced each other and reverted to their earlier political conflict.

The Trauma of 9/11 and Resurgence of Prejudice and Discrimination against Iranians

The horrific September 11, 2001, attack on America was another sad turning point in the migration history of Iranians in the United States. Despite their innocence and lack of a single piece of evidence regarding their involvement in this hideous act, once again Iranian immigrants in the United States were subject to new forms of discrimination and prejudice and civil rights violations. As indicated earlier, immediately after the 9/11 attack, President Bush labeled Iran a terrorist sponsor country and part of an "axis of evil." To combat terrorists and avoid any similar actions in the future, the U.S. government initiated a series of actions that had major consequences for Iranians as well as Arab and/or Muslim Americans. Although these federal initiatives were not designed exclusively for any particular ethnic or religious group, Arab and/or Muslim immigrants suffered the most from these policies. On June 5, 2002, the attorney general announced the National Security Entry/Exit Registration System (NSEERS), reminiscent of the reporting requirements for Iranian students to the INS during the hostage crisis. NSEERS required noncitizens from twenty-six designated foreign countries—predominantly Muslim countries, including Iran—to submit fingerprints and photographs upon their arrival in the United States; report to INS field offices within thirty days; report to the INS annually for reregistration; provide additional information that might include their addresses in the United States and in their countries of origin, information about both parents, points of contact in the noncitizen's country of origin, intended activities in the United States, and more; and notify INS agents of their departure.[70] On November 6, 2002, the INS required men older than sixteen from twenty countries, mostly in the Middle East, who had entered the United States prior to September 10, 2002, to register with the INS. Iran was among the first five countries whose nationals were subjected to special registration. Hundreds of Iranians in Los Angeles were among the one thousand registrants who were arrested and detained when they appeared to register with the INS in California.

Overall, after 9/11 Iranian immigrants in the United States, most of whom are U.S. citizens, encountered new waves of discrimination, hate crimes, employer and government profiling, and violations of their civil rights by both public and private actors. Due to the 9/11 crackdown and the ongoing U.S. terrorist sweep, many Iranians experienced being fired from jobs, improper workplace background checks, unwarranted FBI interrogation and surveillance, and security clearance denials and revocations.[71]

Despite my U.S. citizenship, thirty years of residence in this country, and professional affiliations and contributions, I feel socially and legally as vulnerable and insecure as I did when I had a student visa and was attending a Dallas high school during the hostage crisis in 1979. Although I have spent two-thirds of my life in this country, developed strong friendship ties with many Americans, and gained a deep appreciation for American culture, I still feel like a foreigner, an outsider on the margins of American society. This feeling is commonly shared by a large number of Iranians in the United States (a topic to be discussed in the following chapters) and is rooted in the ongoing complicated and cumbersome U.S.-Iranian relations, the distorted image of Iran and Iranians, the profiling of Iranians, and various forms of subtle and blunt discrimination against them. Ethnic profiling of Iranians as a suspected group, among other Middle Eastern immigrants in the United States, took me back to 1979 and evoked bitter memories of Americans' distrust of Iranians and their anti-Iranian rhetoric during and after the hostage crisis. Once again I felt under a spotlight and compelled to prove everyone wrong about the stereotypical images of Middle Eastern Muslim men that had been fixed firmly in the minds of most Americans, including some of my educated colleagues, students, and neighbors. For the first nine months after 9/11, during every other of my air travels I was selected for "random" enhanced screening. On one particular occasion at Reagan National Airport in Washington, D.C., after passing airport security checks I was removed from the waiting area at the boarding gate by two airport security guards, searched thoroughly, and asked to remain seated in a designated area until my departure. Similar incidents were experienced by some of my friends often. During a trip to a professional conference, one of my friends who is the chair of his department at a prestigious university was embarrassingly removed from the airplane. Fifteen minutes after his flight took off, it returned to the gate, where he was deplaned for interrogation because a flight attendant saw him moving to another empty seat in the plane. After intensive questioning that proved his innocence of any wrongdoing, he was left at the gate without any apologies.

Although nearly three decades have passed since the hostage crisis, unfortunately the story of Iran and Iranian immigrants remains unpleasant, and the distorted generalizations and stereotypes about Iranians persist and are widespread in the United States. The Iranian government is still viewed as a fanatic and terrorist state and part of an "axis of evil" and as a threat to the international community. As long as U.S.-Iranian relations remain entangled, Iranian immigrants in the United States will be subjected to prejudice, discrimination, and profiling; and as long as Iran continues to experience its current inflation, population growth, and political repression, Iranians in the diaspora will continue the paradoxical life of double exile, a fragmented and conflicted life that has made them ambivalent about living both in Iran and in the United States. Theirs is a kind of purgatory; they are neither happy in exile nor looking forward to returning home. Their identities are marginalized in the societies of both their host and their home countries.

2 To Be or Not to Be an Iranian
Politics, Media, and the Paradox of National Identity

*Within a week after the embassy occupation took place on November 4, pictures of a scowling Ayatollah Khomeini were as frequent and unchanging in what they were supposed to be telling the viewer as the endless pictures of vast Iranian mobs. The burning (and selling) of Iranian flags by irate Americans became a regular pastime; the press faithfully reported this kind of patriotism. Increasingly, there were frequent reports showing the popular confusion between Arabs and Iranians, such as the one carried by the **Boston Globe** on November 10 of an angry Springfield crowd chanting "Arab go home."*

Edward Said,
Covering Islam

In a poll of mainstream Americans conducted in 1981, 56 percent of the respondents cited hostages as coming to mind when Iran was mentioned; also commonly cited, after Khomeini, oil, and the shah, were anger, hatred, turmoil, and troublesome country. Moreover, 50 percent of the respondents described "all" or "most" Muslims as "warlike and bloodthirsty," 49 percent described them as being "treacherous and cunning," and 44 percent as "barbaric" and "cruel." . . . When asked what comes to mind when the words Muslim or Islam are mentioned, the two most common responses—which received an equal number of votes—were Muhammad and Iran.

Fawaz Gerges,
"Islam and Muslims in the Mind of America"

The Hostage Crisis, American Media, and Emergence of Anti-Iranian Narratives and Stereotypes

Although U.S. officials in the first stages of the Iranian revolution supported Ayatollah Khomeini's new government, their perceptions of that government underwent a radical shift after pro-Khomeini militant students seized the American embassy and took fifty-two Americans hostage for 444 days. As indicated by Gary Sick (2001), the principal White House aide for Iran during the Iranian revolution and the hostage crisis, the invasion of the U.S. embassy in Tehran marked Iran as a dangerous, unpredictable, and unreliable state in the international community. Nowhere was this truer than in the United States, where 97 percent of Americans watched the evening news and read daily newspapers for almost fifteen months to seek information about the conditions of hostages and political developments between the United States and Iran.[1] This information provided by American media on Iran, however, as noted by Edward Said (1997:83), was a "poorly defined and badly misunderstood abstraction" that represented Iranians as "militant, dangerous, and anti-American." In his view, headlines like "An Ideology of Martyrdom" and "Iran's Martyr Complex" in *Time* and *Newsweek* represented Iranians as "non-rational," "hungry for martyrdom," and "unwilling to compromise." According to Said, the analysis of the Iranian revolution by reporters, government officials, academic Middle East experts, and guests from corporations on major television news programs such as *The MacNeil/Lehrer Report* was unsatisfactory, superficial, imbalanced, inaccurate, ethnocentric, ideologically driven, non-investigative, and lacking in depth. Furthermore, the reaction of Americans to postrevolutionary Iran was rooted in the "longstanding" "Orientalist" attitude of the West toward "Islam, the Arabs, and the Orient" that related Islam to war, murder, and conflict and portrayed Muslims as anti-American and uncivilized.

Said is not the only one critical of media stories of the hostage crisis. Scott (2000) notes how mainstream American media presented Khomeini as a "cagey," "fanatic," tyrannical leader and Islam as an "irrational," "arbitrary," and "crazed" religion. In her view, these images characterized the crisis as a "contest between civilization and barbarism" and a battle between Christianity and Islam. Furthermore, the dramatic and sensational coverage of the cruel, humiliating, and inhumane treatment of hostages by militant students reinforced the "heroic resistance" elements of the classic American captivity narrative. This sensationalism emotionally inflamed Americans and evoked support for the U.S. government and outrage toward the "enemy government."

The threats faced by hostages in Iran, Scott notes, had been firmly grounded in American mythology and national memory since colonial times, when Puritans confronted Native Americans. Just as Puritan "captivity narratives" served as a tool for "articulating Puritans' special mission in the New World" and rationalized their actions toward the "devilish" barbaric Indians, the hostage crisis narratives influenced America's mission in the world and justified actions taken by the Carter administration against the "devilish savages" of Islam. Referring to works of other authors, Scott explains how the "captivity narratives" functioned as propaganda tools against the French, justified colonial expansion as the fulfillment of scriptural prophecy, shaped the identity of colonists as captives during the American Revolution, and forged American identity. As an updated captive narrative, the hostage crisis circulated and echoed identifiable and recurring Puritan captivity themes of confrontation with the "other," fears of innocents being violated, danger faced by America, threats to American identity, and heroic leadership and rescue, all of which had been demonstrated during other crises. Thus, Scott contends, the hostage crisis not only had a mythological significance in America's national memories of settlement, expansion, survival, and conquest but also shaped U.S. foreign policy challenges. Moreover, the hostage crisis, Scott remarks, reverberated with fervent American patriotism and replayed the cold war rhetoric of "prophetic dualism"—moral and religious superiority of America—in stories, editorials, songs, T-shirts, and comic strips about Khomeini, Islam, and the hostage takers. Finally, Scott observes, the hostage crisis and the media's powerful representation of Iran and Islam as enemies, as well as the tormenting of captives and the perpetuation of recurring myths of heroism, patriotism, and freedom, provided an opportunity for America to assert its identity as a strong, united nation in a hostile world.

News media were not the only sources of anti-Iranian propaganda. The film industry in the United States had a *major* destructive role in creating and conveying stereotypes and shaping attitudes of Americans toward Iranian immigrants in the United States. As Jane Campbell notes (1997), all the motion pictures released between 1978 and 1991 in the United States that portrayed Iranians, whether comedic or action-adventure, depicted them in an insulting, stereotypic manner similar to the ones perpetuated by television and print media. Without offering any background or understanding of Iranian society and culture, these ethnocentric movies ignored diversity within Iran and the Iranian community in exile and constructed a distorted homogeneous image of Iran in the minds of millions of American. Iranians appear in very few American movies. When Iranians do appear, Campbell finds, they are predominantly portrayed as "terrifying, alien, irrational, cruel, barbaric people who threaten our national economy and our very safety in the United States" (180).

Unfortunately, the distorted images presented in these movies reinforced the same disparaging stereotypes emanating from television and print media. Such distorted and destructive stereotypes—that Iranians are untrustworthy terrorists, illogical, fundamentalist Muslims, and patriarchal, fanatic, demonic, primitive, evil, and criminal—stigmatized and devalued Iranians. These stereotypes functioned as a means of justifying prejudice and discrimination against Iranian nationals, thus encouraging their harassment in the United States. These widely held unfavorable images alienated Iranian immigrants from their community and increased the level of social distance and decreased intimacy between Iranians and Americans. The images marginalized Iranians socially, hindered their integration into American society, and led inevitably to low personal self-esteem as well as fragmented and distorted collective identities for Iranian immigrants. Furthermore, the highly focused "demonization" of Iran and Iranians (Said 1997), derogatory images, and strong, widespread anti-Iranian, anti-Muslim narratives constructed by news media and Hollywood posed a serious threat to Iranians' national and religious identities and pushed them to conceal those identities. This has particularly been the case for Iranian practicing Muslims.

The extent of prejudice and discrimination against Iranians since the hostage crisis is unknown. However, according to the executive director of the National Iranian American Council, after 9/11 as many as five cases of discrimination per day have been reported to that organization's office in Washington, D.C. Due to the extent of reported instances of abuse and discrimination against Iranians, in 2003 Congressman Marty Meehan sponsored House Resolution 367 condemning discrimination and bigotry against Iranian Americans. As described earlier, discrimination and prejudice against Iranians began during the hostage crisis and has continued until today. Based on a random sample of about seven hundred Iranian heads of households in Los Angeles in the late 1980s, Bozorgmehr and his associates gathered valuable quantitative and qualitative data on discrimination against Iranians during and after the hostage crisis (Bozorgmehr 2000). As expected, the findings reveal that Iranians in Los Angeles experienced more discrimination during the hostage crisis than when it subsided. Surprisingly, Bozorgmehr did not find a significant difference in the rate of discrimination between Iranians who left Iran as exiles for political and religious reasons and economic migrants who left Iran for educational and economic reasons. However, given that a large number of Iranian exiles are non-Muslim members of religious minorities, they seem to have experienced less prejudice than the economic migrants with a larger share of Muslim population. This indicates the unfavorable stereotypes associated with Islam in America and the double jeopardy experienced by many Iranian Muslims. His findings also suggest that the level of perceived prejudice was much higher than the rate of discrimination experienced by Iranians. Although 50 percent of Iranians in his sample reported that they had felt prejudice, less than 20 percent indicated that they were discriminated against mainly in finding jobs and obtaining promotions.

To estimate the level of discrimination against Iranians, I asked respondents in my survey if they had experienced discrimination because of their nationality before or after 9/11, or both. Overall, 40 percent of the respondents indicated that they experienced some form of discrimination because of their Iranian nationality. While half of the respondents experienced discrimination both before and after 9/11, the remaining half was almost equally divided between those who had experienced discrimination either before 9/11 or after it. In a related question, 45 percent of Iranians pointed out that after the 9/11 attack, they felt socially and politically insecure. Another survey, conducted by an Iranian Studies Group at MIT (2005), found the same rate of discrimination against Iranians. In a sample study of 3,880 relatively young, educated, first-generation Iranian immigrants conducted online, 32 percent of respondents said they "sometimes" experience discrimination. The proportion of Iranians who were "often" and "always" discriminated against were 8 percent and 2 percent, respectively.

In a recent telephone survey of eight hundred Iranians in California, conducted by the Institute of Government Studies at the University of California–Berkeley (2007), 25 percent of the respondents indicated that they experienced discrimination by being singled out for special searches or questioning at an airport since 9/11. Another 43 percent reported denial of visas for family members or friends who intended to visit the United States after the 9/11 attack, 5 percent of the respondents stated that they had been turned down for jobs, and 12 percent reported general hostility from members of their local communities.[2] In a multilingual study of one thousand ethnic Californians, conducted by Bendixen and Associates in 2002, nearly 60 percent of Iranians in the sample stated that they had been the victims of racial or ethnic discrimination more often after the events of 9/11.[3] In the same survey, 50 percent of Arab, Iranian, Pakistani, Afghani, and Asian Indian participants indicated they experienced racial or ethnic discrimination and more depression after 9/11.

The widespread discrimination and prejudice created a wide social gap between Iranians and Americans and increased the level of social distance between the two groups. Sparrow and Chretien's (1993) research among 415 college students gives a clear indication of the low degree of affinity Americans felt toward Iranians and the low degree of social interaction Americans desired with Iranians. Applying the seven-item Social Distance Scale developed by Emory Bogardus (1926), University of Chicago sociologists Sparrow and Chretien asked a sample of 132 blacks, 271 whites, and 12 Asians and Hispanics whether they would be willing to admit members of thirty-one different ethnic groups into the following associational networks—1) kinship by marriage, 2) club as personal chums, 3) street as neighbors, 4) company as employees, 5) country as citizens, and 6) country as visitors—or 7) would exclude them from the country. The score of 1 for any group would indicate no social distance and therefore no prejudice, and the score of 7 would indicate greater social distance with more prejudice between themselves and the ethnic groups. The researchers found that most college students would be willing to have more intimate social contacts and closer interactions with most racial/ethnic groups other than Iranians. Overall, most minority groups were ranked at a lower level of social distance and were accepted as personal chums in clubs or as neighbors, while Iranians were consistently given the greatest social distance and not tolerated any closer than as citizens of the country. Ranking all the thirty-one groups in the study, Sparrow and Chretien found Iranians to acquire the last and lowest score. This disturbing finding clearly indicates the extent to which degrading stereotypes perpetuated by the media repelled Americans from accepting Iranians as a group, marginalized them in the United States socially, and increased conflict between the two groups (a topic to be discussed in the next chapter).

Coping with the Stigma of Being Iranian: Identity Politics, Identity Crisis, and the Emergence of a New, Less Threatening "Persian" Identity

The importance of groups and the extent to which they exert influence over our lives and constrain our behavior has been well documented by social scientists. Groups shape our self-concept and social identity. How we behave and what we experience is shaped by groups to which we belong. In short, groups shape nearly all aspects of our lives—perceptions, emotions, beliefs, motives, identities, and behavior—and regulate our interactions (Turner 2006).

Sociologists make a distinction between in-groups and out-groups. In-groups are the groups to which "we" belong and for which we have a sense of loyalty, attachment, and respect. Out-groups, on the other hand, are "those people," that is, other groups to which we do not belong. Often members of out-groups are collectively devalued, even disliked or scorned. Research on group dynamics indicates that individuals tend to value, trust, and discriminate in favor of their in-group members. Moreover, people identify very strongly with their in-groups and use their membership as a source of pride and self-worth (Jones 2002). If groups are the principal source of our self-worth and social identity, then what happens to members of devalued groups such as Iranians? How do stigmatized groups maintain relations with other groups in society? How do stigmatized groups perceive the dominant groups? What is the impact of stigma on the collective identity of stigmatized groups? How do discredited groups and their members, such as Iranian immigrants in the United States, cope with their devalued identity and the shame of stigma? How do they minimize the injuries caused by the stigma, prejudice, and discrimination associated with it? To answer these questions and to understand the predicament of Iranians and the impact of unfavorable stereotypes perpetuated by media on their in-group and out-group relations, it is important to understand the concept of stigma and its effects on stigmatized individuals and groups developed by Goffman (1963) and Allport (1958).

In a classic analysis, sociologist Erving Goffman traces the meaning of the word "stigma" to its Greek origin, which denotes "bodily signs designed to expose something unusual and bad about the moral status of the signifier" (1963:1). As Goffman suggests, stigmas can be based on membership in devalued racial, ethnic, or religious groups or what he called tribal stigma; abominations of the body such as physical disabilities; or blemishes of individual character such as addiction and imprisonment. Once an individual is discredited and stigmatized in the eyes of others, the person is perceived only in terms of that stigma. Thus, the stigma determines the person's overall position in society and assumes a "master status" that pervades all aspects of the individual's interaction in society. As explicated by Goffman, "an individual who might have been received easily in ordinary social intercourse possesses a trait that can obtrude itself upon attention and turn those of us whom he meets away from him" (3).

Besides discrediting the individual and assuming master status, stigmas can have many other harmful effects on stigmatized individuals and groups and create certain traits among them. Allport (1958) terms these 55 "traits due to victimization" or "persecution-produced traits" and enumerates the varieties of damaging social and psychological effects of stigmatization including 1) deep feelings of anxiety, suspicion, and insecurity; 2) denial of belonging to and membership in the minority group; 3) passivity and withdrawal from social interaction; 4) jesting and making facetious remarks in order to be accepted by the dominant group; 5) slyness and cunning; 6) self-hate and a tendency to identify with the dominant group; 7) hostility against one's own group and blaming it; 8) passing on of the prejudice and discrimination by using it against other minorities; 9) excessive neuroticism; 10) self-fulfilling prophecy brought about by internalization and acting out of the derogatory social definition and stereotypes; and 11) excessive urge to strive for status to compensate for the feelings of inferiority.

To minimize the extent of injury or suffering, Goffman maintains that stigmatized individuals or groups respond in a number of ways. They can correct what they see as the main source of the failing and difficulty, as when a physically deformed individual undergoes plastic surgery. Although such a strategy is just a transformation of self and not an acquisition of fully normal status, it indicates the painfulness of the situation that leads the stigmatized person to take such extreme measures. Another coping strategy Goffman finds is withdrawal by encapsulating oneself within a group of individuals who share the same stigma. Finally, a stigmatized person may employ the strategy of identity control so that the stigma will not be perceived by others and the stigmatized person is able to "pass." Disguising identity through information control may or may not be effective. If it is not effective, the person may attempt to convert the stigma into a lesser form.

Many first- and second-generation Iranian immigrants in the United States experienced some of the social and psychological effects of stigmatization specified by Goffman and Allport in varying degrees during the hostage crisis and to some extent after the 9/11 attack and adopted the coping mechanisms outlined by Goffman. The most terrible outcomes, however, were social isolation and marginalization; lessening of social interaction with Americans beyond work; deep feelings of social and political insecurity and vulnerability; denial of being Iranian; development of pessimistic and cynical attitudes toward other Iranians and the Iranian community; and strong feelings of social and psychological detachment from

American society. These feelings and experiences are best captured in the following words from Ali Behdad, an English and comparative literature professor at the University of California–Los Angeles. Behdad expresses his feelings about being Iranian and explains the protective and survival strategies he utilized during the hostage crisis:

> For so long I did not have a sense of national identity. You know that the Iranians of my generation who came to the United States have a particular kind of shame. . . . To be Iranian was marked for people of my generation in this country by the hostage crisis, the way we were ashamed of our Iranianness. I did not cook anything Iranian until about four or five years ago. I didn't have any Iranian things as I now do anywhere in my apartment. It was not until two or three years ago that I celebrated Norooz and put out the Haft Seen. Those are elements of culture that were being repressed. When I wanted to go out and socialize with people during the hostage crisis I would say I was Afghani, I was Italian—anything so as not to say I was Iranian. I was ashamed to own my Iranianness. (In Sullivan 2001:249)

To manage their stigma and feelings of self-hatred, shame, inferiority, and insecurity as well as the deep American antipathy toward Iran and Iranians in the United States, Iranians exercised many of the strategic options outlined by Goffman and Allport and described by Ali Behdad in the foregoing quotation. Some Iranians, including many young immigrants of the "1.5 generation" (second-generations who immigrated under the age of thirteen), opted to alter of their physical appearance. Others altered their Iranian names or adopted second, Americanized versions of their names. Still many others repressed their cultural and national identity, avoided public practice and display of their culture, maintained very low ethnic and national profiles, minimized collective visibility as a group, and escaped from participation in and public support of community events on various occasions. Furthermore, they either lied about their national origin or started to call themselves "Persians" or "Persian Americans."

Ansari's field observations (1992) during his research indicate that because of all the negative characterizations, many school-aged Iranians asked their parents to buy them green contact lenses so they would look like non-Iranians. "Acting white" to blend in and altering one's physical body to cope with the stigma attached to being Iranian in a "racialized" society have not been limited to young Iranian children. In a more recent study among Iranians in Southern California, Mostofi (2003) finds that

Iranians alter their bodies through plastic surgery, tinted contact lenses, and diet and various other cosmetic changes such as dyed hair and plucked eyebrows so they can "whiten" their bodies and construct a new identity to facilitate their assimilation and economic success. Although Mostofi does not provide any tangible statistics to show the extent of cosmetic surgery among Iranians in Southern California, she says that "for Iranian-Americans, the 'whiter' the body, the more attractive the appearance, and the greater the ability for assimilation of the public face, which translates to success" (694).

Adopting Americanized names has been another stigma management strategy for many Iranians. Blair's study "Personal Name Changes among Iranian Immigrants in the USA" (1991) reveals that although traditionally Iranians seldom change their names, many in Los Angeles, especially women, adopt an unofficial American name. A significant factor affecting the Americanization of their names, Blair notes, is competition against Americans in the mainstream job market. In addition to changing their physical appearance and adopting American names, many Iranians have either masked their national identity and constructed a new, less stigmatized, and more esteemed identity such as Persian or presented themselves to others in terms of their subnational and subreligious heritage such as Armenian or Baha'i rather than their Iranian national origin. Flora Keshishian, an Iranian professor of Media Studies at Queens College of the City University of New York, expresses this experience and strategy in an autobiographical account (2000). As a member of a religious minority group in Iran, Keshishian describes the dilemma of masking her national identity during the hostage crisis:

> When asked about my nationality, I often told people I was Armenian. I did not lie to them because I am Armenian by ethnicity. But, sadly, I did leave out the Iranian part of my identity, even though Iran is the country where I was born and grew up. I found it too isolating to associate myself with the image I knew people would have as soon as they heard the word Iran. (101)

Although nearly three decades have passed since the hostage crisis and the anti-Iranian backlash, Iranophobia—although in a new context and under a different pretext—is still prevalent in the United States. Therefore, Iranian immigrants in the United States are still victims of the same old stereotypes and stigmas, suffer from the same emotional and social fears as they did before, and rely on the same self-protective strategies for survival. After the 9/11 attack and media propagation of unsubstantiated political charges against Iran as part of "the axis of evil," sponsoring terrorism, failing to cooperate with international atomic energy agencies for the development of its nuclear energy technology, and interfering with the peace process in the Middle East, there was a resurgence of anti-Iranian sentiment in the United States. Once again, the U.S. government targeted Iranians as a suspect immigrant group and, along with immigrants from twenty-nine other Muslim countries, subjected them to a special registration procedure with the NSEERS procedures of the INS. Reminded of their situation during and after the hostage crisis, Iranians as a group continue to feel insecure and detached from American society in general and uncomfortable being associated with Iran and identified as Muslims. Nearly half of the 507 Iranian respondents who participated in my Texas survey indicated that since 9/11 they have felt socially and politically insecure.

Today, many Iranian immigrants continue to opt to conceal, misrepresent, or lie about their national origin and ethnic identities. They have disassociated from the Islamic Republic of Iran and all it represents, including the Islamic faith, and have altered their presentation of self so as to exclude claims or acknowledgment of Iranian and/or Islamic identity. As a young day care teacher in Dallas put it, "Iranians don't want anyone to know that they are Iranian. Some of them get offended if you ask them whether they are Iranian or not." A fifty-eight-year-old Iranian schoolteacher from Dallas said,

> Iranians are very kind and warm-hearted, but unfortunately they try to keep distance from other Iranians. They avoid speaking Persian in public stores, so they can hide their identity.

A forty-three-year-old Iranian restaurateur who had been living in Houston since 1978 spoke of Iranians' loss of identity and added,

> I don't care for the Iranian community in Houston. Since the revolution, Iranians have changed their national and cultural identity. They are no longer the same people as they were before the revolution.

Concern about ethnic and religious identity loss was also expressed by a thirty-five-year-old Iranian medical student from Houston:

> We will never be accepted by Americans, particularly after the 9/11 event. Unfortunately, many Iranians have lost their cultural heritage and pride. Opposi-

tion to the Islamic Republic of Iran has mistakenly led many Iranian nationals to be alienated from their culture, country, and religion.

Finally, the feeling of many of the respondents was summed up by a thirty-five-year-old married Iranian who had been living in Houston for four years:

> Most Iranians in Texas are uneasy about being identified as Iranians. In fact, they prefer to be more identified as Iranian American than just Iranian.

As reflected in the foregoing comments, Iranian immigrants use a variety of strategies to cope with their "tribal" stigma and protect themselves. While some members of the Iranian community continue to identify themselves as Iranian, an increasing number identify themselves as Persians. Still others alternate among Iranian, Persian, Persian American, Iranian American, and American Iranian, depending on the situation and the audience. A little over 21 percent of respondents in my sample of 510 Iranians in Texas identified themselves as Persians. Another 8 percent chose a Persian American or Iranian American ethnic identity in their interactions with non-Iranians. Similar findings have been reported by other Iranian scholars and study groups in the United States. In an online survey of 3,880 Iranian men and women ages thirty-five to forty-nine conducted by the Iranian Studies Group at MIT from January to March 2005, only 44 percent of respondents indicated that they identified themselves as Iranians. Another 46 percent identified themselves either as Persian (26 percent), American (2 percent), or a combination of Persian/Iranian American (18 percent). The remaining 10 percent had a flexible and fluid identity and switched among Persian, Iranian, and Iranian/Persian American "depending on the situation."

Although despised by many community members, ethnic switching and veiling national identity among Iranians has been such a common practice that it is now the subject of jokes and a punch line for Iranian stand-up comedians like Maz Jobrani. In one of his shows a few years ago, widely circulated among Iranians through the YouTube Internet site,[4] Jobrani, a second-generation Iranian, provoked laughter in his audience by indicating how Iranians mask their national identity:

> It is not a good time to be from the Middle East. Iranians have learned how to deal with it. We have learned how to trick Americans. We say we are Persians. It sounds a lot nicer and exotic and it confuses Americans, you know. We are

always like, I am not Iranian, no, no, no. I am a Persian. . . . I am not axis of evil, no, no I am Persian, like the rug, I am soft.

Political Opponents, Iranian Exile Media, Anti-Islamic Narrative Construction, and Birth of a Non-Islamic Persian Identity

Although Jobrani's comic punch line about switching national identity from Iranian to Persian appears to be a novel self-protective practice for many Iranians that confuses and deceives Americans, it is nevertheless a conscious political and ideological statement made by many opponents of the Islamic Republic of Iran in exile. In other words, veiling ethnic or national origin by adopting the "Persian" or "Persian American" ethnic label by many Iranians is not just a coping strategy for protection against any potential social and psychological harm in the United States. It is also part of a new narrative framing and a political reaction to the consequences of the "cultural trauma" of the Islamic revolution in Iran in 1978 and Islamization of the Persian/Iranian culture. This narrative has been constructed, conceived, narrated, and perpetuated by disenchanted Iranians in exile—mainly royalists and supporters of the former regime of the shah. Before I discuss the link between the Iranian revolution and construction of a new, non-Islamic Persian identity and narrative in exile, it is important to provide a brief overview of "cultural trauma" theory.

In *Cultural Trauma and Collective Identity* (2004), Alexander and his colleagues define cultural trauma as "a horrendous event that leaves indelible marks upon the consciousness of members of a collectivity, and changes their identity fundamentally and irrevocably" (1). Cultural traumas can be generated in multiple ways: peaceful or violent encounter of diverse cultures; spatial mobility of people as emigrants and refugees; fundamental institutional or governmental changes through reforms or revolutions; and change of ideas, beliefs, creeds, and doctrines through acquisition of new knowledge. Revision of established historical accounts and exposure to new ideas can result in tension and the breakdown of cultural stability, continuity, and identity of a people. In developing a social constructionist theory of cultural trauma, Alexander et al. maintain that regardless of its source, events do not in and of themselves create collective trauma. What makes an event traumatic is not so much the experience of pain. Rather, it is the acute, socially constructed discomfort that enters into the core of the collectivity's identity and threatens its identity, past, and future. In other words, for any traumatic event to emerge at a collective level, it first must be constructed, represented, and conceived as a social crisis, a cultural crisis, or both.

The social construction of trauma is carried out by collective actors through cultural and institutional processes in a way that signifies the threatening impact of the trauma on the collective identity of the group. While social/structural traumas massively affect arenas of social structure and lead to the breakdown of social institutions, cultural traumas undermine or overwhelm one or several essential ingredients of a culture such as values, norms, outlooks, beliefs, and ideologies. As indicated by Sztompka (2004), the cultural domain is more sensitive to the impact of trauma because culture contains the heritage, tradition, and identity of human communities as well as injuries inflicted upon a culture that are most difficult to repair and emerge as cultural scars. The normative chaos, or "anomie,"[5] caused by cultural trauma tears the social fabric of a group and creates a dramatic loss of identity and meaning for them. It leaves indelible marks upon the consciousness of the group and marks its members' memories permanently in irrevocable ways.

The social construction of cultural trauma involves telling a new, compelling story or "master narrative" to the audience-public by "cultural carrier groups"—collective agents or specialists of the trauma process—about a horrible, destructive social process and a demand for reparation and reconstitution. Carrier groups may be elites, politicians, intellectuals, journalists, moral entrepreneurs, leaders of social movements, denigrated and marginalized classes, prestigious religious leaders, or groups whom the majority has designated as spiritual pariahs. Given both their ideal and material interests, the carrier group deliberately establishes a claim of traumatic cultural damage and persuades the wider audience members that they too have been traumatized by an event. Moreover, the carrier group needs to provide compelling answers to the nature of the pain, the nature of the victim, the relation of the trauma victim to the wider audience, and an attribution of responsibility. In creating a compelling trauma narrative it is critical for the carrier group to establish the identity of the perpetrator, the "antagonist." In most cases production of a master narrative of social or cultural suffering is a contested process that involves debates among various political groups regarding the legitimacy of the trauma, its meaning, and the kinds of feelings—pride, humiliation, rage, guilt—it should arouse. As indicated by Smelser (2000:38), "Once a historical memory is established as a national trauma for which the society has to be held in some way responsible, its status as trauma has to be continuously and actively sustained and reproduced in order to continue in that status." The creation, representation, and perpetuation by carrier groups of a master narrative of cultural trauma can occur in various institutional realms mediated by the distribution of material resources and the social networks available to them.

Acting as a carrier group, opponents of the Islamic Republic of Iran from various political backgrounds not only played a crucial role in constructing a historical memory and a compelling traumatic master narrative of the Iranian revolution but also represented it as a horrendous event that destroyed the cultural stability and national identity of the Iranian people inside and outside of Iran. In their struggle against the Islamic government, political dissidents and critics of the Iranian regime, particularly the pro-shah royalists and advocates of monarchy, criticized the postrevolutionary Islamization of Iran and praised Reza Shah and Mohammad Reza Shah Pahlavi for modernizing Iran in the twentieth century. In their view Pahlavi's social and political reforms accelerated Iran's progress toward modernization. These reforms not only reestablished Persian national identity, resurrecting the pre-Islamic civilization of ancient Persia, but also glorified Iran and modernized the country. Since the revolution, opponents of the Islamic government assert, the government has Islamicized Iran, promoted the religious ideology and an Islamic identity of Iranian society, made Iran a backward country, destroyed the glorious Persian culture and heritage, and damaged the Iranian national identity domestically and internationally.

Mediated through the Iranian exile media, especially Iranian television networks in Southern California financed by monarchist political activists and elite members of the previous government, the Iranian carrier group has played a major role in narrating the Iranian revolution as a horrendous event, portraying the Iranian regime as an enemy government, and manufacturing, revitalizing, and promoting a non-Islamic Persian national identity among Iranian expatriates. As Naficy suggests (1998), exile ethnic pop subcultures have a dual function of guiding exile communities to make a transition from liminality to incorporation into the host culture and of providing a means for the preservation of ethnic culture and the expression of resistive, subversive, and oppositional ideas. Dominated by secular anti-Khomeini royalists who support a form of constitutional monarchy, Iranian television and radio programs produced in Los Angeles have served as an important ideological tool against the Islamic Republic of Iran and the chief purveyors of the non-Islamic Iranian national identity. As part of constructing a secular national identity, Naficy finds, recurring images of a pre-Islamic or prerevolutionary Iran are frozen into icons and continuously circulated in television program titles and logos, in music video images, and in the programs themselves. Discussions about the increasing deterioration of social and political conditions in Iran, treatment of political dissidents, and loss of national dignity and international respect under the Islamic government are a central feature of Iranian media in exile.

The interplay of politics, media, and ethnic identity formation as well as the link between the political forces in Iran and the United States and the deliberate construction of an anti-Islamic narrative both in American and Iranian media in exile point to the complexity of Iranians' ethnic identity. This interplay indicates that the question of ethnic identity is not only a contested and problematic issue for many Iranians but also a politicized issue that is far more complex than something rooted simply in national origin. For many Iranians, particularly the pro-monarchy opposition group, ethnic identity is linked to and shaped by culture but perhaps more importantly by political orientation toward the current and the prerevolutionary governments in Iran. The 1978–1979 Iranian revolution seems to have been the most important historical event in shaping Iranians' collective memory and ethnic identity in exile. Although not all Iranian immigrants suffered from the postrevolutionary changes or experienced anti-Iranian actions in the United States, there is a notion that every Iranian living abroad is a political or economic refugee who has been a victim of the 1978 Iranian revolution and the political relations between the United States and the Islamic Republic of Iran since then. As discussed before, the anti-Islamic images perpetuated by Iranian media in exile, the deterioration of postrevolutionary Iranian society, and the rise of political opposition and activism against the Islamic Republic of Iran have contributed to the emergence of Persian ethnic identity among Iranian immigrants in the United States. The amplification of Islamic values and rituals or Islamization of Iranian culture by the new government has enhanced Persian ethnic consciousness and Persian pride among Iranians. Thus many Iranians in exile have chosen to undermine Islamic traditions and celebrations, highlight the pre-Islamic Persian heritage, and opt for a non-Islamic Persian ethnic identity.

Social scientists have argued that ethnic identity is contextual, situational, socially constructed, and fluid.[6] As noted by Nagel (1994), ethnic identities and ethnic boundaries are influenced by external political, economic, and social forces and formed through a dialectical process between internal and external forces as well as the subjective ethnic identification and labels designated by outsiders. The shift between subjective "optional" (internal) and objective "mandatory" (external) ethnic identification and the relationship between the two depend on the audience and the availability of socially and politically constructed "ethnic options" or labels for ethnic groups. Lyman and Douglas (1973) find that this process involves ongoing individual negotiations and strategies in the production of ethnic boundaries or mechanisms of group differentiation. They note that as a "mental state" and a strategy in social encounters, ethnicity, ethnic identity, and ethnic boundaries must be invoked and affirmed by the "ethnic actor" in order to retain social relevance in social situations.

Considering the fluidity of ethnic identity and its construction in response to external political and social forces as discussed by Nagel (1994), it seems plausible to argue that such a powerful, traumatic political event as the hostage crisis and the subsequent widespread discrimination and prejudice against Iranians were the impetus for the birth and popularity among Iranians in the United States of a set of ethnic labels including Persian, Persian American, and Iranian American. As audiences changed, so did Iranians' ethnic choices. In other words, Iranians' presentation of ethnic identity has been fluid, particularly with the element of religious affiliation, depending on where and with whom they were interacting.

Politics, Ethnic Identity Renewal, and the Iranian Community in Exile

Political construction and perpetuation of a non-Islamic or anti-Islamic Persian national identity by opponents of the Iranian government coupled with the continued Islamophobia of American society has had an impact on Iranians, particularly Iranian Muslims, and their community in exile in a number of significant ways. First, there has been a sharp rise in the number of nonpracticing Iranian Muslims and Iranian-born Muslims who have converted to Christianity.[7] Nearly half (46 percent) of Muslim respondents in my survey indicated that they are nonreligious and do not practice Islam. MIT's 2005 Iranian-American Community Survey results indicate the same secular shift among Iranian Muslims in exile. One of every three Iranians in MIT's survey self-identified as agnostic (33 percent) and another 9 percent as atheist. The proportion of respondents claiming to be spiritual with no organized religious affiliation was 21 percent. Moreover, of the 49 percent Muslim participants in the survey, slightly more than half of the respondents indicated that they did not practice Islam, and another 10 percent said they were not comfortable practicing Islam in the United States. In a study of Iranian immigrants in Los Angeles, Sabagh and Bozorgmehr (1994) attribute the secularization of Iranian Muslims to the marked selectivity in their urban origin, high social class, exile status, and secularism in Iran before migration.[8] A large number of Iranians in the current study were secular and shared some of the selective secular traits identified by Sabagh and Bozorgmehr. However, I believe the diminishing religiosity and neglect of religious habits and conventions among them have been more an adaptive response to a combination of the prevailing Islamophobic and anti-Iranian attitudes in the United States than a function of their selective premigration characteristics.

In addition to an increase in the number of nonpracticing Iranian Muslims, many Iranians, notably the anti-Khomeini critics, not only have become resentful of Islamic teachings and faith but also confess their strong, blasphemous, anti-Islamic sentiments ostentatiously and openly in various regular television shows and print media. They condemn and attack Islam as a fanatic religion that is inconsistent with modernity and progress, they look down upon practicing Muslims in exile, and they are suspicious of Islamic centers and their activities. They believe these centers are financed by the Iranian government and run by sympathizers and faithful supporters of the Islamic Republic of Iran. During my fieldwork in Houston in 2004, I witnessed a demonstration organized by pro-shah royalists to protest the Iranian regime in front of an Islamic mosque where religion and language classes are offered regularly and a small number of Iranians occasionally attend during important religious holidays. Many whom I interviewed told me that the Islamic mosque in Houston should be shut down because it is financed by the Iranian government and gathers supporters of the Islamic Republic of Iran.

The tendency for anti-Khomeini critics to link Islamic centers and devoted practicing Muslims with the Iranian government has prevented those who do not particularly defend the Islamic regime in Iran from supporting these centers financially and participating in their gatherings and activities. Therefore, despite their rejection of the current agenda of the Islamic Republic of Iran, practicing Iranian Muslims as a group have less visibility in the community. Practicing Iranian Muslims who attempt to maintain their religious identity and faith, particularly women who wear the *hijab* (traditional Muslim hair covering), worry about being labeled *hezbolahi* (Shiʿa fundamentalist) and sympathizers of the Islamic government. Fear of hostile reactions by anti-Khomeini critics and concerns about being viewed as sympathizers of the Iranian government have consequently impelled many practicing Muslims to suppress and withhold public expression of their religious identity. Furthermore, these concerns have marginalized practicing Muslims and pushed them into the periphery of the Iranian exile community, as if there are two unequally distinct Iranian communities—one subordinate Islamic and one dominant secular—in exile.

Another detrimental impact on the Iranian community in exile of the construction of a new, non-Islamic, Persian national identity by opponents of the Islamic Republic of Iran has been the intensification of political and ideological conflicts and debates over national identity among various Iranian interest groups and a major setback in the emergence of solidarity among Iranians in exile—the single most frequently expressed complaint by Iranian immigrants. Opposition to the Iranian government and to Islamization of Iranian society in the past thirty years has had a dual consequence. This opposition has heightened Iranians' sensitivity to Islamic teachings and practicing Muslims; it also has led many community organizers and opponents of the Islamic Republic of Iran in exile to deemphasize Islamic celebrations and rituals and criticize or condemn participation in Islamic gatherings and support for Islamic centers and their activities. For most opponents of the Iranian regime and critics of Islam, Persian rituals and folkways, not Islamic rituals and celebrations, are central features of Iranian national identity and cultural heritage. As such, instead of recognizing and commemorating all Iranian ceremonies including the Islamic holidays and celebrations, community organizers and secular ethnic associations selectively glorify and publicize the communal celebration of non-Islamic Persian cultural festivals and deliberately promote a non-Islamic Persian national identity.

The intentional discrediting of Islam and devaluation of its overall impact on Iranian society and culture by pro-monarchy opponents of the Islamic Republic is not only a form of cultural and political resistance against the hegemonic Islamic policies of the Iranian government but is also a critical element in the creation of a master narrative that legitimates their claim regarding reconstruction and reconstitution of the prerevolutionary monarchy and serves as a political tactic to discredit other alternative political organizations in exile with an Islamic ideology, including the *mujahedin*.

Unlike the Persian nationalists who advocate a national identity based on Persian heritage devoid of Islamic roots, other Iranians define themselves through a combination of religious (Islamic) and cultural (Persian) features. They believe that irrespective of the current practices of the Iranian government and the outcomes of the Islamic revolution, Islamic values and teachings have been part of Iranian culture for the past 1,400 years and Islam is inseparable from Iranian culture. To them, Persian cultural traits and the Islamic religious practices are distinct but indivisible dimensions of Iranian collective identity. Therefore, being a Muslim and participating in Islamic rituals is as meaningful to them as celebrating non-Islamic Persian festivals.

The debate concerning the basis for Iranians' ethnic and/or national identity between the advocates of non-Islamic Persianists and those who endorse an ethnic and/or national identity based on a fusion of Islamic tradition and Persian cultural heritage on the one hand and political rivalry between supporters and opponents of the prerevolutionary monarchy government of the shah on the other hand has divided the Iranian community and contested ethnic identity designation and representation of Iranians in exile. During my fieldwork in 2003-2005 an Iranian center for religious and cultural activities in Houston where weekly Islamic lectures and forums, Persian language instruction, and music classes were offered was closed down because of a serious dispute between some board members concerning the extent and nature of Islamic activities and identity fostered by the center. After months of public confrontations (often aired on local Persian radio) between advocates of an entirely nonreligious cultural center and those who endorsed a multifunctional religious-cultural center and accusations on both sides of wrongdoing that led to a lawsuit, the court ordered the board of directors to sell the property and divide the assets equally for establishment of two distinct centers in Houston—one Islamic and the other cultural. Based on the court order, two separate foundations—one Islamic and one cultural, each with a completely different purpose and an independent board of directors—were created in 2007.

As indicted in its bylaws, the mission of the Iranian Islamic Foundation of Houston is to improve the understanding of Islam, shape the religious identity of second-generation Iranians by introducing them to Islamic values and cultural heritage, organize public events for the Iranian community in Houston, educate the public on Persian and Islamic civilizations and traditions, and engage in interfaith dialogue to promote Iranian Muslims as progressive, educated, and peaceful people. By contrast, as a secular organization, the mission of the Iranian Cultural Foundation of Houston is to promote appreciation of Persian culture, provide social and charitable services to the Iranian community, assist disadvantaged Iranians, celebrate Iranian holidays, and promote a deeper mutual understanding between Iranian and American communities.

These presumably religious and cultural divisions as well as debates over national identity and political and ideological clashes embedded in the

Iranian community have had considerable harmful consequences for Iranians and their communities during the past thirty years. These deep-seated tensions not only have divided the Iranian community but also have led to a strong sense of disappointment in and repugnance for their community among many Iranians. They have generated a feeling of hopelessness and apathy about the political future of Iran and about improving the social status of Iranians in exile, promoted and justified an extremely damaging and self-defeating belief about Iranian immigrants, and discouraged many Iranians from participating in and supporting community events and interacting with other Iranians beyond family and friendship circles.

3 Double Ambivalence and Double Detachment
The Paradox of Living in the United States

Making it in America is a complex process, dependent only partially on immigrants' motivation and abilities. How they use these personal resources often depends on international political factors—over which individuals have no control—and on the history of earlier arrivals and the types of communities they have created—about which newcomers also have little say. These complex structural forces confront immigrants as an objective reality that channels them in different directions.

Alejandro Portes and Ruben Rumbaut,
Immigrant America: A Portrait

To Love or to Hate Americans: First-Generation Iranian Immigrants and Images of the United States and American People

The prevailing anti-Iranian stereotypes in mainstream media and the discriminatory immigration policies against Iranians that began during the hostage crisis, coupled with the ongoing political tension between Iran and the United States since then, have had several damaging social consequences for Iranian immigrants and their interactions with Americans. First and foremost, they damaged Iranians' confidence in the American government and people and pushed many naturalized Iranians to be less interested in social issues of U.S. society and less involved in its politics. Second, they created a strong backlash among a majority of Iranian immigrants against Americans and made many of them ambivalent about American society and culture. Many Iranians became enormously disappointed in Americans and developed reverse prejudice and ethnocentrism toward them, denounced the American culture and way of life, and sharply criticized U.S. society on almost every level. Third, they heightened Iranians' social distance from Americans, discouraged them from developing close relationships with Americans and embracing their culture, and encouraged them to resist assimilation into U.S. society. Finally, they motivated many second-generation Iranians who were born and raised in the United States to self-identify less as Americans (a topic to be discussed in Chapter 4).

Research findings of my survey in Texas provide a telling description of Iranians' attitudes toward Americans and their feelings about living in the United States. When asked, "Do you feel attached to American society and culture?" 80 percent responded "never" or "very little." Only 20 percent of first-generation Iranians felt strongly attached to their host society. Consistent with this finding, two out of every three Iranians in Texas felt like foreigners and outsiders in the United States. Thus, it is no surprise to realize that close to two-thirds (62 percent) of Iranian immigrants in the survey pointed out that they had no or very little friendship association with Americans outside of the workplace. The acknowledged feelings of marginality and detachment of respondents in the survey—developed partly as a result of prevalent anti-Iranian attitudes of Americans—have provided fertile ground for the development of strong reverse prejudicial attitudes toward the United States and the American people among many Iranian immigrants in exile.

As indicated above, there are three distinct images (positive, very negative, and mixed) of the United States and its people in the minds of Iranian immigrants. With the exception of a minority of *optimist* Iranians who harbor a positive perception of the United States and view Americans as kind, warm, sociable, informal, honest, hardworking, and patriotic citizens, most Iranians are either deeply *ambivalent* and conflicted or bitterly hostile and *cynical* toward the United States and its people. While the ambivalent Iranians perceive Americans as honest but simple-minded, kind but misinformed, hard-working but wasteful, and resourceful but irresponsible, the cynical Iranians generally view American people as stupid, ignorant, naïve, selfish, hollow, unaffectionate, superficial, credulous, gullible, callous, ethnocentric, overconsumptive, and materialistic. These negative, often racist and ethnocentric assumptions, however, are politically motivated. The Iranians who harbor such negative sentiments toward Americans find them politically immature and unsophisticated, ignorant about global political issues, and continuously manipulated and misinformed by their government. It is noteworthy that most of these Iranian immigrants are themselves easy prey for conspiracy theories concerning the "invisible hands of the powerful elites" that are responsible for controlling and "brainwashing" Americans.

Cynics: Iranians Who Categorically Indict Americans

The following quotations, culled from extensive interviews and open-ended survey questions with Iranians in Dallas, Austin, and Houston, illustrate the frame of mind of Iranians who are bitterly critical of the United States.

A sixty-two-year-old woman from Houston who had lived in the United States since 1980 mixed her resentment of the country with a generous dose of conspiracy theories about the origins of the Iranian revolution of 1979:

> In my opinion Americans are the most foolish and ruthless people in the world. The closest thing they have to liberty is the Statue of Liberty, and even she has turned her back to the New York Harbor. As a professional woman who has worked in both Iran and the United States, [I can say that] I never felt as much sexism in Iran as I have experienced in this country. . . . I believe that as long as the CIA exists, this world will never be a safe place. If it were not for the American malicious foreign policy, we would have never had this dirty revolution imposed upon us.

The same anger toward the U.S. government and American people is expressed by a twenty-two-year-old female student who describes them as "people who have killed the Native Americans, Mexicans, blacks, and then the Japanese and Vietnamese and now the Arabs. These people are mostly savages."

An Iranian middle-age naturalized citizen and structural engineer presented a similar perception. He portrayed Americans as "TV-bound, closed-minded, unsophisticated, and wasteful." A young professional viewed Americans as

> very optimistic toward their government and their president. They do not want to accept that their elected officials in the past and present have made diplomatic mistakes in other societies and have harmed other countries politically. Television plays a vital role in forming their views.

Another Iranian informant pointed to what he perceived to be intractable racial problems in the United States: "Ultimately, this country is the territory of the white Europeans, and our place is not much above slaves. Political ignorance and insensitivity toward global problems is a major social issue here."

An Iranian artist who had been living in the United States for more than three decades describes the people of the United States as "uninformed about other societies and cultures. Money and only money plays the biggest role in their lives and most Americans consider money as the only source of happiness. It is a wasteful consumerist society."

Besides reproaching the American government for unfair and hostile treatment of minorities and imperialistic ambitions, many Iranian immigrants in this research accused the U.S. government of distorting the political news and using the media propaganda to keep Americans unaware of domestic and international political issues. Ignorance and manipulation of Americans at the hands of the government and media was the single most important disappointment the majority of Iranians expressed in their comments. The cynical Iranians perceive the U.S. government as a hostile, duplicitous, malevolent superpower with racist policies and imperialistic ambitions; they found Americans to have a very "young," "low," "decaying" culture obsessed with materialism and individualism and devoid of humanitarian and family values. The strong anti-media sentiments of many Iranians are reflected in comments such as in the examples that follow. It is noteworthy that even those Iranians with favorable sentiments toward Americans distinguish between the American society and American people, criticize the U.S. government, and critically reflect on the powerful role of media in shaping American public opinion. For example, an Iranian from Austin opined:

> Altogether Americans are good people. American society, however, is dominated by media's brainwashing power. There is no hope for Americans to be-

come informed about political realities outside of their country. They should not be blamed for being so closed-minded and racist.

A self-employed Iranian from Houston echoed this view:

> Americans are kind and simple people. Their simplicity, however, is a weapon in the hands of the politicians and benefits the capitalists. By controlling the television and other forms of media, politicians control Americans and shape their political views.

An Iranian from Dallas expressed the same viewpoint: "I believe the American people are very gullible and blindly faithful to their country and flag. They are indifferent towards other countries, and I think the U.S. government should be blamed for failing to educate Americans about other nations."

A fifty-three-year-old automotive engineer who had been living in Dallas for the previous twenty-nine years noted how Americans' ignorance caused by cliché TV images influenced their perceptions of foreigners and other nations and "makes them think all Iranians are terrorists." Many Iranians criticized Americans' disinterest and misunderstanding of the American political processes and democracy as well. A thirty-nine-year-old Iranian woman from Austin commented that the "American people are incredibly gullible; they blindly follow the so-called democratic laws, which are in reality capitalistic and autocratic. Americans are slaves without knowing it."

Another, from Dallas, said, "On the surface the United States is a democratic and free society, but in reality there is no democracy; and political freedom exists only for the elites and upper-class Americans. Americans have a very limited outlook on the global events and other cultures." The same view was expressed by a middle-age Iranian woman who had resided in Houston for the previous twenty years. She found Americans "chaotic, without any moral and humanitarian values . . . Americans have little knowledge regarding their own country."

As these comments illustrate, many Iranian men and women from various socioeconomic backgrounds and lengths of residence in the United States have a fairly unfavorable view of Americans in general and believe they are uninformed about their government and political processes both at home and abroad. An implicit assumption in these judgments is that Iranians are not only more mature and sophisticated but also politically astute. This naïve political arrogance is best captured in a comment by a forty-two-year-old manual worker from Houston:

> The American people have no desire to learn about political issues or issues and problems concerning other countries. A ten-year-old child from Iran is more familiar with global politics, political issues, and geography than an American with a graduate degree.

What perplexes and disappoints Iranians most about Americans' political amnesia is that despite the endorsement of freedom of speech, protection of democratic principles, and provision of vast amounts of intellectual and educational resources in the United States, Americans remain politically naïve and uninformed. American people's lack of political sophistication takes recent arrivals by surprise. A middle-age Iranian store clerk in Dallas stated:

> The American people are completely different from what I had imagined. Before I came to the United States, I thought Americans are well informed, insightful, and aware of political issues due to all the freedoms they have. Now that I am here, I am surprised to realize that they are completely uncultivated and clueless about what is going on in their country and in the world.

Optimists: Iranians Who Categorically Praise Americans

Not all Iranians are cynical toward the American government and mainstream media. In fact, there are other Iranians who focus on economic, social, civil, and technological advantages of the United States and perceive it as a land of economic opportunity, democracy, pluralism, individual freedom, religious tolerance, and material comfort based on the rule of law and protection of civil rights. Moreover, unlike the cynics, the optimistic Iranians view the American people as warm, sociable, informal, kind, and patriotic with a gracious attitude toward foreigners. They ignore or discount American foreign policy errors. A young professional woman from Houston described her positive experience:

> In my opinion the American culture is comprised of various cultures. Fortunately, in this country, we can adhere to our culture to any extent and any way we want without anyone stopping us. American people show interest in other cultures and religions and respect other cultures and religions. I am person-

ally glad to be living among these people. While I have my veil, I have a feeling of comfort and calm living in this society.

A young professional man who had been living in Dallas since 1995 said, "In general I like the American culture because of the individual freedom which exists in the society. People do not interfere in each other's business and respect each other's rights. American people, in general are gracious and patriotic people."

Finally, a young Iranian nurse from Houston compared the United States with Europe:

> I am happy that compared to European countries, racism and hatred towards foreigners does not exist in this country and I am happy to see that my children are able to achieve their goals and accomplish all they wish for. In general, Americans are good people and accept foreigners easier. In my opinion, this is a good country to live in. There's always an opportunity for advancement for everyone.

Ambivalents: Iranians Who Have Paradoxical Feelings toward Americans

Between the two extremes, the cynical and the optimistic views of the United States and its people, lies another significant group of Iranians who perceive both negative and positive qualities in American society and are, thus, ambivalent about the USA. Unlike either the cynics, who highlight only the negative features of American society, or the optimists, who see the United States as a great land of economic and social opportunities and political innocence, the ambivalent Iranians balance their political skepticism and distrust of the U.S. government with democratic principles, protection of individual and religious freedom, and opportunities for advancement provided in the United States. On the one hand, much like the politically disenchanted critical Iranians, the ambivalent Iranians are disappointed at American ignorance of domestic and global political issues and blame the media for keeping them in this state of mind. While the cynical Iranians are highly critical of the U.S. government and mainstream media, the ambivalent Iranians express more repugnance toward American culture and way of life. Many Iranians, particularly the refugees, repeatedly highlighted political and religious freedom as the best feature of American society. A forty-four-year-old Iranian woman from Houston who left Iran four years earlier commented:

The law is respected in the United States. In fact, America is the country of laws, and this is striking for Iranians because in Iran there is a vast discrepancy between legislation and enforcement of the law. Laws in Iran are written only in the books, and when it comes to maintaining, practicing, and enforcing them, there is a disparity. American culture is not rich, and Americans are uninformed about the rest of the world and domestic news. Media influence their thoughts and opinions easily and effectively.

A forty-six-year-old male said, "I like the execution of law in this country, but I don't really like American culture and way of life." A young professional woman who had been living in Houston since the Iranian revolution in 1978 stated:

I think the freedoms that people have in the United States is a feature that attracts people from all over the world to this country, and this is why people migrate to the U.S. in any way they can. American culture is not a very rich culture, and Americans express no humanity and kindness. This is getting worse with each generation.

A middle-age professor from Houston who had been in the United States for twenty-seven years expressed her ambivalence by saying, "Like other cultures, there are good and bad aspects. Americans have high standards of living but lack political awareness. That is why they are overpowered by their government."

Besides the views on civil liberties and individual freedoms, many ambivalent Iranians alluded to the economic opportunities and advanced technology as major strengths of the United States as well as to the general shallowness and gullibility of the populace as a serious problem of this society. A young homemaker from Dallas stated, "The United States is an advanced society with a strong economy. American culture, on the other hand, is empty and shallow. Americans are devoid of feelings and emotions." A sixty-year-old retired Iranian man from Dallas shared the same sentiment: "The United States is an advanced country, but the general population's level of political information is incredibly low."

A fifty-two-year-old insurance agent from Austin said, "The United States is a society based on the rule of law and respect for human dignity with unlimited opportunities for growth. Unfortunately, lack of discipline among the new generation and the availability of guns have made America increasingly unsafe."

As indicated in these comments, the attitudes of Iranian immigrants are far more critical—often ethnocentric—and ambivalent on the cultural level than their perceptions of U.S. society. Besides media propaganda and a lack of political awareness, materialism, consumerism, violence, excessive individualism, and erosion of family values were among other sources of Iranians' sense of ambivalence toward the United States. A young accountant from Austin commented:

> There are positive and negative aspects. Respect for human rights and legal protection of civil rights by the government are the most positive aspects of American society. Negative features include deterioration of family, dominance of capitalism, culture of consumerism, and overemphasis on individualism.

A female architect with fifteen years' professional experience in Houston said, "American people, as a whole, are good and honest people. American society, however, is diseased and wasteful. American culture seems to be lost as a result of being young [as a nation]."

A graduate student and electronics technician who also detested American culture reiterated that view:

> Americans are very decent people, but unfortunately, they are influenced by political propaganda in the news. They view foreigners through the eyes of conservative media and politicians, not their own eyes. I do not particularly like the American culture. There is too much waste and spending.

Concerns about materialism and consumer debt were also frequently voiced by many Iranian professionals in the study. A young nurse who moved to the United States more than fifteen years earlier referred to Americans as

> good people who accept foreigners easier, except for the ones who are racists. . . . The United States is a good country to live in. There is always an opportunity for advancement through legitimate means. Nevertheless, American society creates debtors; you have to be very careful and not use credit cards often.

A young computer engineer focused on inequality:

> American society suffers from a major class division. This is a capitalist society with an extremely materialistic population, encouraged to go after

money. American culture is made overnight and it is empty. Americans are very kind but are not very compassionate towards other human beings unless it is beneficial to them.

Abhorrence of materialism was echoed in another professional Iranian's comments: "American society is open and accepting, and Americans are generally kind people. I love the melting pot aspect of American culture but not the aggressive pursuit of materialistic goals."

A graduate student from Dallas touched upon another negative aspect of American society with views shared by a large number of ambivalent Iranians. Admitting that "societal freedom is the most positive aspect of the United States," he concluded his comment by specifying "individualism and the lack of family values as the most significant negative features" of American society. Finally, the ambivalent attitude of Iranian immigrants—regardless of their gender, age, professional status, and social class—in this study was summed up by a young Iranian from Austin:

> In general, I like American society because of the individual freedom which exists here. People do not interfere in each other's business and respect each other's rights. On the other hand, these people are very lonely and gullible. That is why I want to be an Iranian in the American society, not an American in the American society.

In addition to the open-ended questions about their feelings and beliefs about the United States and its people, a sample of which is presented above, I asked Iranian participants about the extent of their interactions with Americans outside of the workplace. Consistent with the noted comments, close to two-thirds of the 510 Iranians in the study indicated that they have no or very little interaction with Americans outside of the workplace. In a related question, about their level of attachment to and social status in the United States, nearly 75 percent of Iranians indicated that they feel like outsiders in America. Political behavior of Iranian immigrants is another noteworthy indication of their relative detachment from and collective apathy toward their adopted society. Despite the increasing number of Iranians who have become naturalized U.S. citizens, when asked whether they voted in the previous U.S. presidential election (in 2000), only 43 percent of the eligible Iranian voters who participated in the Texas survey responded "yes." Most first-generation Iranian citizens

in the sample who did not vote listed lack of interest in U.S. politics or belief in the conspiratory and ineffective nature of the voting process as their
main reasons. The number of Iranian citizens who participated in the political processes at the local and state levels was slightly higher, at 45 percent. The same reasons were listed again for refraining from casting their
votes. In the past several years, however, the number of Iranians who have
become more active in local politics has increased. Recent political mobilization of Iranians is discussed in the concluding chapter.

To Love or to Hate Iranians: Iranian Immigrants and Images of the Iranian Community in the United States

Does Iranians' sense of detachment and estrangement from American society, condemnation of American culture, and disengagement and alienation from the political affairs of American society suggest their commitment to the Iranian community in exile or a willingness to return to Iran?
Does it mean that Iranians have remained more "ethnic" in their orientation, and by staying on the periphery of American society they are preserving Iranian cultural heritage and resisting assimilation and integration?
Does Iranians' condemnation of the U.S. government and its discriminatory immigration policies against Iranians since the revolution mean that
Iranian immigrants have become united and developed an ethnic solidarity to protect their legal rights and promote their political interests? On the
contrary, as the following testimonies of respondents demonstrate, many
Iranians are as critical, prejudiced, and disappointed, if not more so, toward their own community and co-ethnics as they are toward the American society and people. Unfortunately, their levels of alienation from and
disappointment with the Iranian community seem to parallel their detachment from American society. With the exception of a small group who
held a sympathetic attitude, a majority of Iranian immigrants said they felt
tremendously dissatisfied and unhappy about their ethnic community in
exile and complain about interacting with other Iranians. A retired Iranian professor expressed his view on the Iranian community in Houston:
"Unfortunately, our social relationships are not good, and we have yet to
form a united organization that would bring all Iranians together regardless of their religious beliefs and political views."

A middle-age engineer from Dallas said:

Iranians are divided, distrustful, and alienated from one another. That is why they feel disinclined to unite, support each other, and work together collectively. Iranians have become politically impotent and are unconcerned about political events in Iran and the United States.

A young, married Iranian woman from Houston echoed the same concern: "The Iranian community in Houston has never been united, and Iranians have never been close to each other. Political and cultural activities are very low here."

One respondent referred to political factions in the community:

There are numerous Iranian groups, and every Iranian is a member of a particular group. Therefore, they will never be united as one single group. One group is pro-monarchy, another group is Mojahed, and the other group apathetic and detached. Everybody is after his own affairs, trying to make more money and improve his economic status. I have never seen any solidarity in the Iranian community.

A middle-age Iranian woman from Dallas also talked about political factions, social cliques, and lack of trust among Iranians:

Iranians don't support each other and refuse to cooperate with one another for the success of the Iranian community, and most of them believe that it is impossible to work with other Iranians. The Iranian community is very disintegrated and disordered, and each person interacts with other like-minded individuals. For example, some are leftist, and others are either pro-monarchy or practicing Muslim. No group accepts, trusts, or tolerates the views and beliefs of another group. They do not collaborate with one another to create an allied association with common goals. All Iranians suffer from loneliness.

The service manager of an auto dealership in Dallas stated, "Small political and social groups with a few members will not take us anywhere. Unfortunately, first-generation Iranians have reached a point that they wish to die in Iran."

The most serious problems Iranian immigrants complain about since the revolution appear to be ideological rivalries and a failure to create a unified political alternative in the diaspora by political opponents of the Islamic Republic of Iran; a lack of solidarity within the Iranian community; and the absence of a single, cohesive, secular, and nonpolitical association that would represent all Iranians and promote and protect their social, economic, and political welfare in exile. Widespread disunity among Iranians in exile, however, is not the only concern. Besides the strongly disparaging and unpleasant comments about ideological conflicts and lack of solidarity and its devastating consequences for Iranians in exile, many respondents in this study expressed dissatisfaction with other social aspects of the Iranian community and described it as unhealthy, lost and aimless, alienating, degrading, unwholesome, disjointed, disintegrated, unorganized, Americanized, materialistic, and undesirable. A young electrical engineer described the Iranian community in Dallas as "a community lost between two cultures." A married, middle-age sales clerk said the "Iranian community in Dallas is very unconcerned, uncertain, lost, purposeless, Americanized, and detached." When a fifty-two-year-old former professor from Houston was asked how he felt about the Iranian community in Houston, he responded bitterly: "The Iranian community is without substance, concerned with material success, and devoid of moral and human values. A hypocritical culture filled with ignorance, lack of knowledge, envy, and enmity has dominated the community."

A former Iranian diplomat who had lived in Dallas since 1977 described the Iranian community as "a lost bundle, up in the air with superficial social relations and no solidarity." A forty-two-year-old restaurant owner from Houston said:

I don't care about the Iranian community in Houston. Actually, ever since the revolution most Iranians have changed their face and are no longer the same people. Other than unrealistic expectations, discord, and in some instances fraud and deception, there is not much to see in the community.

An Iranian professional in Austin complained about Iranians' ungrateful attitudes toward the United States:

Most Iranian immigrants in the U.S. act as if America is indebted to them. Despite all the social and economic welfare that is available for Iranians in the U.S., people still talk bad about the U.S. in Iranian circles. In my opinion, ungratefulness is one of the worst traits of Iranians.

The pervasive critical attitude, discountenance, and disappointment of Iranian respondents in the survey were not limited to their community in general. When asked how they felt about other individuals in their local communities, except for a small minority of respondents who praised Iranians for their remarkable educational success, economic accom-

81

plishments, and friendly social manners, the vast majority of first- and second-generation respondents expressed the same, if not more, levels of pessimism, frustration, and disappointment about personal social relationships with other Iranians. Unlike the optimistic Iranians, who viewed their co-ethnics as successful, hardworking, educated, professional, entrepreneurial, socially conscious, caring, friendly, kind-hearted, determined, hospitable, vigorous, intelligent, eager to live a high-quality life, and devoted to and concerned about education and the manners of their children, pessimists expressed an exceedingly unpleasant feeling about other Iranian immigrants. They viewed Iranians as closed-minded individuals who were either culturally alienated and Americanized or lost between two cultures and described them as ill willed, two-faced, insincere, inquisitive, distrustful, unsupportive of Iranian businesses, uncooperative, disingenuous, rumor-mongering, emulous, untruthful, pretentious, judgmental, divided, self-indulgent, selfish, charlatan, uncaring, apathetic, unconcerned about social and political conditions in Iran, lost, ambivalent, suspicious, uncertain, dubious, confused, contentious, and disbanded. The pessimistic Iranians not only were discouraged about the attitudes and wary of the behavior of their compatriots but also avoided interacting with them.

These Iranians' negative feelings about their communities and compatriots are reflected in their stated preference to dissociate from other Iranians and avoid participation in community events. Describing why he refused to interact with other Iranians, a fifty-year-old professor who had been in Houston since 1976 stated:

> Iranians suffer from identity crisis. They feel no responsibility toward Iran and other Iranians. They only think about themselves. They have become a petrified, opportunistic group unconcerned about everything except their self-interest.

A young dissident, professional Iranian man described the Iranian community as a superficial, chaotic community and indicated that he preferred to "dissociate with other Iranians in Dallas because they are insincere and ostentatious." If some respondents had minimal interaction with other Iranians because they found them insincere, egocentric, and unconcerned about the feelings of other community members, many more preferred to distance themselves from other Iranians because of their opportunistic attitudes, ethnic identity concealment, and loss of cultural heritage and national identity—traits that are frequently associated with intra- and interethnic relations in public. A practicing Muslim Iranian woman from Dallas summarized her experience with other Iranians:

> Unfortunately, the Iranian society, with its rich and valuable culture, has forgotten everything, and it seems that they are ashamed of being Iranian. Individually all Iranians are successful, but why can't they work alongside each other to improve their situation and maintain a high status? If they see an Iranian woman wearing the veil, they keep their distance from her without even knowing her views. This is why, although I am Iranian and Muslim, my motto is "Bravo to Americans!"

An Iranian businessperson from Houston said:

> Upon entering Houston, most of the individuals I knew advised me not to have any contacts with Iranians as much as possible and to keep to myself and to not go to an Iranian to buy a car, a house, insurance, and avoid doing business with them. Each of them had interesting stories about the different ways they were cheated.

An Iranian woman who was very concerned about Iranians' loss of identity said, "Iranians are being pulled in two opposing directions by two completely different cultures, and they have lost or are on the way to losing their cultural identity."

Although many of the respondents' negative comments reflected general criticisms of Iranians and their communities in Texas, when specific questions were asked about Iranians in other parts of the country, California—where close to 50 percent of Iranians reside—bore the brunt of more criticism. A significant number of respondents in the survey stated that compared to those in Texas, Iranians in California, particularly in Los Angeles, were more crooked, phony, thick-headed, shallow, superficial, wealthy, assimilated, and Americanized. A substantial number of respondents said that although less educated and less affluent, compared to those in California, Iranians in Texas were less Americanized and more caring, authentic, and hardworking, with more respect and appreciation for Iranian cultural values. Many Iranians in Texas firmly believed that most Iranians in California were pro-shah royalists and monarchists who resembled the prerevolutionary upper- and upper-middle-class Iranian subculture and had benefited either from inherited wealth or from money taken out of the country when they fled the revolution. A middle-age Iranian woman from Dallas who had lived in several states shared her views:

"I think Iranians in California are not as kind as Iranians in Houston. Most of them are wealthy pro-shah individuals who are upset because they lost their power and wealth after the revolution." An Iranian man from Houston described Iranians in California as "very superficial" and added that "they have fallen in the trap of materialism and like to show off to other Iranians."

Double Ambivalence and Double Detachment: Cultural Clash or Political Conflict?

Why do so many Iranian immigrants have a feeling of double detachment from both American society and their own ethnic community? Why do so many Iranians with a relatively long-term residence in the United States have such a low opinion of their host culture and feel detached from the American society and people? What makes them so distrustful of the American government? How can we explain Iranians' reverse prejudice and ethnocentrism against Americans and their culture? What accounts for the blatant, sometimes racist, comments about the United States that were reiterated by numerous Iranians? What accounts for the ambivalence of Iranians about the United States, the coexistence of attraction and re-pulsion, acceptance and rejection, love and hate? Why, despite their im-pressive professional success, upward mobility, remarkable educational achievements, and residential integration into predominantly middle- and upper-middle-class neighborhoods, do so many Iranians feel marginal-ized or detached from American society and perceive themselves as out-siders in the United States? What are the consequences of detachment, ambivalence, and perceived marginal status on their relations with Ameri-cans? Furthermore, why do so many Iranians detest and renounce their ethnic community and hold other Iranians in low esteem and refuse to in-teract with them? What makes the Iranian community so repulsive that it is so unappealing to many first- and second-generation Iranians? Finally, what are the effects of this double loss, double marginality, and double re-pugnance on Iranian ethnic institutions, cultural heritage, community structure, and social status; and how do Iranians cope with this serious dilemma?

These and related questions have a long history in the race relations and migration literature and were among the central themes pursued by Robert Park, a major sociological analyst, and his students at the Univer-sity of Chicago in the 1920s and 1930s. Park's pioneering work on the race relations cycle and the marginal status of immigrants guided the scholarly research on immigrants' assimilation into their new society for several decades. Since Park's pioneering work, many race/ethnic relations scholars in the United States have adopted and made new and significant contributions to the assimilationist perspective. According to Park and his colleagues and students at the University of Chicago, new immigrants would eventually lose their cultural distinctiveness, gradually adopt the customs and attitudes of the prevailing culture, and "assimilate" into the host society. Park asserted (1964) that assimilation is a "progressive" and "irreversible" process that would remove "the external signs" such as patterns of speech, dress, manners, and food preferences that would distinguish immigrants from Americans. First-generation immigrants probably would not be able to make a complete transition to the new way of life, but their grandchildren, the third generation, eventually would make "progress" and become full members of the host society. Social problems of immigrants such as finding jobs, family and community disorganization, and conflict with members of the host culture, the Chicago social scientists argued, were inevitable temporary conditions on the path toward assimilation that would ultimately disappear.

Another inevitable outcome of a clash between the conflicting cultures of immigrants and the host culture is the emergence of the "marginal man." Marginal man is a new personality type, Park notes (1928), that struggles to live in two diverse conflicting cultures, to neither of which he quite belongs. Marginality, according to Park, results from a clash of cultures when migrants from one culture encounter another. Barred by prejudice from complete acceptance into the host culture and unable to sever ties with his own, the marginal man as Park saw him is betwixt and between his own culture and the new culture. For Park, the marginal man is a stranger and a cosmopolite with an unstable and "divided self." He is a "mixed blood" caught in permanent inner turmoil, instability, restlessness, and distress. He is in a marginal predicament because he is "a cultural hybrid, a man living and sharing intimately in the cultural life and traditions of two distinct peoples; never quite willing to break, even if he were permitted to do so, with his past and his traditions, and not quite accepted, because of racial prejudice, in the new society in which he now sought to find a place." A marginal man, Park continues, is a "man on the margin of two cultures and two societies, which never completely is interpenetrated and fused" (892).

Framed differently, Merton and Barber (1976) assert that ambivalence emerges not because of inner conflicting emotions, thoughts, and actions of individuals or their distinctive history and personality but because of social structure—a particular network of locations in social space. That is, the more distal causes of ambivalence are contradictory demands inherent in incompatible expectations, attitudes, beliefs, and norm-mandated behaviors. The status of Iranian Americans embodies a disjuncture between socially approved social roles and cultural values and the means for achieving them. According to Merton and Barber, "The ambivalence is located in the social definition of roles and statuses, not in the feeling-state of one or another type of personality" (7). They make a distinction between psychological and sociological ambivalence and note that unlike the psychological ambivalence that focuses on the inner experiences and psychic mechanisms released by efforts to cope with conflicting emotions, thoughts, and actions, sociological ambivalence focuses on the ways in which ambivalence is rooted in the structure of social statuses and roles. For Merton and Barber, a sociological theory of ambivalence is foregrounded in that psychological experiences mediate the causal impact of social structure upon ambivalent actions. Incompatibilities and inconsistencies in the social structure and the social situation in which the actors are located, not the personality, create ambivalence and engender personal tendencies toward contradictory feelings, beliefs, and behaviors.

Some major sources of ambivalence, Merton and Barber maintain, are incompatibilities and contradictory expectations embedded in social structure of a single status or a set of statuses, a particular role associated with a single social status, several roles associated with a particular status, cultural values held by members of a society, and culturally prescribed aspirations and socially structured means for achieving them. Another form of sociological ambivalence that can best be exemplified in the lives of immigrants, according to Merton and Barber, is orientation to differing sets of cultural values and normative expectations among people who have lived in two or more societies. In the past twenty years, many scholars have examined the experience of Iranian immigrants in the United States in light of theoretical assumptions of marginal man, assimilation perspective, and cultural differences and incompatibilities between the Iranian and American cultures. Iranians may exhibit some of the social and psychological symptoms of marginality as described by Park and Merton. Nonetheless, neither Park's "marginal man" and Merton's "sociological ambivalence" nor the various assimilation approaches adopted by scholars who have studied Iranian immigrants seem fully plausible explanations for understanding the double ambivalence of many Iranians about the U.S. government and people and the Iranian community in exile.

Despite their convincing theoretical explanations and potential application, these theories are inadequate and have limited relevance to the experience of Iranians in the United States for two main reasons. First, applying these theories would reduce the marginal status of Iranian immigrants and the ambivalence toward and detachment from their host society to differences in cultural values and norms, and it would overlook the powerful impact of political conflict between Iran and the United States and the external political conditions in Iran or hostile conditions triggered by the hostage crisis against Iranians in the United States to which I alluded in previous sections. To elaborate on this statement, a few points highlighted previously should be reiterated here. Immediately after the hostage crisis, the Iranian government was defined as deviant. Therefore, because of their ascribed national identity and affiliation with Islam and the Islamic Republic of Iran, Iranians' "spoiled identity," to use Goffman's terminology (1963), discredited and disqualified them from full social acceptance, assimilation, and complete integration. Furthermore, the insults, attacks, humiliations, racist agitations and restrictions, and propaganda against the Iranian government during and after the hostage crisis threatened the social identity of Iranian immigrants and excluded them from full participation in American society. Despite their impressive and remarkable educational, professional, and financial accomplishments, negative stereotypes and various subtle and unsubtle forms of discrimination and prejudice against Iranians not only separated them from the mainstream society but also created an "us versus them" feeling among them. Ignoring these harsh, macroscopic, sociopolitical conditions and their impact on almost every aspect of Iranians' life in the United States and relegating their intense feelings of ambivalence or detachment to divergent cultural practices would be an overly simplified approach concealing subtleties of politics as an influence on the integration of Iranian immigrants that has yet to be adequately explored and explained.

The second reason for the inadequacy of the marginal man theory and an assimilation approach in general and the theories of Park and Merton in particular with regard to the experience of Iranians in the United States rests on two sets of discrepancies. One is the discrepancy between the fundamental assumptions of these theories and the existing demographic profile of Iranian immigrants. The other is between the theoretical views of the assimilationist paradigm and the scholarly research findings regarding Iranians' level of assimilation and material success in the United States. For example, education, employment, length and pattern of residence, earning level, proficiency in the host language, and immigration status are important variables that traditionally have fostered the assimilation and integration of immigrants into their new host society. Migration scholars have traditionally used a combination of these indicators to measure the level of assimilation and integration of immigrant groups.

As indicated in the U.S. Census reports and findings of the data collected for this study, Iranians score high on almost all of these variables. As indicated in the 2006-2008 American Community Survey (ACS) reports produced by the Census Bureau, a remarkable characteristic of Iranian immigrants in the United States is their high rate of economic activity and labor force participation. About 65 percent of Iranians sixteen years and older are employed in the civilian labor force.[1] Except for approximately 4 percent unemployed, almost all the remaining 61 percent are in the civilian labor force, with more than 53 percent concentrated in management and professional occupations. The pattern of occupational concentration for Iranian men and women, however, is considerably different. Slightly over 55 percent of Iranian men were employed in managerial, professional, and related occupations. Next come sales and office occupations at almost 26 percent; production, transportation, and material moving occupations at 7 percent; construction, extraction, maintenance, and repair occupations at about 6 percent, and service occupations at 6 percent, as the largest concentrations of employment for Iranian men. Similar to men's employment, almost 51 percent of Iranian women in the labor force were engaged in management and related occupations. Unlike men, however, a much larger proportion of Iranian women was concentrated in sales at 31 percent and service occupations at 15 percent and a much smaller proportion, not quite 3 percent, in production and transportation.

Overall, slightly more than half of all Iranians in the United States were employed in management and professional occupations such as computer sciences, architecture, engineering, health care, and legal, educational, and community and social science occupations. The high concentration of Iranians in professional occupations is consistent with their remarkable and unusually high level of educational training. Almost 59 percent of Iranians over twenty-five years of age had a bachelor's degree or higher, and another 18 percent had either an associate's degree or some college education but no degree. This exceptionally high level of education is largely a result of the heavy influx of Iranian students to the United States in the late 1970s and early 1980s.

Furthermore, as revealed by the 2006–2008 ACS reports, many Iranians in the United States were affluent enough to make comfortable lives. The median household income for Iranians in 2008 was $69,377, while the national median was $52,175. The family incomes of Iranians were even more impressive than their household incomes. With a median family income of $86,087 in 2008, Iranian families ranked among the most affluent immigrant groups in the United States.[2] The fairly high income has affected Iranians' settlement patterns in the United States and has led to home ownership in predominantly middle- and upper-middle-class neighborhoods of major U.S. cities. As described in the 2006–2008 ACS reports, nearly 62 percent of Iranian immigrants were home owners and lived on properties with a median value of $553,800.

As for their language fluency, Iranians show a remarkable degree of English proficiency, undoubtedly linked to their high level of education. Although nearly 75 percent of Iranians spoke a language other than English at home, only 28 percent of Iranians over the age of five claimed that their level of English proficiency was less than "very well." The demographic data collected from a sample of Iranian immigrants in Dallas, Houston, and Austin are very consistent with the 2006–2008 ACS reports and reveal the same impressive findings about the socioeconomic status of Iranians in Texas.

The 2006–2008 ACS demographic reports suggest that as a group, Iranian immigrants either have successfully acculturated and assimilated into American cultural norms and values or have the potential and all the necessary resources and requisites for assimilation but refuse to do so. The first scenario does not seem to be plausible at all. If Iranians had already successfully assimilated and integrated into their host society, they would not only have had a deeper commitment to American society and the core values and beliefs of its culture but would also have felt less detached and marginalized in the United States. As discussed earlier, the research findings in this chapter suggest otherwise. In light of this paradox, the second scenario seems to be more probable and convincing. It seems that despite their impressive human capital, cultural familiarity, English proficiency, and potential for assimilation, Iranian immigrants spurn assimilation into the American way of life and embrace of its core values. This is particularly the case in their family relations, a topic to be discussed in detail in chapters 4 and 5. Instead, it appears that Iranians have selectively adopted and blended certain traits and patterns of American culture with Iranian culture and have created a unique hybrid Iranian American culture that resembles neither the Iranian nor the American culture.

Consistent with my argument, the disjuncture between the outstanding assimilation potential of Iranian immigrants and their detachment from American culture has been reported by a number of scholars. Using Gordon's model of assimilation, Barati-Marnani's research among Iranian immigrants in southern California (1981) indicates that they had low levels of cultural as well as identificational assimilation.[3] Although proficiency in English is instrumental for integration into American society, Barati-Marnani finds no correlation between English proficiency and level of assimilation among Iranians. In another study, Diane Hoffman (1990) explores the relationship between language use and acculturation among first-generation Iranians in the United States. Contrary to the common belief that immigrant groups that master the language of the host society lose at least some of the original cultural patterns and experience more acculturation, Hoffman's research reveals that high English proficiency among Iranians is linked neither to their greater acculturation nor to inner, deep commitment to "becoming American." Iranian immigrants, Hoffman maintains, use English more as a tool for participation in daily life and for avoiding "the culturally undesirable effects of standing out or drawing too much attention to oneself in the context of U.S. society."

Chaichian's in-depth interviews (1997) with first-generation Iranians in Iowa reveal the same disarticulation. He points out that despite their educational and professional success, appreciation for American secular and religious events and rituals, and socialization and intimate interactions with Americans of non-European origin, Iranian immigrants refuse to internalize the core values of Americans and blend into American culture, be acknowledged as Americans, or raise their children based on American cultural values. Another study conducted by Hoffman (1989) reveals the same findings. Iranians had a positive experience in adapting to American culture but were very selective and eclectic, while feeling detached from the host culture.

A more recent study by Mostofi (2003) among Iranians in Southern California regarding the perplexity of Iranian American identity suggests that Iranians in exile do not fit neatly onto a linear, American identity continuum. In her view, Iranians have successfully and selectively melded specific elements of Iranian and American cultures and constructed a mixed, dual, Iranian American identity based on notions of liberty and democracy rooted in American civic nationalism and Iranians' concept of family. While the Iranian component of this dual identity manifests itself in the private domain of the home through food and Iranian hospitality among close friends and family members, the American component is carried out in public interactions. Although many first-generation Iranians have established roots in the United States and have no desire to return to Iran, they still regard Iran as their "ideal home" and feel strongly connected and committed to Iran. Mostofi attributes the successful fusion of these two cultures among Iranian immigrants to the cultural links between Iran and the West since the late nineteenth century and the emergence of Westernized, middle- to upper-middle-class professionals in Iran before the revolution.

So, if these demographic variables are major indicators of assimilation and integration and if as indicated in the census data Iranian immigrants in the United States have an impressive and remarkably high achievement level on almost all of them, then why do so many Iranians feel marginal, detached, disconnected, and removed from American society and its people? Considering their overall high level of education and professional and financial success, high naturalization rate, proficiency in English, and residence in predominantly affluent non-Hispanic white neighborhoods, one would expect Iranians to have greater appreciation for American culture and be less contemptuous and scornful about American society. By the same token, if as postulated by advocates of assimilation theory immigrant groups with high levels of language fluency, residential integration, and successful adaptation suffer less from ambivalence, marginality, and cultural conflict, then it would also be reasonable to expect Iranians to experience less cultural conflict, ambivalence, and cynicism and to feel more attached to American society and its people.

What accounts for Iranians' retarded assimilation, selective blending of Iranian and American cultures, relative marginality, and ambivalence toward the United States and its culture? If as indicated in the literature, Iranians have relatively adapted and assimilated to some of the most general aspects of American culture, then why are they so conflicted about American society and living here? On the other hand, if most Iranians feel socially marginal and detached from American society and have infrequent interaction with Americans outside of their workplace, why do they not return to Iran or strengthen their ties with other Iranian immigrants and the ethnic community in exile? Finally, if cultural tension or orientation to differing sets of cultural values, as suggested by Park and Merton, respectively, does not seem to be the source of Iranians' cynicism and ethnocentrism toward American society and its people, then what is causing most Iranians to be so contemptuous and scornful about American society and their own exile community?

In my view, the marginal status and mixed feelings of love and hate for ambivalent Iranians toward American society as well as distrust of the U.S. government and strong beliefs about Americans' political ignorance and Iranians' detachment from their community in exile and dissociation with other Iranians are two sides of the same coin. Contrary to the fundamental premises of Park's assimilation and Merton's ambivalence theories, Iranians' double ambivalence appears to be linked neither to a collision between the Iranian and American cultures, cultural incompatibility between the two, the lack of assimilation, and cultural transition nor to simultaneous orientation to different sets of cultural values and normative expectations. Rather, the real source of Iranians' double marginality seems to be related to simultaneous rejection by both societies. If Iranians are members of both Iranian and American societies and participate in them and yet do not wholly belong to either, it is not because they are in transition but because they are simultaneously repelled from two hostile societies due to concurrent political confrontation and exclusion from each without options for either return or integration.

As indicated by Portes and Rumbaut (2006), policies of the receiving government, conditions of the host labor market, and characteristics of the ethnic community as well as the combination of positive or negative features experienced at each of these levels are the most relevant contexts of reception that can greatly shape the mode of incorporation for new immigrants. Government policies not only determine the immigration flows and the forms they take but also affect the likelihood of successful immigration with economic opportunities and available legal options. Governments can exclude immigrants and force them into an underground existence, passively accept and grant immigrants access without impeding or facilitating the migration process, or actively encourage a particular inflow or facilitate a resettlement of immigrants. Government support, Portes and Rumbaut maintain, is crucial because it provides newcomers with access to an array of resources that are not available for other immigrants. The interaction of government support with labor-market conditions of the host society and characteristics of the immigrant community can lead to very different outcomes. Government support and resettlement assistance and a generally positive public perception and reception can facilitate economic mobility and creation of a cohesive community for immigrants. By contrast, official persecution combined with widespread discrimination, hostility, and negative public contexts of reception can hinder upward mobility and lead to creation of impoverished communities with no social or material resources.

The hostage crisis and subsequent bitter political relations between Iran and the United States and the 9/11 attack on Americans demarcated Iranians' limit to inclusion and integration into American society. These events not only provided a negative official and public context of reception and disqualified Iranians from integration but also discredited and distorted their social identity. Moreover, the antagonistic political relations between Iran and the United States have disempowered Iranian immigrants socially and politically and subjected them to various subtle and unsubtle forms of prejudice, discrimination, and social injustice. The strong anti-Iranian attitudes of Americans and disparaging media images have suppressed the tendency and desire for integration among Iranian immigrants and retarded their integration. It was not possible for Iranians to be accepted and integrated in the United States or to return to Iran and tolerate the postrevolutionary conditions of war, economic disaster, and political crisis. Similarly, the ambivalence of many Iranians toward members of their own ethnic group and detachment from their community has been a reaction to their despised social status and intra-ethnic political tensions in exile. As indicated before, to cope with their "spoiled" identity many Iranians have concealed their ethnic background, minimized their social interaction with other Iranians, kept a very low ethnic profile, and remained detached from the community. Furthermore, the postrevolutionary political conflicts and ideological rivalries between various factions in exile have divided the Iranian community and fostered intra-ethnic hostility and wariness, particularly between opponents and supporters of the government. Intra-ethnic political tensions coupled with a stigma attached to Iranian identity have pushed many Iranians to avoid active participation in the community except for major national holidays such as the New Year celebration.

Psychologists contend that when people are constrained to staying in two undesirable situations, they will become immobilized partway between the two. Movement in either direction increases anxiety, and such decisions invite postponement and procrastination. The conflict of choosing between two options that are simultaneously attractive and repellent has been the predicament for many Iranian immigrants since the Iranian revolution.

4 To Be an Iranian, American, or Iranian American
Family, Cultural Resistance, and the Paradox of Ethnic Identity among Second-Generation Iranian Americans

Throughout the history of the United States, immigrants have seldom felt "as American as everyone else" because differences of language and culture separated them from the majority and because they were made painfully aware of that fact. Being "in America but not of it," even if they wished to, represents an important aspect of the experience of most foreign groups and a major force prompting ethnic identity in subsequent generations. The rise of ethnic pride among children of recent arrivals is thus not surprising because it is a tale repeated countless times in the history of immigration.

Alejandro Portes and Ruben Rumbaut,
Immigrant America: A Portrait

Three Life Stories
Jairan's Story

Jairan is an Iranian. In response to the question "Where are you from?" she promptly and concisely responds: "Iran." The equation (if we may call it such) is more complicated than that, however; to be precise, Jairan was born in 1983 in Ireland to a mother who finds her roots in the Bakhtiari Province of Iran and a father from a small village outside of the central city

of Isfahan. She was raised mostly in postrevolutionary Tehran with spo-
radic visits and slightly more prolonged stays in the United States until the
greater portion of her immediate family made two consecutive efforts to
move permanently to the United States. The second effort was successful,
and she moved to Pittsburgh to pursue a nursing degree.

If we had approached Jairan as recently as three or four years ago she
would have informed us, with a certain self-assuredness that hinted at an
underlying pride, that she had found it remarkably easy to adjust to each
move from one country to another. In fact, she would even claim to relish
the idea of packing up one night and shuffling out of Iran and arriving
halfway around the world within twenty-four hours. All major changes in
lifestyle and environment aside, the idea of literally *going* to another country fascinated and excited her. She was not a stranger to travel, either; her
father spent long expanses of time in other countries or en route to various
places on the globe. After his marrying and having children, his wife and
daughter (and eventually, son) became occasional cohorts, companions,
and tag-alongs in his travel routine. The fact that Jairan was born in Ireland became something of a hallmark, an odd idiosyncrasy that informed
some of the decisions she made later in life (like the yearning to learn Irish
step dancing, for example), and became a small factoid that others would
find amusing and surprising.

Near the time of Jairan's birth, her mother left Iran for Istanbul, Turkey, where Jairan's maternal grandfather was living at the time. This was
on the way to Dublin, the ultimate destination and also where one of Jairan's paternal aunts was, conveniently enough, living with her Irish husband and young son. After her birth and a brief four-month tenure in her
aunt's home in Ireland, Jairan and her mother returned to Iran, where her
Irish passport was immediately confiscated at the airport since she was already considered a citizen of Iran by proxy, and dual citizenship was not
permitted in the relatively young Islamic Republic. Coming back to Iran
meant that the family would have to adjust to the normal swing of things,
resuming a social life as well as beginning a new familial one. Naturally,
the constant exposure to Farsi through friends and relatives resulted in
Persian being Jairan's first spoken language. The critical years for infant
language acquisition were filled with the utterances of a mother and an
army of relatives (mostly paternal and coming from Isfahan for long stays)
who visited frequently and peppered the air with gossip, anecdotes, and utterances in general.

The somewhat curious aspect of Jairan's early childhood was the lifestyle led by her parents, specifically her father. His career mandated him

to be very mobile and a frequent traveler. This resulted in long periods of his absence and in many hours spent with her mother and grandmother. Her father's return would often signal a kind of abundance, with new toys, children's books, pockets full of strange currency, and (literally) foreign objects to explore and arouse curiosity. She specifically recalled a kimono-clad Japanese doll and a children's book about a kitten that experienced difficulties in trying not to wet her bed at night, also in Japanese. As a young child she was moved from place to place quite frequently. One particular trip to a foreign country may have indeed saved her life, as during the Iran-Iraq war, the neighbor's pool became the unwitting recipient of an Iraqi missile, which created tremors that caused a sizable chunk of ceiling to break off and fall onto the crib where she would have been sleeping.

In 1987, when Jairan was four, her family welcomed the addition of her brother. At the decision of her parents for medical and logistical reasons, her brother was born in the United States in a suburb of Washington, D.C., that would later become a place of annual visits throughout her life and eventually, a permanent residence. As the time for Jairan to attend kindergarten and elementary school approached, her parents enrolled her at an early learning Montessori school and later at Westbriar Elementary. Travel and other factors had made English something of a mainstay in her parents' household while living in Iran. This familiarity with the language made it possible to pick up English and proceed smoothly into the American preschool system. Television was also a factor, as Jairan's mother was a steadfast fan of *Sesame Street* and *Mr. Rogers' Neighborhood*. This presented its own difficulties, however. As is typical with many children who are born and raised in exile or who are very young immigrants, the initial spoken language may be lost or may develop as an entirely different language altogether. Her mother sought to remedy her daughter's constant babbling in English and seemingly utter disregard for her first language by responding only in Farsi and refusing to answer questions asked in English. This undoubtedly helped, even though what remained of Jairan's Farsi was laced with an intense American accent that sounded somewhat like Armenian.

When Jairan was between the ages of four and six, her family lived in northern Virginia in a suburban neighborhood. For Jairan, attending school there and becoming acquainted with the American elementary school system soon resulted in a social and psychological attachment to the system, its structure, and individual teachers and classmates. Before long, the family started to mobilize for another major relocation to Iran. This significant change in environment and lifestyle was spurred by eco-

nomic reasons and bolstered by the fact that the children of the family were still quite young and unlikely to sustain any developmental blows or culture shock as a result of the move. When Jairan was four, particu-
larly loquacious, and speaking full-blown English, the family completed the move to Tehran and settled in a northern, residential area of the city. At that time, Iran was in the throes of recuperating from a still new and unseasoned revolution. The government of the Islamic Republic had experienced several permutations and changes in policy in addition to losing many of its key leaders, and it was recovering from internal unrest and an incredibly costly war with neighboring Iraq.

Jairan did not particularly remember the move itself. The journey and arrival in Tehran are no longer images served up by memory. Instead, the most accessible recollections are those of a distinctly juvenile nature. For example, the seemingly sudden addition of doting relatives and extended family members struck a major chord. So did the structure of the homes and streets, where there were different social codes dominating public visibility and social engagement. While in the United States it was entirely possible to visit the neighbors living two floors down or travel across a neighbor's lawn to retrieve a runaway toy, here the runaway toy had to be tossed back over the neighbor's wall, and the children were often heard but not seen. Jairan remembers the amazing surplus of stray cats and that the only available ice cream (Keem or Kim brand ice cream, which had a single vanilla popsicle variety) was impossibly watery and tasted nothing like the ones available in the United States. The only chocolate bars on the market were Turkish and came in comparatively tiny portions, and there was no cereal to be found. These concerns were clearly trivial compared to many others present in this particular household, as with any migrant family. But for the children, especially the young Jairan, who was left with memories of a somewhat American childhood, what was quite commonplace in the United States (gleaming commodities, endless television programming, encouraging and engaging teachers) became reevaluated as luxuries.

Life in Iran boasted a totally different kind of social interaction. It was somewhat more difficult to associate with young children of the same age and almost entirely impossible to interact with people of vastly different racial or cultural heritage. However, being in Iran meant exposure to grandparents, aunts, uncles, cousins, and further extended family who became frequent faces in the home or at family gatherings, parties, and holidays. It is customary in Iran to repay visits, and therefore Jairan often became a companion to her mother as she made the cyclical rounds to her own extended family. Needless to say, many of these relatives were quite old, and most of the time during those visits was devoted to talk and gossip. The result of being privy to many of these gatherings and what went on in them was a calmer, focused, and more sedentary lifestyle for Jairan, her mother, and to some extent her brother.

Introduction into the Iranian school system was inevitable, and soon Jairan was enrolled at a public school in northern Tehran. As it became common in postrevolutionary Iran to name institutions and thoroughfares after religious figures or martyrs, the school bore the name of Sheikh Fazlollah Noori, a notoriously hard-line cleric. The name would become a testament to what went on within the walls of the establishment itself. Noori Elementary, like all other Tehran schools, was segregated and required its students, all girls, to wear the veil and raincoat ensemble that would be mandatory all through high school, college, and beyond. This did not prove very cumbersome to Jairan; indeed, the implications of wearing government-sanctioned Islamic garb would not register with her for a number of years. She was enrolled in the first grade and would remain at the very same school for seven more years. Soon her English accent was swiftly disappearing.

Jairan credited the Iranian school system and the environment in her particular school with many of the sentiments and sensibilities that she harbors to this very day. Her middle and high school years were spent mostly in the Islamic Republic, punctuated briefly by a short tenure at a middle school in Virginia, and culminated in the eventual move that occurred during her third year of high school. The comparatively frequent moves presented a "culture shock" factor and a greater likelihood of experiencing confusion between vastly different cultural norms and value systems. This was not such a problem for Jairan at the very beginning of each move. She found that making additions to her vocabularies to facilitate interaction with her peers and complete school work was relatively easy and required little effort. The most difficult parts involved sympathizing with the vast stores of pop culture and childhood nostalgia that her peers, both in Iran and in the United States, accrued over the years while growing up in the cultural spheres within their respective geographic and ethnographic locales. For example, she found Iranian public television to be abhorrent in terms of programming and subject matter, and therefore she refrained from watching the situation comedies that were forming much of the prevalent sense of humor and popular culture references in the lives of her peers. Similarly, in the United States, she found much of the programming packed so densely with rapid-fire exchanges and American historical references and cultural material that they might as well have been inside jokes that she never got. She found it simply impossible to respond to them and felt hopelessly excluded when they were evoked in the daily exchanges of her peers.

Although some of the cultural confetti that peppered the air around her was largely alien to her, at any given point in time or location, some of her favorite anecdotes arose from her ignorance of them and the slightly embarrassing situations that ensued as a result. In her later years in high school she became less embarrassed about not catching on to quotes and quips from such Iranian cultural favorites as films featuring prominent actor Akbar Abdi or the *Green House* or their American counterparts in *Animaniacs* and *The Simpsons*. Instead, she began to acknowledge that feigning cultural savvy was far more likely to result in a humiliating situation. Her approach became either to remain silent about the cultural topic at hand (in Iran) or admit ignorance and stock up on as much pop cultural material as possible in her free time (in the United States). During her college career, especially after she declared art as one of her areas of study, she became so immersed in Western history and political and artistic movements that she found it hard *not* to absorb the same culture her peers had been reared on and trained in. The reason for the greater investment in her cognizance of American popular culture can be traced to the fact that while growing up her ultimate destination for eventual higher education and adult life was posited as the United States by both herself and her parents. In that sense, attempts to equate oneself with the pervasive attitudes and social norms of the United States struck her, subliminally, as somehow a wise investment.

While in high school, both in Iran during the first two years and in the United States during the latter two, Jairan confronted her own burgeoning sexuality in the social context of her adolescent cohort. She experienced a piqued sense of sexual Puritanism in Iran where, unlike her peers, she refrained from discussing matters of sexuality, and while she partook in activities and became the willing audience of jokes and conversations that involved sex, she abstained from actively seeking out members of the opposite sex. She even went so far as to pass silent judgments that, while never uttered, were not particularly favorable toward those of her contemporaries who had chosen to take significant others or allow pursuit by neighborhood boys.

Upon her arrival in the United States, Jairan remained uninterested in matters of sexuality and "steady" relationships until the final year of her high school career, when she became involved with a young American man of Jewish descent. Many Iranian and Iranian American families would agree that the relationships and romantic aspects of the lives of Iranian youth are often filled with familial clashes and exchanges that debate and even contest the national, religious, and ethnic backgrounds of the youths in question. Often, immigrant parents do not find the joining of their children with "foreigners" to be desirable. But in the case of Jairan and her relationship, her family made no such contest. Her preference for Western men has been regarded by her family and relatives as an idiosyncrasy or even a little harmless quirk. She counts this to her fortune, although she has faced mild pressure from her grandmother (who has been known to be a proponent of marriage) to seek an Iranian mate for future marriage.

When the time for college drew close, Jairan took her cues from her classmates and began applying to universities. She did not have much guidance in this process, and her family was more or less detached from it up until the very end of the college application season, when her prospective schools had already been nailed down and her applications were complete. Her parents did not apply any particular pressure to her at that time and at the same time made no suggestions for possible alma maters or majors. The entire process was very much left up to her. A reason for that may have been that Jairan had envisioned her life in America as largely having the purpose of higher education, a goal about which she talked often. Therefore, there was no real doubt that she would pursue college. But as is the case with many college freshmen, she decided to attend a university in a different state, in this case Pennsylvania, as opposed to one near her mother and brother in Virginia. At first, this did not present much of a problem, and her mother expressed satisfaction that Jairan was well on her way to experiencing a life away from home. Later, especially when she received her bachelor's degree, her mother began hinting and sometimes insisting on her moving closer to the family in Virginia or at least considering a state or graduate school where her mother and brother could move as well. She has found this difficult to do, as there are not many colleges in the vicinity of her Virginia home that offer master's degrees in art. She found herself having to move farther away in the United States. This has been a cause for anxiety for both her and her mother.

While attending Carnegie Mellon University for her undergraduate degree, she remained without a declared major until her sophomore year and eventually chose to double-major in fine arts and linguistics. She admitted that her father expressed greater faith in her career as an artist, and her mother appeared partial to her prospects in the field of linguistics. She often traces these preferences to the fact that her father had tried his hand at being a painter and always admired Jairan's handiwork. Her mother, on the other hand, had studied political science and developed a soft spot for the humanities and social sciences. Jairan also said she believes, personally, that her mother is prone to thinking of the arts as a notoriously uncertain career path, a notion with which many people (including artists) would agree.

Jairan has an art degree and while studying nursing in Pittsburgh also spends much of her time producing artwork in various media. Her artworks center almost exclusively on the situation and mentality of female youth living in Iran and the mindset and behavior of female Iranian immigrants in the United States. She spent two weeks in Iran in January 2009. She found that trips to Iran have usually had a cumulatively beneficial effect on her; each trip to Iran serves as a sentimental reminder from her past as a student there and revisits some of the things she misses most about Iran, such as the topography, traditions, food, local culture, and hearing Farsi spoken around her. She is also mindful that trips to Iran have a negative aspect; she finds the political climate and human rights situation in Iran to be in severe need of change. She is concerned for the youth of Iran for a number of reasons: first, how their prospects for entertainment and achieving their academic and personal goals are often hindered, and second, how many have taken to glorifying the West and the United States as the ultimate bastion of freedom and expression (which she feels is a misconception). She cooks Iranian food often and visits her family fairly frequently. Her father lives in Tehran, her mother in Texas, and her brother is finishing his college course work in Atlanta. She communicates with her father on a somewhat regular basis and speaks with her mother daily.

Cindy's Story

Cindy is a twenty-six-year-old Iranian woman with big eyes and long, black hair. Unlike her only, younger sister, who was born and raised in Houston, Cindy was born in Iran and migrated to America when she was eight years old. She grew up in an educated, affluent family. Both of her parents were educated in Iran before they immigrated to the United States. Like thousands of other Iranian families who have waited for several years to be reunited, it took Cindy and her mother five years to be reunited with her father. At the time of her interview, Cindy and her family lived in one of the (nice) suburbs in Houston. She worked as a preschool teacher during the day and attended school in the evenings. Her mother worked at a department store, and her sixty-year-old father has remained self-employed after two previous business failures within the previous fifteen years. Turning to self-employment unwillingly after so many years of a highly prestigious professional career has been a very frustrating and unsuccessful shift for Cindy's father. Cindy's mother and father were unable to find professional jobs related to their skills and education after they moved to the United States. Consequently, Cindy's parents suffered from a long period of unemployment and sharp downward social mobility from which they have yet to recover. Unlike her extended family members who are wealthy and live trouble-free lives in big houses, Cindy's parents have a modest life filled with financial troubles and family conflicts. In addition to financial stress, Cindy's family continues to bear the constant quarreling between her parents that sometimes turns physical, which started prior to their migration and worsened after they moved to America. Having witnessed family fights for so many years, Cindy has become repulsed by her parents, especially her mother. In addition to tiresome family fights, her mother's cynicism, distrust, and overprotective attitude pushed Cindy to move out at age twenty-five. She resented her mother's refusal to let her do anything and attempts to control her. When Cindy was in high school, interacting with the opposite sex, even her best friend's brother, was a big issue for her mother and would lead to major conflicts.

Cindy's decision to move out made her parents unhappy initially. They resisted her decision and were afraid that she would leave them permanently. Even though Cindy's relationship with her father has improved, she has remained annoyed with her mother and still has a bitter relationship with her. They disagree "on almost everything." Despite her education, Cindy finds her mother critical, controlling, uncompromising, and backward, particularly with regard to gender and sexuality. To make her mother happy when she was living at home, despite her interest in literature she changed her major to dentistry. Soon afterward, she realized that her personality is more compatible with literature and decided to pursue her literary desires regardless of her family's opinions. With all its challenges, Cindy's independent life away from home has been a very positive experience, and she enjoys living alone very much. When she lived at home, Cindy acknowledged, her mother would not let her learn how to do things. She did not even know that she had to call to connect the electricity for her apartment. Given that this is her first time living alone, she has adjusted well with no problems except for killing the cockroaches in her apartment without calling her dad. Distancing herself from the family fights and disputes with her mother has given Cindy serenity and peace of mind.

After sixteen years of living in the United States, Cindy has yet to receive her permanent residency or green card. She had just turned twenty-one when her mother became a permanent resident and received a green card. Therefore, unlike her sister, who automatically became a permanent resident as a dependent child through her mother, Cindy was unqualified to get her permanent residency. Despite her deep love for Iran and her longing to visit, Cindy's lack of a green card has prevented her from returning to Iran since she left the country. Having been in the United States since she was eight years old, Cindy quickly adapted to living conditions and lifestyle here. Soon after the move to Houston, Cindy's fluency in Farsi became frail and gave way to half Farsi, half English, or what she calls "Fenglish." Interaction with Americans at school gradually damaged Cindy's Persian fluency so gravely that she signed up for Persian reading and writing classes at Khanehghah, the Islamic Sufi center in Houston where she began improving her Persian language skills again when she was sixteen. Taking Persian classes has not only made Cindy more fluent in speaking and reading Persian but also strengthened her ties to Iranian culture.

Cindy's overall beliefs about life in general and sex and intimacy in particular have profoundly been influenced by teachings of Islamic mysticism taught at the Sufi center where she has been taking language lessons. Unlike that of her father, who discontinued Islamic religious practices and became antireligious after he moved to the United States, Cindy's interest in Islam grew so much that she began taking Koran classes regularly several years ago. At first, her father objected to Cindy's attendance at Khanehghah and opposed the teachings there. Realizing the big impact of Sufi teachings on Cindy's life, however, has made him less resistant to her participation at Khanehghah.

Cindy's gradual involvement at the Sufi center for several years has provided an opportunity for her to know more about Islamic mysticism and its philosophy. The essence of mysticism in a nutshell, as described by Cindy, is "to live in the world but not be of the world." She does not find any contradiction between Sufi teachings and a worldly life, as long as one is not deceived and obsessed by material needs. She has learned that the best belongs to the believer. She believes that genuine Islamic mystic teachings, not ideological propaganda, would have a very positive, influential, transformative impact on the lifestyle of young Iranian boys and girls in the West by giving them a more powerful perspective for distinguishing between transitory worldly fun and everlasting eternal satisfaction. Cindy feels that had it not been for the teachings of Khanehghah, she would still be the same naïve, gullible, and passive person with no discipline to continue her graduate work. The new lifestyle she has embarked upon has made Cindy very selective in choosing friends. She has very few American friends with whom she finds much in common. Given Cindy's strong self-identification as 95 percent Iranian, not an Iranian American, she is keen to associate predominantly with Iranians of her age. Besides studying and listening to traditional Persian music, Cindy and her friends keep themselves busy with going to Persian concerts and movies whenever they get a chance.

Unlike many of her friends who had boyfriends and experienced physical and sexual intimacy, at the time of her interview Cindy indicated that she had not had a boyfriend in an American sense. Although she had many male friends and dated many Iranians in the past, she had not kissed a man. Cindy's ideal relationship was one that would eventually lead to marriage. She began looking for her ideal Iranian marriage partner when she was nineteen years old. Cindy's views about relationships and marriage set her apart from many of her Iranian peers. Cindy's relationship with her sister is very warm and open, with a great sense of responsibility and concern for her well-being. She openly talks with her sister and her sister's friends about relationships, and they seek her advice on various issues. Instead of endorsing abstinence from relationships and suppressing natural feelings, Cindy advised her sister "to know her worth and not just get involved with anyone."

Kevin's Story

Kevin was a twenty-one-year-old second-generation Iranian American who was born and raised in the United States. He had visited Iran twice, once when he was a baby and another time when he was twenty years old. Kevin's parents were in their twenties when they left Iran. They both finished their education in the United States and strongly reinforced the importance of educational achievement in Kevin's upbringing. They were in their late forties at the time of his interview and had professional jobs related to their educational degrees. Kevin's parents, particularly his father, have been very protective of their only child. They observe Islamic practices and rituals moderately. As "spiritual Muslims" they mention God although neither one prays regularly in a traditional Islamic fashion or attends an Islamic mosque or religious center. Unlike his father, who strongly abhors drinking, Kevin's mother drinks occasionally. Despite their moderate religious convictions, Kevin's parents did not impose their religious viewpoints on their son and left it to Kevin to decide his religious beliefs. Kevin regrets that he did not take the time to familiarize himself with the Islamic faith. His knowledge of Islamic teachings is very rudimentary, and he would not be able to talk about Islamic principles or quote from the Koran or the Prophet.

Kevin's relationship with his parents has been very bumpy, particularly during his teenage years. Growing up in a rigid, unyielding family in which everything had to be done in a very specific way created some friction between Kevin and his parents. At times, Kevin's uncles, aunts, and grandparents would call from Iran to intervene and ask Kevin's parents to be a little more flexible in their relationship with him.

Kevin finds the United States a much better place to live permanently, but he wanted to go back to Iran and visit his relatives. Although he grew up in a home with a completely Iranian cultural ambiance, he feels more attached to American culture and lives his life almost completely based on American values and standards. However, he identifies himself mostly as a Persian or Iranian American to his friends, not because he accepts and holds the Iranian way of life but mainly because his roots and his parents are Iranian. In his mind, Kevin sees himself as an Americanized Iranian or an "American in every sense with Iranian roots." Identifying himself as Persian or Iranian has not been an issue for Kevin. Kevin does not deny that he is an Iranian, and his friends and acquaintances know his ethnic roots and affiliation. Despite his ethnic pride, after the 9/11 attack and subsequent media coverage of Muslims and Middle Easterners, Kevin has kept a very low identity profile and avoids situations in which he would have to bring up his Persian/Iranian ethnic identity.

Despite his strong Persian identity, his recent visit to Iran, his relative fluency in the Persian language, and his exposure to Iranian culture in exile, Iranian society and culture remain relatively unknown to Kevin. Other than what he reads in newspapers or watches on television, he does not know what real life in Iran is like. Even when he traveled to Iran in 2003, partying, visiting friends and relatives, and sightseeing got in the way of seeing the normal daily life in Iran. By contrast, having lived in Texas all his life, Kevin not only appreciates and embraces many aspects of the

American way of life but also has a much more real sense of life in the United States than in Iran.

His embracing of American cultural norms and values and his unintentional lack of attention to and disregard for Iranian cultural practices have created some tension between Kevin and his parents. Kevin sees Iranian and American cultures religiously, socially, culturally, ethically, and in almost every other way to be not only incompatible but polar opposites. It would be very difficult, Kevin asserts, to grow up and live in the United States based on Iranian ideals and cultural beliefs. During his high school years, Kevin and his parents argued mainly about his whereabouts with his friends, partying with friends, and dating. His parents' cultural beliefs regarding education, friendship, and family obligation were in sharp contrast with what Kevin believed and wanted to do as a teenager. His parents reminded Kevin constantly that he was only born in the United States but not raised as an American. Such expectations as staying home and studying six to eight hours after he would get home from school created major conflicts between Kevin and his parents. Most of the time Kevin's parents would dominate. Other times, however, Kevin would persist in what he wanted to do, and they would come to terms with his point of view. Dating was never accepted by Kevin's parents. Every time Kevin brought up the issue of dating with them, the answer was a straight "No" without any explanations.

Despite their confidence in their son's academic performance, Kevin's parents initially objected very seriously to his choice of a college outside of the Dallas area. Following a series of arguments, Kevin made a deal with his parents and agreed to attend a local college in return for their financial support. After the initial resentment experienced by Kevin's parents regarding their new financial obligation, their relationship with him improved gradually after Kevin moved out and lived independently. His moving out was not easy for Kevin or for his parents, and it was a turning point for all of them. For Kevin, working and paying for tuition was a big financial adjustment, while for his parents, losing the company of their only child was a major emotional adjustment. Instead of spending their whole lives arguing, Kevin and his parents have learned to compromise and develop mutual respect from different perspectives.

After completing college Kevin gained more respect from his parents and their acceptance of his views and lifestyle. He feels this respect and mutual understanding has been achieved in part because of his ability to live independently and in part because of his parents' greater tolerance for

American cultural values and lifestyle. For example, compared to his teen-age years, Kevin's parents became more liberal in their views toward dating. Albeit dating Iranian girls was what they preferred, they objected less to his dating Americans. A few years earlier, it would have been very difficult for them to accept Kevin's interethnic dating. Today, however, they have really changed, Kevin affirms. They accept many more things than before and respect what he is going through.

Unlike his writing, Kevin's comprehension of the Farsi language is perfect. He can only write his name in Farsi, which to him is like drawing a picture. Although his comprehension is strong, he does not speak excellent Farsi, and sometimes his words sound strange. Therefore, he speaks either in a mixed Farsi-English or mostly in English with his parents. When he is around other Iranians, he is a little embarrassed to speak the language. Kevin and his friends, Iranian and American, get together at least once a week. Their gatherings are usually mixed with men and women from different nationalities. Culture and ethnicity has not been an issue for Kevin in his friendships and interactions with his peers. He feels as comfortable with his Iranian friends as he does with his American and non-American friends. Nevertheless, unlike the attitudes of his American friends, Kevin finds that more of his Iranian friends are judgmental and have a tendency to impose their ideas and views on everything. On rare occasions, to avoid any major conflict, criticism, mockery, or admonishment, he finds himself more reserved with some of his Iranian friends. Not all of Kevin's Iranian friends are judgmental and opinionated. There are some who are more "laid back" and nonjudgmental. Like his American friends, they just want to party and have a good time.

At the time of his interview, a typical gathering for Kevin and his friends consisted of meeting up at someone's house and either staying home and listening to music and having casual conversations about school, work, and what was going on in their lives or going out to the movies, having a drink, or smoking a *ghelyoon* (water pipe) at a local Middle Eastern café. Kevin's drinking is no secret to his parents. In fact, sometimes Kevin and his mother go out for a glass of wine without any serious objection from his father. Out of respect for his father, however, Kevin does not drink in front of him. Sometimes Kevin goes out with his Iranian friends, some of whom bring their non-Iranian friends along, and other times he goes out with his non-Iranian friends, most of whom are not American. The few American friends that Kevin hangs out with accompany him to these ethnically mixed gatherings and enjoy themselves. Sepa-

rating his Iranian from his non-Iranian friends has occurred unintention-
ally. The dynamics of Kevin's relationships with his Iranian and American
friends are typically the same. The only difference is who the people are.

Occasionally Kevin and his Iranian friends discuss the political situation in Iran or the presidential election in the United States. He voted in
the U.S. presidential election for the first time in 2004. His enthusiasm
for participation in the American presidential election was mainly due to
his concerns for the sociopolitical situation and future of Iran. He does not
want to see a military invasion of Iran by the United States. His concerns
about political events in Iran are mainly personal and emotional, owing to
the fact that his parents are Iranian and all of his relatives live in Iran. In
addition to parents, relatives, friends, and news sources, Kevin finds online sources a very effective way to keep up with the news about Iran.

Kevin's last visit to Iran before his interview revived his feelings for and
sense of attachment to Iranian culture and nationality, motivated him to
be more involved in the Iranian community in Dallas, and made him interested in knowing more about Islam and Iranian society. Soon after his
return from Iran, Kevin got involved with the Iranian student association
at his college and organized a New Year's celebration. His feelings toward
Iran and his involvement with the exile community later subsided. Nevertheless, he continued to enjoy attending family gatherings either at his
parents' house or the homes of family friends, whether there was anybody
his age or not, without feeling alienated, out of place, or marginalized.

Subsequently, Kevin's major challenge has been to advance professionally in his career. He was free of any overwhelming, unmanageable issues
in his private and public life. His relationship with his parents improved
significantly, and they have an uncomplicated, trouble-free connection.
Even though Kevin's parents still interfered with his career choices and
advised him frequently on money management, there was no real conflict
between him and them. In 2005, Kevin's parents agreed to support his decision to move out of state for a couple of years and experience living and
working in other places.

As indicated in these life stories, like children of most other immigrants,
children of Iranian immigrants are a very diverse group in terms of birthplace, age and life stage at arrival, length of residency in the United States,
extent of socialization into and internalization of American cultural values, blending of Iranian and American cultural norms and values, and
fluency in the native Persian language. Many like Kevin are second-generation Iranian Americans who were born and entirely socialized in the

United States. They completed their entire education in the United States, lack firsthand, deep experience of their parents' native culture, and can only speak broken Persian with an English accent. Others like Jairan and Cindy are 1.5 generation who were born outside of Iran and immigrated to the United States when they were either elementary school age or in their adolescent years. They attended elementary school in Iran, learned to read and write in Persian and are very fluent in speaking the language, and were partly socialized in and still retain memories from Iran. Some of these young 1.5- and second-generation Iranian Americans are children of foreign-born Iranian parents who have visited Iran several times, and others still are children of mixed, interethnic marriages with at least one foreign-born Iranian parent who has never visited Iran and can barely speak Persian.

According to the 2006-2008 American Community Survey report, there were 422,664 individuals of Iranian heritage living in the United States in 2008. This constituted 0.14 percent of the total population of the United States. Close to 36 percent of Iranian immigrants could be classified as second-generation, having been born in the United States. Young people are disproportionately represented in the Iranian population in the United States. Due to the recent migration of older Iranians, however, the age composition of the Iranian population is changing gradually. Based on the 2009 ACS report, one out of every four Iranians in the United States was under the age of eighteen.

A majority of second-generation Iranian Americans in the United States were born within the past twenty years, are too young to have established their own families, and are far from procreating a third generation. Therefore, Iranian parents play a vital role in managing interpersonal relations and social interactions of their teenage sons and daughters within and outside the family unit. They also play a significant role in the development of self-identity that is part of a larger identity with the family and preservation of the family's reputation and honor in the local community. Thus, most Iranian parents try to instill in their children the core values of the Iranian family, such as obedience, loyalty to parents and older relatives, and cooperation with and respect for family members. They are deeply concerned about the ethnic and cultural identities of their children. Their concerns, however, are more about the behaviors and actions of their children and not what ethnic labels they use to identify themselves in their interactions with non-Iranians.

A large number of parents in my survey commented that they had a number of concerns about their children, with loss of Iranian cultural heritage as the topmost among them. The results of my Texas survey of 507 first-generation Iranian Americans reveal that 72 percent of Iranian parents are concerned about the upbringing of their children in the United States. When asked to specify major sources of their concerns, 36 percent of Iranian parents in the survey marked lack of knowledge about Iranian cultural values, and another 30 percent designated disrespect for Iranian family values and sexual freedom as equally important causes for worry about the upbringing of their teenagers in the United States. Americanization and the adoption of an American lifestyle, drugs and alcohol, and lack of religious beliefs and values were listed as the other major worries for 25 percent of Iranian parents in the survey. Americanization for most Iranian parents implies dating and sex, individualism, lack of respect for family and family members, and disregard for the family's welfare. Most Iranian parents reject behaviors and norms of dating, clothing, and entertainment practiced by American adolescents. Most dogmatically refuse to allow their young sons and daughters to date and tightly control their sexual behavior. They perceive such behaviors as dating and premarital sex, especially for their girls, as not only disrespectful and inconsistent with Iranian cultural values and practices but also shameful for the family. Other major concerns of Iranian parents in the survey related to children's educational achievements, individualism and separation from the family, and interethnic marriage. Discussions about children's educational plans and achievements recur in Iranian gatherings regularly. While some Iranian parents view education as social capital that brings honor to the family and makes it respectable in the community, others think education is imperative to financial success in the United States. Therefore, children are expected to do their best and do well in school so they will avoid bringing shame or dishonor to parents in their circles of friends and the ethnic community. For Iranian parents, involvement in the educational decisions of their children is an indication of their full support and concern about their children's future, but for teenage Iranians their parents' behavior indicates restrictive authoritarianism of the Iranian family (Shavarini 2004).

In general, all these concerns of Iranian parents pertain to the single issue of ethnic identity for their children. For most Iranian parents, Iranian identity of children is best manifested and maintained in native language competency, respect and obedience toward their parents, and conformity to ideal gender roles and norms of the Iranian family. As long as children can speak relatively fluent Farsi, abstain from premarital sex (particularly girls), respect their parents, and maintain their link with the family and

Iranian community, they are considered Iranians. The strong emphasis of many Iranian parents on sexual abstinence, native language competency, and family respect, as indicated in interviews, is partly because these components are traditional ends in themselves and partly because they are significant strategically in creating a cultural ambience that would minimize intergenerational cultural conflicts and reinforce the boundaries between Iranian and American cultures.

Despite their efforts, however, as with most other second-generations, Iranian American youth have variably adopted the values and behaviors of Americans in one form or another. Therefore, most Iranian parents worry and complain that their teenage sons and daughters have become too Americanized and are losing the Iranian culture. Consequently, like most other first-generation immigrants, Iranian parents experience socialization conflicts when their native cultural values and practices collide with values of their American-reared children. Iranian parents have a different set of child-rearing practices and values that are distinct from American child-rearing styles. Thus, to learn about the main sources of intergenerational conflict between Iranian immigrant parents and their teenage sons and daughters, it is important to understand the ideal family norms of Iranian culture, the perceptions of Iranian immigrant parents toward American families, and the intersection of these two. It is equally important to understand who second-generation Iranian Americans are and what ethnic labels they use to identify themselves.

The Ideal Iranian Family and the Perceptions of Iranian Immigrants about the American Family

The Iranian family has been shaped by such factors as level of education, social class, urban or rural residence, ethnic membership, and religious orientation. This range of social variables has long existed. Despite this diversity the most significant institution in Iranian society remains the family. Family relations have been guided and shaped by a set of ideal cultural norms and values that dominate every aspect of an individual's private and public life. An individual's entire life is shaped extensively, even dominated, by the family, family obligations, and relationships and responsibilities toward other family members. Individuals rely on family networks for support, security, power, influence, and position. The importance of the family as a social unit for Iranians dates back to the pre-Islamic period and is rooted in Zoroastrian teachings,[1] which emphasize the sacredness of rearing children and familial obligations of children toward their parents (Jalali 1982). With its heavy emphasis on the collective physical, financial, and emotional protection and preservation of family, even after children leave home or marry and establish their own families, Iranian culture encourages family members to stay as physically close as possible and to remain loyal and committed to their family and its well-being. As such, family members are expected to maintain solidarity, remain loyal, and sacrifice their individual desires and interests for the good of the entire family.

In addition to valuing family attachment and strong ties, like all other cultures the Iranian cultural ideal specifies clearly defined norms of behavior based on age and gender that govern an individual's actions within the family and society. The traditional Iranian family is dominated by the visible, undisputed authority of the father as head of the family. The relationships among family members are structured hierarchically along age and sex. The father, as head of his household, expects to be obeyed and is responsible for the unification of the group and the resolution of internal conflicts. He exercises incredible influence and power. The wife's status within the family is defined by religious laws. As a wife, a woman is expected to be submissive and live under the guardianship of her husband. As a mother, she is expected to take care of the children. She is particularly close to her children and devotes most of her time to them. The father is responsible for the public domain of family life, and the mother is responsible for the home and domestic matters such as food preparation and child care. While the father's power is direct, the mother has a more subtle and indirect power that depends in part on the kind of relationship that she has developed with her husband, sons, brothers, and the other women in the family (Jalali 1982). Nevertheless, the roles and activities of women are limited to familial and domestic spheres in the home. Older sons accept the responsibility of looking after their mother and young unmarried brothers and sisters in the absence of the father. Children are expected to be submissive, polite, and respectful toward parents, older relatives, and older siblings and to address them in a formal fashion. Gender role socialization starts from childhood by teaching boys to protect and command and teaching girls to obey, be beautiful, and become good mothers (Nassehy-Behnam 1985).

Iranian culture, like other Middle Eastern cultures, has been typified as one in which the social and economic activities of women are shaped by the Islamic ideology of sex, for example, sexual modesty, virginity, strict marital fidelity, veiling, and segregation. The Islamic ethos emphasizes that women's sexuality is inherently dangerous and can create social chaos and disorder. Men are, therefore, charged with authority and protection over female sexual behavior. The control of the sexual behavior of women-folk is closely tied to a male's honor, or *namus*. Namus can be lost through such misconduct of women as premarital sex and marital infidelity. There-fore, to protect the family namus or honor and maintain a good reputation it is better for women to stay home or minimize their interactions and con-tacts with outsiders and unrelated men. As such, Iranian parents are typi-cally more permissive toward their sons and endorse restrictive behavior, particularly regarding sexual behavior, among their daughters. Premarital sex for women is looked down upon and scorned, and women are expected to remain virgins until they enter a marital relationship. Regardless of the children's gender, Iranian parents are deeply concerned with and involved in their lives. Despite the changes experienced by the modern urban fam-ily, the traditional gender roles within the family and attitudes toward women have remained conservative and relatively unchanged.

These ideal images about the structure of the Iranian family and the cultural norms governing gender roles, as well as the relations between parents and children, stand in sharp contrast to the structure of the Amer-ican family. This contrast has significantly added to the complexity of the Iranian family in exile. These cultural differences have increased the ex-pectations of Iranian parents for their teenage sons and daughters without their understanding the everyday realities and challenges facing second-generation Iranian American children and thus have created serious fam-ily tensions between parents and their children. The ideal family norms of Iranian culture, relentlessly viewed as superior by almost all Iranian par-ents, have profoundly shaped the negative perceptions of Iranian immi-grants about the American family and have made them more inflexible in interacting with their children who have become "Americanized." As in-dicated in the following sample of comments, single and married Iranian men and women of all social strata interviewed for this project reject the American family lifestyle because they find it deteriorated and dysfunc-tional, with weak emotional bonding among its members. A large number of respondents to my survey commented that many behavioral problems and most major social problems of Americans related to sex, violence, drugs, and emotional troubles are deeply rooted in the erosion of fam-ily and of family values in the United States. Others criticized the exces-sive individualism of American society and how it poses a threat to fam-ily stability and cohesion. Unlike Iranian women for whom family loyalty and the welfare of children have a higher priority than individual needs, many Iranian female respondents commented that American women are

self-centered and put their own desires ahead of those of their families.
A twenty-four-year-old graduate student from Dallas who had been in the
United States for seven years shared some of her views:

> One of the most significant negative features of the American society is the
> emphasis on individualism and the lack of family value.

A middle-age Iranian professor who left Iran twenty-two years earlier said:

> Altogether, I like this country. However, I believe the American people are
> unaffectionate and irresponsible towards their children, and in general they do
> not value marriage.

An Iranian parent echoed the same view:

> American culture is very different from the Iranian culture. American children
> are not brought up the right way, and there is no mutual respect between
> children and parents. The family affection that exists in Iran does not exist in
> any other culture.

A forty-year-old professional Iranian woman who had lived in Austin since
1983 noted:

> The American culture is not really digestible for me, particularly with regard to
> family and raising children.

A forty-four-year-old Iranian receptionist with five years of experience living in Houston expressed a very unfavorable view of the American family:

> The sexual freedom that exists in this society is absolutely unacceptable to
> me. Family has no value here. Families easily break up and separate without
> even thinking about the consequences for children. In general, the way we de-
> fine family in Iran does not exist here. Married couples separate easily as soon
> as they grow tired of each other.

The same concern was reiterated by a young Iranian housewife who was
reunited with her family in Dallas six years earlier:

> I am not pleased with the freedom that exists for the youth at all. For example,
> it is not cool for them if they do not have a boyfriend or girlfriend. Families
> leave everything up to the kids once they get to be eighteen years old.

Concerns about family and children's upbringing were also expressed by a young Iranian mother from Dallas:

> I never liked living outside of my homeland mainly because of my children. I wish I could raise my children in Iran because I do not accept the excessive sexual freedom and lack of moral boundaries in this culture.

A young married mother of two said:

> In my opinion Americans are completely consumed by work and try very hard to make a living. Therefore, a majority of Americans take the great responsibility for upbringing of their children as a very unimportant task. Most Americans care less about family values and have become so self-centered.

The same negative sentiment about family was shared by a forty-four-year-old educated mother with nineteen years of marital experience. In her view, "Due to their financial and economic ambitions, American families have developed a new structure with less emotional bonding. Emotional fulfillment has no place in American society and family."

Another Iranian woman commented, "American family values are very low, and there is almost no respect for the elderly and adult family members." Rejection of American family values and practices is equally if not more shared by Iranian immigrant men. Much like their female counterparts, most Iranian men in the study found the American family to be very weak, with deteriorated moral values. As indicated by a young Iranian physician from Houston, "Weakness of the family institution is one of the most significant problems of American society." These negative perceptions coupled with two vastly different cultural beliefs regarding family not only have created tension between Iranian immigrant parents and their children with conflictual outcomes but also have contributed to an identity crisis among second-generation Iranian Americans.

Second-Generation Iranian Americans and Identity Crisis

For many second-generation Iranian Americans, the question of ethnic identity is a contested and problematic issue. Some of these young participants in the study regarded second-generation Iranian Americans as a confused generation that either has lost its Persian identity and ethnic and cultural pride or suffers from identity crisis. Others indicated that second-generation Iranian Americans either do not know where they have come from and are completely divorced from their roots or are torn between two divergent cultures. Still others viewed second-generation Iranian Americans as a Westernized group engrossed in negative aspects of American culture such as sex and materialism and that has turned its back on such a rich culture and is ashamed of its heritage and ignorant of its current sociopolitical conditions.

A young female college student in Dallas expressed her view:

> Second-generation Iranians seem to be as interested in Iranian events and gatherings, though I think their struggle comes in when feeling that they have to choose between the identity of being solely American or Iranian.

A young Iranian American male born and raised in Houston indicated,

> I think most second-generations avoid their culture and try to dissociate themselves from their ethnic heritage as much as possible. They don't have enough pride in their ethnic background.

A twenty-three-year-old second-generation who was born in Iran and moved to Houston when he was ten reflected,

> For some Iranians, losing touch with their culture or not knowing where they come from is a major problem. This is mostly for Iranians who have not had the opportunity to visit Iran. I have many friends who were brought here as babies or born in America and are constantly searching within themselves to discover their origin and ethnic roots.

The widely held view of many respondents regarding the seeming cultural confusion that second-generation Iranian Americans exhibit was summed up by a twenty-two-year-old college student from Austin:

> I think that second-generation Iranians are confused. They want to assimilate and participate in American culture, but their parents go to great lengths to shield them from this. They then inadvertently become rebellious and generate negative thoughts about their own culture. I think they try too hard to show they are Americanized.

As indicated in the last comment, many second-generation Iranian Americans blame their identity crisis and lack of ethnic or cultural pride on their parents and their primary socialization process at home. A twenty-one-year-old college student from Dallas spoke of second-generation Iranians' identity crises and loss of cultural identity:

> Second-generation Iranians are very superficial. Not all, but most. Major problems are the different values between American and Iranian cultures. The source is most likely the parents' lack of effort to instill Iranian values from a young age and keep their kids closer to the culture and traditions.

Concern about identity crisis and parental responsibility was also expressed by a twenty-four-year-old Iranian medical student from Houston:

> I think second-generation Iranians are torn between the American culture they've grown up with and the closed-minded Iranian customs and beliefs that their parents want them to follow.

This view was shared by another college student:

> I am a part of the second-generation Iranians because I was born in Houston, Texas, but the number one problem I always encountered while growing up was that my parents put a lot of restrictions on me that my American friends never understood. It was very difficult growing up in America with my parents insisting that I respect the Iranian culture and traditions.

A second-generation female expressed her views regarding the role of Iranian parents in the identity crises of their children:

> Second-generation Iranians are confused and unable to balance Iranian culture and American culture. Parents tend to be very strict, almost alienating their child from his/her American surroundings.

As demonstrated in the above comments, the relationship between first- and second-generation Iranian Americans is strained and tense, and often Iranian parents and their teenagers cannot relate to each other. Most second-generation Iranian Americans in the study said the cultural gap between the two generations was widening and each generation is moving in a different cultural direction with no desire to compromise. They found it difficult if not impossible to communicate with their parents, and they expected their parents to be more sensitive to their sexual needs and need for freedom. Some complained that their parents treated them as though they were living and growing up in Iran and wanted to inculcate

Iranian cultural values in them. Others blamed their parents for being closed-minded, tunnel-visioned, old-fashioned, controlling, incapable of open communication, obsessed with saving face in the Persian community, holding everything to Iranian standards, and not understanding their children's mannerisms.

For some second-generation Iranian Americans the root cause of the intergenerational tension was cultural incompatibility. They believed clashes occurred because of inherent differences between Iranian and American ways of life, language barriers, upbringings in two different cultural backgrounds and value systems, and cultural misunderstanding. For others, the tension was generated by lack of communication. Parents lacked full integration and adaptation into the mainstream American culture; they insisted instead on retaining traditional Iranian cultural values and thus failed to respect the social activities and values of their children.

Irrespective of what second-generation Iranians perceive to be the source of intergenerational conflict and tension, their ethnic identity formation and the ethnic labels they use to identify themselves seem to be most deeply shaped by the interplay between their parents' socialization practices, perception of Iranian immigrants as a group, perception and level of involvement with and participation in the Iranian community, and the degree of their exposure to and attitudes toward American culture and people. Though any typology implies simplification, to understand what ethnic options or labels second-generation Iranian Americans use to identify themselves and to explore how these subjective ethnic identities are formed, I constructed such a classification based on three ideal types of ethnic identities and the degree of ambivalence they experience. This typology may help us to understand why some second-generation Iranian Americans define themselves as American and others, particularly those born and raised in the United States, choose the Iranian ethnic option. What compels many Iranian youth to construct a dual ethnic identity and define themselves as either Iranian American or American Iranian? How are these ethnic options constructed and maintained? What factors contribute to the creation of one or the other? And what mechanisms and parameters do children of Iranian immigrants use to construct and maintain their ethnic identity and ethnic boundaries?

These types are constructed from interviews, field observations, and the surveys. They include the disillusioned, the sympathetic, and the ambivalent second-generations. Within the typology outlined below, second-generations use different ethnic labels to identify themselves. The disillusioned are more likely to identify themselves as American, the sympathetic are most likely to identify as Iranian, and the ambivalent second-generations tend to refer to themselves as Iranian Americans.

Disillusioned Second-Generations and American Ethnic Identity

The disillusioned second-generations are very critical of first-generation Iranian Americans. They find the first-generations to be closed-minded, strict, controlling, annoying, old-fashioned, uptight, nosy, stereotypical individuals who are not only too set in their beliefs but forcibly apply Iranian ideals to their children. The biggest frustration of this group from the first-generation Iranian Americans is their inflexibility and failure to accept and adjust to American cultural values and their inability to compromise with their American-raised children (who arguably live in a totally different culture). As indicated by many informants, Iranian parents need to realize that they no longer live in Iran and it would be unrealistic to ask second-generation Iranians to behave like teenagers in Iran. They expect their parents to be less dogmatic, insular, and ethnocentric and more receptive to the American way of life and the freedom imparted to young people living within the American cultural schema.

One participant responded to how Iranian parents treat their children:

> I think a lot of them try to force their ideas on their children when in fact the children are in a totally different society and need different guidance.

Another respondent said:

> Most Iranian parents happen to be closed-minded when it comes to a lot of things. They moved to America by choice, so they need to know how to adapt to the American culture and tradition.

The same concern was echoed by another participant:

> It is like we are from two different planets. Things in Iran are not like things in America, but parents still hold everything to Iranian standards.

A young female from Austin also noted the cultural clash between the two generations:

> The biggest issues between the first- and second-generations is that the kids
> are Americanized and liberal and want the freedom that all their friends have
> but can't because of the close ties to their Iranian culture and parents.

Compared to their parents and other first-generation Iranian Americans, the antipathetic second-generations perceive Americans to be open-minded, liberal, good-hearted people who appreciate and accept diversity. The liberal attitudes of American parents toward sex and dating as well as their respect for the freedom of their children makes them far more relaxed and less controlling than Iranian parents. These second-generations believe the United States is a great society that provides many opportunities for upward mobility, and they very proudly identify themselves as Americans.

A college student compared her parents with American parents and expressed how she feels about Americans:

> My parents and I argue about dating all the time. They think we are living in
> Iran and no pre-marital dating or anything of the sort is allowed. They are
> basically narrow-minded. I think Americans are liberal and so am I. However,
> my parents are closed-minded and think Americans are loose and free, while I
> think that Americans are just good-hearted and open-minded people.

Another second-generation also spoke of how different and open-minded American parents are:

> Americans' views are different than my parents'. They give their children more
> freedom than the Iranian parents do. Also, they are more open-minded about
> dating than Iranian parents.

In addition to the perceived closed-mindedness of Iranian parents in comparison with Americans and unrealistic cultural expectations (as claimed by second-generations), many antipathetic second-generation Iranian Americans feel very unhappy and distanced from the Iranian community. Unlike the ambivalent second-generations who will be discussed in the following section, the antipathetic Iranians have a very strong feeling of repugnance toward the community either because they feel their Americanized or non-Iranian behaviors are unaccepted by community members or because they do not find the community activities worthwhile. In their view the Iranian community is boring, inactive, disorganized, fragmented, condescending, pretentious, incongruent, insular, xenophobic, bigoted and prejudiced toward "nonconformists," and incoherent, with no political leverage to promote and protect the interests of Iranians in exile effectively. They find the quality of community events either poor or irrelevant to their concerns. As such, they feel distant from the community and its members, they deliberately stay detached from the community, and they refuse to participate in community gatherings. Their interactions are limited to relatives and a few close friends. Therefore, they feel more American than Iranian and identify themselves as such. When asked "Do you think of yourself as Iranian or American?" a twenty-three-year-old Iranian responded:

> I feel American for the most part. I feel Iranian because of my family members, and I do things in certain ways to appease them at times. Otherwise, my entire lifestyle is American. I enjoy and value being able to make decisions independently. I appreciate the diversity and accepting nature of American culture. I love the food, music, and fashion. My views are radically different from my parents'. My mother would like for me to dress more conservatively, but since she has a weird taste I don't listen to her and then get nagged. My parents dislike the television shows I watch and the music I listen to because they think it is immoral and a bad influence. My parents, more so my father, dislike my belly button ring.

A sixteen-year-old Iranian from Houston who also identified himself as an American stated:

> I consider myself American. It is all I know myself as. I am definitely not like my cousins in Iran. They all think I am cool because I am American. They are kind of weird. I feel sorry for them because living in Iran would suck. You cannot do anything fun in Iran. I only socialize with Iranians when I am with my parents. My dad always makes me shave and hates the way I dress. My jeans are torn up and my boxers shine.

Sympathetic Second-Generations and Iranian Ethnic Identity

Sympathetic second-generations see the first-generation Iranian Americans as educated, hardworking, smart, friendly, passionate, ambitious, persistent, quick-learning, and nice individuals with many opportunities for success. Unlike the antipathetic "Americanized" second-generation

Iranian Americans, the sympathetic second-generations admire the first-generation Iranians for their successful cultural adaptation to the American way of life while keeping the core Iranian cultural beliefs and values intact and staying in touch with their roots. They also empathize with them for having gone through so many challenges and experiencing financial and cultural struggles in exile. The most important attribute of first-generations for this group is their concern for the well-being of their families and sacrifices they have made for the education of their children. These second-generations are very optimistic about the future of Iranians in exile and see the migration of their parents as a beneficial step with more opportunities and better life chances to come. Overall, their positive attitudes toward first-generation Iranian Americans and their ethnic community give them such a strong feeling of cultural pride and attachment that they would be more inclined to maintain their Iranian ethnic identity and label themselves as either Iranian or Persian.

A young Iranian female college student who thought of herself as completely Iranian expressed her positive views toward first-generation Iranian Americans and the ethnic community:

> I think first-generation Iranian immigrants are wonderful people. Many of them are people who came to a completely foreign land and, after many years of hard work and study, are now successful. This is something that makes me proud. . . . I am Iranian because my mother and father are Iranian. I was raised as an Iranian, not as an American. I do not hesitate to let someone know where I am from and that I am proud of it. I have also never hesitated to stand up for Muslims and advise that No, you are not a terrorist just because you believe in Allah.

This feeling was shared by a twenty-two-year-old second-generation male who was raised in Sweden:

> I admire first-generations' persistence and motivation. Not many people can come from an unfamiliar country and assimilate so quickly and successfully. I think they have done a great job. I would describe them as cultural chameleons.

In describing his identity he added, "I am Iranian in the sense that I love, respect, and enjoy spending time with my family. I love our food, culture, and language."

Another participant spoke of how proud of her Iranian heritage she is: "I think of myself as mostly Iranian. I am fascinated by my culture and the history of my ancestors. I am very proud of being an Iranian."

Compared to the antipathetic Iranians, the sympathetic second-generations view Americans as too carefree, unwise, spoiled, uneducated, conservative, easily manipulated, and ignorant of world issues, with a twisted worldview and a fixated pop culture that pressures individuals to conform to the daily capitalist work routine. The following comment by a sympathetic second-generation clearly indicates reservations about being identified as an American:

> I feel the American culture is one of ignorance—ignorance of the world, of their surroundings. They are not concerned about what happens outside their own community. They truly take for granted what they have.

Another second-generation stated:

> I am really not a fan of American culture. American culture to me means Levis, Coca-Cola, and Bruce Willis. Americans tend to think they are superior and for the most part have a twisted worldview. Contrary to what they believe, Americans are usually closed-minded and inflexible. I don't mean to generalize; there are always exceptions to everything.

The same negative view was expressed by another second-generation:

> American culture is a large melting pot of others; I am less judgmental than my parents, but I often consider [Americans] to be superficial, uncultured, and often lacking morality.

Lack of respect for family values was another undesirable aspect of American culture that was repeatedly mentioned as a reason for many second-generations to identify themselves as Iranian. A twenty-five-year-old woman from Austin remarked:

> I think family is more important in our culture. Values also play an important role in our culture. Americans are not as caring as us, and they do not have the same views of the importance of family and values that Iranians have.

Another respondent said:

Americans are a little too carefree and unwise; they are very liberal and don't really value life and its simple things. My parents are more emotion-filled.

The sympathetic Iranians think very highly of the Iranian community and would like to be more involved in community events. They are impressed with educational and occupational achievements of first-generation Iranians and believe the community is very active and offers numerous cultural activities. While acknowledging its slow growth and shortcomings, the sympathetic second-generations are proud of the development of the Iranian community and its ethnic institutions. Cultural pride and a feeling of respect for Iranians as warm, welcoming, and family-oriented are incentives for the sympathetic second-generations to be more involved and visible in the Iranian community. Therefore, most sympathetic second-generations also actively participate in Iranian gatherings including concerts, dances, music and art classes, fund-raisers, and meetings, and they frequent ethnic restaurants. They are also active on college campuses, and through celebrations of Iranian cultural events they find opportunities to introduce the rich heritage of Iranian tradition to Americans. Many of them see themselves as representatives of the Iranian community and feel responsible for helping to improve the community's status. Hence, they contribute to the community financially and volunteer to organize community events and gatherings. Overall, they feel very attached to their families, have many Persian friends, and interact mostly with other Iranians.

Ambivalent Second-Generations and Iranian American Ethnic Identity

Between the disillusioned and the sympathetic lies a third category, ambivalent second-generations with mixed feelings about Iranian and American cultures and an inclination toward being identified as Iranian American. A majority of second-generation Iranians in the United States fall into this category. They feel neither detached from nor completely attached to the Iranian community. They have mixed feelings about the community. On the one hand, they find the Iranian community rewarding for providing ethnic food, sponsoring Persian concerts and other cultural events, and preserving and promoting Persian cultural heritage through celebrations of Iranian holidays and other festivities. On the other hand, they are highly critical of the Iranian community for its adversarial structure and

"rumor mill" mentality, its lack of unity, solidarity, coalescence, and organization, its exclusiveness, and its minimal skill when it comes to either
educating Americans and other ethnic groups about Iranian culture and
society or connecting and associating with other ethnic communities.
In their view, the Iranian community is very caring and prosperous with
material and intellectual potential for advancement. Nevertheless, also
in their opinion the Iranian community limits Iranians' integration into
American society and their advancement toward upward social mobility.

Although the Iranian community has come a long way, these ambivalent second-generations believe, it needs to grow more, mainly by purging
gossip. Their ideal community is one in which "positive" aspects of Iranian and American cultural values and practices are blended together. Although they like to be more visible in the community, they avoid active involvement and participation due to the gossip. This is particularly the case
for second-generation Iranians with families that are respected and well
known and that have a good social reputation (*aaberu*) in the community.

Despite their grievances over community structure and social relations
among Iranians, they selectively participate in major events and cultural
celebrations such as the Iranian NoRuz (New Year). Insecure about their
Persian language competency, they interact mostly with family members
and close friends and attend private parties. They visit ethnic restaurants
and stores infrequently and devote more time to school and career than to
community affairs.

The feelings of the ambivalent second-generations toward American
society and culture are at least as mixed and conflicted as they are toward
the Iranian community. They find ethnic diversity and the "melting pot"
culture as well as respect for individual freedom and opportunities for social and economic advancement to be the most distinguishing features of
American society. However, they are critical of the excessive materialism
of American culture and the imperialistic ambitions of the U.S. government. In their view, Americans are self-centered, uncultured, ignorant,
and gullible individuals who take everything for granted.

These mixed, contradictory feelings toward both the Iranian community and American society have created divided selves filled with feelings of
love and hate, attraction and repulsion along with a dual Iranian American
identity. To cope with their ambivalent feelings most second-generations
in this category have innovatively selected bits and pieces of both cultures
that are meaningful to them and have created reconciled, harmonious cul-

tures of their own that are neither Iranian nor American. The following comments illustrate the challenging task of balancing the two cultures for most ambivalent second-generation Iranian Americans. Interesting is that they are all cognizant of their divided selves and the tensions of living in two incompatible cultural realms. A female college student from Dallas wrote:

> My hospitality is very Iranian. I welcome people (friends and family) to my home, serve them tea, food, fruits, etc. I go out of my way to be of some assistance to others. I date but have very Iranian traditional goals for marriage (i.e., I don't date just to "have a good time"). I have intentions of finding a suitable spouse. My independence makes me very American. I have learned not to rely on my family's financial support as of working age. I also respect the privacy of others as well as my own. In Persian culture intrusion is a more popular concept than privacy.

Another student from Dallas commented:

> Other than the density of hair on my body, and my nose, I don't know what is Iranian about me. I have been told the way I view the world is Iranian, but I am not sure if that is Iranian boosterism or reality. What makes me American is easy. My attachment to all things TV, my addiction to media, and my impatience for things to happen quickly.

Speaking of her divided self and divided social life, a high school student from Dallas stated:

> I am Iranian when I am at home with my family. I eat Persian food for dinner. When I go anywhere with my family or my Iranian family friends, I am Iranian. When I am at school or with my American friends I am American most of the time. This gesture is one I never really thought about ever. It is just the way I live. I suppose I am used to it. I consider it to be normal behavior.

The mixing of two cultures and its challenges was noted by a second-generation Iranian American from Houston:

> I have done most of my growing up away from Iran. Therefore, I feel I belong to a different culture (not so much Iranian or anything else) but a mixture. I

believe I have taken the better parts of each culture I have been exposed to and left behind the parts I did not like. This practice has made me to be more different than if I had been exposed to only Iranian society/values. My parents did not have the opportunities which I was given, and therefore have a hard time relating to some of me being distant. Sometimes they feel rejected even because I might not share the same point of view. But, overall, we all have found our comfort zones, regardless.

A college student from Austin wrote:

I am a teen lost between both cultures. I love being Iranian and going to Iranian events, and Persian music is what I listen to most. Yet, the American part of me is liberal, likes to party, date, and drink. Yet, I do all this without my parents' consent. However, I consider myself more Iranian and am very proud to be Persian, so I blend these two cultures together by making sure I live up to my parents' educational standards, yet having fun and being very liberal to all issues that I come across (drugs, drinking, sex, etc.).

The contradictory expectations of Iranian and American cultures and their emotional toll was repeatedly mentioned by many second-generation Iranian Americans in the study. A twenty-three-year-old college graduate from Houston expressed this contradiction succinctly:

Being constantly occupied with what society thinks of my behavior is the most Iranian feature, and wanting to be an individual and a person of myself is a very American feature. They often clash for me.

The same view was echoed by a second-generation Iranian American from Austin:

I have to suppress most of my beliefs when I'm in Iran, in order to keep peace with everyone. I don't feel the reverse when I'm in the USA. Mainly because I live alone for the most part, and really nobody cares how others live around here so long as it does not affect them. My Iranian experience drives me constantly to want to know about events around me and the world. I make this part of my daily life, but the indifference which I see from the American life regarding everyone else and world events puts me in direct (course of clash) with the society, especially southern culture such as Texas.

A teenage Iranian spoke of the main difference between her Iranian self and American self:

> I always thought the caring part of me was Iranian, but I'm finding that that's not true. The part of me that constantly feels guilty is Iranian. Good Americans are just as caring as good Iranians; they're just not obsessive about it. I can be very co-dependent and melodramatic and clingy, and I think that part of me is Iranian. What is American about me is that I am deeply interested in myself as a person and believe deeply in my right to be independent and grow and learn. I also have a capacity to live in the moment, instead of constantly thinking about the future, that I feel is very American.

A twenty-five-year-old female from Houston talked about balancing the two cultures:

> I want to engage myself in some American pastimes that my parents do not approve of. They expect me to be too Iranian. The best thing I have done is to balance these two cultures in my life. I love Persian food, gatherings, my family, my religion, my strong values that I have been brought up with. I love attending football games, barbecues, and the Houston rodeo.

A student from Austin outlined her attitudes, values, and behaviors that are Iranian and the ones that are American in detail in two columns, as if they were polar opposites. She considered her background, morals, family values, future outlook, views of God and religion, pride, ability, intelligence, honesty, truth, goodness, judgmental and opinionated nature, and sensitivity to be rooted in Iranian culture. Her American self consisted of open-mindedness, good nature and humor, freedom and liberties, understanding, sexuality, interest in music, partying, drinking, style, demeanor, "stupidity, bullshit ability, lies," and harshness.

Finally, the experience of having a divided self and the challenges of reconciling and blending the two selves together were best summed up by a twenty-year-old female from Houston:

> My morals and values, closeness with my family are Iranian. I love to speak Farsi and embrace my culture and am very proud of it always. My American side is a bit more on the liberal side. As an American, I have learned to enjoy

my life to the fullest and laugh out loud, be myself always. Iranians tend to
keep to themselves and not express their emotions and feelings. They are too
uptight.

It has been a difficult road to blend these two together, but still I had to
blend [the two, and I did so]. I have maintained my Iranian morals and values
but have also learned to enjoy my life without being concerned with who is
watching or what they would think of me.

Iranian Family, Cultural Resistance, and Second-Generations' Ethnic Identity Dilemma

As indicated in the above comments, first-generation Iranian immigrants
are not the only group in the Iranian community who suffer from an identity crisis and ambivalence. As with their parents, ambivalent feelings and
a contested ethnic identity are also problematic issues for many second-
generation Iranians in the United States. However, rooted in a different
origin and directed in a different orientation, the ambivalence and ethnic
identity crisis of second-generation Iranian Americans are fundamentally
different from their parents' in two important ways. First, unlike their parents' experiences, the primary ambivalent and mixed love-hate feelings
and relations of most second-generation Iranian Americans are directed
more toward the Iranian ethnic community, not American society. Second, while the ethnic identity dilemma of first-generation Iranians was a
direct political outcome of Iranian-U.S. conflict and the widespread prejudice and discrimination of Americans toward Iranian immigrants during
and after the hostage crisis, second-generation Iranians' ethnic identity
crisis has been an unforeseen and latent cultural by-product of their parents' cultural resistance against the political consequences of Iranian-U.S.
relations and the subsequent, prevailing anti-Iranian stereotypes.

As indicated by Moghissi (1999), to cope with racial discrimination,
prejudice, and cultural stereotyping, often a minority group retreats from
association with the dominant culture and the values it represents and en-
closes itself within the traditional cultural heritage, turning it into a pole
of resistance. Cultural resistance and oppositional culture can take different forms and can be articulated through various institutions. It can be
expressed openly through major institutions such as religion or disguised

in art and music. Another form of cultural resistance is cultural nationalism and enhancement of cultural identity. For example, religious-spiritual songs and Afro-Christianity among the enslaved African Americans in the late 1700s and the flowering of writing and arts among African American intellectuals known as the Harlem Renaissance in the 1920s were major sources of resistance and cultural nationalism (Feagin and Feagin 1999).

As described earlier, stereotyping of Iranians was a dehumanizing experience for thousands of Iranian immigrants in the United States that led to enormous disappointment among many Iranians and the denouncement of American culture and way of life at all levels, including family values and norms. To cope with the ongoing widespread stereotyping of Iranians and the prejudice and formal and informal discriminatory practices against them, many Iranian parents retreated from American society and presented very low cultural and ethnic profiles in public. Consequently, the ethnic community and institutions, particularly family, were the safest grounds where Iranians could bolster their ethnic pride and cultural values, particularly family values, maintain and reinforce their cultural norms and beliefs, and express and continue their cultural resistance. Articulation of cultural resistance through the institution of family had three crucial manifest and latent cultural outcomes for young second-generation Iranian Americans and their perceptions of and participation in the Iranian community. First, it intensified the cultural collision between second-generation Iranian American youth and their parents. Second, it eventually alienated second-generation Iranian Americans from the first-generations and the Iranian community due to a deep intergenerational cultural gap. Third, the cultural clash between the American-born and -reared Iranian youth and their parents minimized the visibility of second-generations in the community, discouraged the younger generation from participating in community affairs and events except for the Iranian New Year celebration and Persian concerts, made them ambivalent about the Iranian community, and contributed to their ethnic identity crises.

With no other individual and in no other social space have first-generation Iranians experienced so much daily tension and conflict than with their children in the family household. Likewise, in no other context in exile have the ideal familial norms of Iranian culture regarding parenting, marital relationship, sexual behavior, dating, and division of labor been so bluntly expressed and manifested than in the Iranian immigrant family.

In addition, in no other setting have Iranian parents gauged and realized the differences between Iranian and American cultures than in the family setting. Finally, in no other relationship have Iranian parents, particularly fathers and husbands, been so stressed and challenged to adjust and change than in their relationships with their young children. Overall, no other Iranian ethnic institution in exile has experienced so many fundamental changes in such a short period than the Iranian immigrant family (a topic to be explored more in the next chapter). This is probably due in large part to the fact that universally, the family is any society's core institution, mediating as it does between the broader culture's macroscopic matrix of institutions and the lived experience of individuals confronting daily social life.

Second-Generation Iranian Americans and Politics: Reclaiming the Iranian Ethnic Identity

As previously mentioned, in the past few decades, a considerable amount of research and theoretical effort have focused on ethnic options and ethnic or national identity formation of immigrants in the United States.[2] Despite their considerable amount of insight, most of these studies have built upon observations of the first-generations, ignoring the experiences of second-generation immigrants and their social adaptation, integration, and ethnic identity formation. Recently, however, more migration scholars have studied patterns and dynamics of ethnic identity formation among second-generation immigrants.[3] It is generally accepted among these scholars that forging a coherent transcultural identity that incorporates elements of both the ethnic or immigrant culture and the host culture effectively (so they can move comfortably between the two cultural domains) is an essential and challenging task for immigrant adolescents. At the same time, incorporating elements of both cultures presents inherent conflicting messages between the American culture they receive from school and the native cultures they receive at home. This conflict is even greater for immigrant adolescents whose group or ethnic origin is subject to pervasive social trauma by prejudice and discrimination. Immigrant adolescents who belong to stigmatized ethnic groups or nationalities with negative stereotypes find it more difficult and challenging to maintain a healthy sense of self-worth and identity (Suarez-Orozco and Qin 2006).

Considering Iranians' "spoiled" and discredited identity due to the on-going mutual political hostility between Iran and the United States and the pervasive anti-Iranian stereotypes and images perpetuated by main-stream American media, one would expect second-generation Iranian Americans to either deny their Iranian heritage or passively withdraw from the American social scene and interaction with Americans. On the contrary, although some second-generation Iranian Americans remain passive and adopt some of the same mechanisms—outlined in Chapter 2—as their parents to cope with the stigma of being Iranian, they have been generally very active and visible with remarkable political accom-plishments. Unlike their parents who remained preoccupied with politics in Iran and for the most part withdrew from the political process in the United States, the grown-up children of first-generation Iranian Ameri-cans have been very active politically, striving successfully to reclaim their ethnic-national reputation as a civilized and peaceful group with a rich culture and a glorious civilization.

Despite the ongoing sociopolitical conflicts between Iran and the United States and the existing anti-Iranian attitudes, as a group, second-generation Iranians actively participate in political processes of their host society, proudly promote and preserve the Persian culture and celebrate cultural events, and organize forums for Iranian Americans to discuss cross-cultural issues and learn more about legal, cultural, and social as-pects of life in the United States. Today, almost all major American cities and universities with a sizable population of Iranian students have Ira-nian American or Persian American clubs, organizations, or cultural as-sociations. While some of these associations are apolitical and avoid po-litical topics, others are political in nature with the aim of protecting the civil rights of Iranian nationals and encouraging first-generation Iranian Americans to take advantage of their legal rights and be more visible and active in American politics (a topic to be discussed in the conclusion). While the political organizations have played an important role in the po-litical socialization of Iranian immigrants, other organizations like the Iranian Alliances across Borders (IAAB) have aspired to educate Iranians and non-Iranians about the experiences of Iranians, particularly second-generation Iranian Americans in diaspora. For example, in collaboration with other second-generation organizations in the past several years, the IAAB has sponsored annual international conferences on both the ac-complishments of and issues facing the Iranian community in exile. In addition to addressing the experiences of Iranians in diaspora, associations like the IAAB try to bring together second-generation Iranians who have grown up in the diaspora so they can share their experiences with one another and form a new discourse about the hybridization of Iranian with American culture and the articulation of the two in exile. With their political activism, educational forums, professional networks, and cultural celebrations, second-generation Iranian Americans hope to dispel and demystify the myths and stereotypes that "spoiled" the social identity of their parents and to regain and retain their ethnic honor.

5 Exile and the Paradox of Gender, Marriage, and Family

Maryam's Life History

Maryam came to Texas in the summer of 1983 to finish her education. When Maryam left, Iran was in its second year of war with Iraq. Although it had been twenty-six years since Maryam left Iran, she still had very vivid memories of the terrifying air raids and deafening emergency sirens. She remembered frightened family members, neighbors screaming and searching for safe shelters where they could hide in the middle of the night, traumatized evacuees from the war zone fleeing to the crowded cities like Tehran, and long lines for rationed food and gasoline. In part Maryam chose to leave Iran because of the impact of war, the deterioration of the status of Iranian women in all aspects of life after the revolution, and the disastrous socioeconomic conditions of the postrevolutionary era. But her primary reason for leaving her home country was to achieve the educational goals that she had cultivated in her mind ever since she was in middle school. Maryam grew up in a semireligious, middle-class family with three older brothers. Except for one of her brothers and a paternal cousin in Texas, both of whom had left Iran before the revolution, no one on either side of her family had ever emigrated from Iran. Unlike many of her cousins and best friends who either dropped out of school or discontinued their education and married right after high school graduation, Maryam was determined to take a different path and go to college. Nevertheless, in April 1980, following Ayatollah Khomeini's order, the new government closed all universities for three years because many university professors and administrators were considered Westernized and the university curricula were regarded as incompatible with Islamic principles. As such, the new Islamic government launched the so-called cultural revolution (*eng-helab-e farhangi*), and formed the Council for Cultural Revolution to de-Westernize the Iranian higher education system and to develop new curricula and course materials compatible with Islamic teachings and the new government's revolutionary mission.

During the three years of the cultural revolution, Maryam had no accomplishments and passed her time "pointlessly" and "futilely" by involving herself in daily routines of eating, sleeping, watching TV, and helping her mother in household chores. Many of her friends either married and settled for a family life or were arrested for political activism. Many more left Iran legally and illegally either to study or to join family members abroad.

With the opening of the universities after three years, Maryam faced new challenges for continuing her educational dreams. Nevertheless, it did not take too long for Maryam to realize that her chances for going to college in Iran were very slim. The number of applicants exceeded the available university seats. Moreover, to ensure that only supporters of the revolution and devout Muslims entered higher education and to promote and perpetuate the ideology of the new Islamic government, universities provided admission priority for applicants from families of revolutionary and Iran-Iraq war martyrs, required rigorous Islamic ideology entry exams, and conducted thorough family background checks on applicants.

The bureaucratic challenges on the one hand and boredom, disenchantment with the new regime, deterioration of the status of women, and the disastrous social and economic conditions of Iran (such as massive unemployment and inflation) on the other hand pushed Maryam to plan for leaving Iran. Iranian parents are more protective of their daughters than sons, and girls are expected to live with their parents until they marry, even those who attend college. Thus, in Maryam's mind, living alone overseas did not seem to be an appealing idea for her parents, especially her father. To her surprise, despite their emotional reservations and the anguish of separation, Maryam's parents were very receptive when she told them about her plans for studying abroad and agreed to support her. Although relieved from the anxiety of making her decision and getting her parents' support, Maryam had mixed feelings about her future. Although she was very excited about the opportunity to complete her education in the United States, she was sad about leaving her family indeterminately. She was tormented by the idea of being separated from family and friends for the first time. She worried about the possibility of being rejected for a student entry permit or visa into the United States and dreaded having to adjust to a new culture and learn a new language.

After a month of preparation, Maryam left Iran with $500—the maximum allowable per passenger—in her purse. Unlike the experience of her older brother, who had come directly to the United States in 1976, closure of the American embassy in Iran after the hostage crisis compelled Maryam to spend two months in Frankfurt, Germany, awaiting receipt of her student visa from the American consulate there. While in Germany, Maryam stayed with a group of Iranian college students who were acquainted with her brother. After several visits to the American consulate in Frankfurt, Maryam eventually received a student visa valid for the duration of her studies in the United States. Although excited about seeing her brother after seven long years and starting this chapter in life independently, much like every new immigrant, Maryam's first reaction upon her arrival in the United States was culture shock and homesickness followed by mild temporary depression and loneliness. To console her, in their weekly letters Maryam's close friends and relatives updated her about the worsening social conditions in Iran, particularly for women, and congratulated her for being so lucky to get an American visa and having the opportunity to study abroad. Contrary to her parents' repeated advice to return to Iran during her initial period of adjustment, Maryam stayed and ultimately reached her dream and attained a graduate degree in 1990.

Today, Maryam, her husband, Amir, and their two American-born children live in Plano, Texas. Maryam and Amir met in college in 1985. Amir is an engineer and worked for a company in Dallas, and Maryam worked part-time for a financial company. Despite the relatively high overseas travel expenses, Amir and Maryam visit Iran at least once a year during the summer to see family members and relatives and to immerse their children in Iranian society and culture as often as possible. Both of their parents received green cards and come to the United States at least once every other year for several months. These periodic visits to and from Iran have helped their children to become more familiar with and appreciative of Iranian culture and more fluent in the Farsi language.

Despite their efforts at maintaining and promoting the Iranian cultural heritage in their family life, one of Maryam's biggest worries is the complete Americanization of her children and their total alienation from Iranian culture. Her concerns about the upbringing of her daughters in an American fashion and a lack of appreciation of Iranian culture were so serious that a few years earlier she contemplated returning to Iran temporarily until her children passed the critical teenage years so they might master the Persian language and internalize Iranian cultural values more completely. After her visit to Iran fourteen months before our interview, however, she realized that postrevolutionary Iranian teenagers were no more immune to many of the same social problems, particularly drugs and sex, than American teenagers were. Although they were continually exposed, albeit in a fragmented way, to Iranian culture and were moderately fluent in speaking and comprehending Farsi, Maryam considered her children to be mostly American and admitted that it was impossible for them to be completely Iranian the way she and her husband desired. Nevertheless, she strove very hard to implant and perpetuate the core values of Iranian culture in their upbringings as best she could. Like many other first-generation Iranian mothers, Maryam's biggest challenge was to balance the cultural expectations of Iranian parents with the American way of life in relationships with her children, particularly her older teenage daughter. In her view, American teenagers gain too much freedom too soon. She disagreed with certain norms and values of the mainstream American family and totally disapproved of many aspects of teenage life in the United States, in particular dating and sexual relationships. At the same time, she valued American parents' emphasis on their children's independence.

Maryam grew up in a family with a moderate religious background and adherence to Islamic rituals and practices. Today, however, she considers herself a secular, unorthodox, and unconventional Muslim who has abandoned most Islamic practices but has retained core dogmas of Islam. For Maryam and her husband, many of the traditional Islamic practices such as praying, fasting, celebrating religious holidays, and observing Islamic holy days have lost their significance and have no relevance to their daily lives. Reevaluation and reconstruction of Maryam's religious beliefs and her disengagement from Islamic practices have been in part caused by her great disappointment in the outcomes of the revolution and the treatment of women by fundamental Muslims as well as by her indignation at the government of the Islamic Republic for manipulating people in the name of Islam and religion. Maryam's disassociation with mainstream Islamic practices has also been an intentional adaptive reaction to the hostile Islamophobic attitudes of many Americans who have ignorantly linked Iranian immigrants with Islamic fanaticism, terrorism, and anti-Americanism. As a secular Muslim, Maryam neither practices veiling nor prays five times a day. Her beliefs about religion are very unorthodox and unconventional. In her view, all religions are essentially the same with a single mission of human salvation. She believes in God and focuses more on moral and spiritual aspects of Islam than its specific religious codes of conduct and daily rituals. Although she is not a traditional believer or practitioner of Islam, she prays once a day in a meditative form in her native Persian language. She sees this praying meditation as a powerful source for spiritual cleansing, guidance for behavior, and connection to a supreme being.

As with many other Iranian parents, one of Maryam's major challenges as a Muslim Iranian mother is to instruct her children about the basic teachings of Islam and to incorporate the fundamental tenets of her faith into the other aspects of Iranian culture in her family's daily life without revealing their religious background publicly. She likes for her children to embrace the core ethical values of Islam, but because of all the anti-Islamic media propaganda and publicity in the United States and the association of Islam with terrorism in the minds of many Americans, she avoids identifying herself and her children as Muslims to her friends and neighbors. Likewise, her children shun identification with the Islamic religion. Unlike many of her friends who have resolved this paradox and challenge by converting to Christianity, Maryam has opted for practicing and teaching her children to practice a subjectively "reformed," unorthodox version of Islam, without branding it as such, that is, a form of Islam that is less socially threatening, more in accordance with universal moral values, and more compatible with living in the United States. Therefore, she has taught the fundamentals of Islamic faith that she finds compatible to life in the United States to her children.

Despite the existence of numerous cultural barriers in her personal and family life, overall Maryam is content with living in the United States. Like most other Iranians, she has mixed feelings about both Iranian and American culture and society. She neither endorses the American way of life and family practices nor embraces her own cultural norms and values. She feels as marginal in the United States as she does in Iran when she visits her family. She finds the United States a land of opportunity for personal and professional development and strongly believes her children will have a better future in this country; but despite her positive attitude toward Americans, she feels that American society is unsafe and unhealthy in many respects. Reconciling her ambivalent feelings and the contradictory beliefs and practices of Iranian and American cultures remains a tough challenge for Maryam. Until then, like most other Iranian immigrant women and parents, Maryam continues her amphibious life in exile.

Although Maryam's life story reveals many of the same forces that pushed many young women out of Iran and uncovers some of the most pressing challenges confronted by most Iranian parents in exile, it presents only one of several modes of entry, conjugal unions, family compositions, and parenting concerns for Iranian families in the United States. Unlike Maryam, who came to the United States as a young, single nonimmigrant voluntarily for pursuit of educational goals, many Iranian women entered the country with their husbands and children as economic migrants in search of better job opportunities, better social conditions, and future educational opportunities for their children. Still others entered the United States either as refugees to escape religious and political persecution in Iran or to reunite with their spouses during their middle or late adulthood. Unlike Maryam, who dated her husband for several months after she finished college and had a professional job, many Iranian immigrant women met their future husbands by family arrangements either through exchanges of pictures or short visits in Iran or another country. While Maryam and her husband live in a nuclear household and are not bearing the burden of caring for their elderly parents in the United States, many married Iranian couples have extended family arrangements and are strained by the social needs as well as the medical and financial responsibilities of their elderly parents.

Aside from variations in their reasons for migration, family composition, and other structural forms, Iranian families in the United States are diverse in terms of interpersonal relations of couples, intergenerational relationships, division of labor within the household, cultural and religious practices, and extent and nature of the family problems they experience in exile. Although some Iranian families have strongly retained core values and traditions of Iranian culture, family values, and religious practices, others ignore some of the central elements of Iranian family values and are completely secular in their religious orientation. Some Iranian parents fail to accept American cultural values and forcibly apply Iranian family ideals on their teenagers born and raised as American Iranians without any compromises. Others are more flexible, insist less on retaining traditional Iranian cultural values, and respect and compromise more with the social activities and values of their children.

Unfortunately, there are no accurate and reliable data regarding the diversity of the Iranian immigrant family. The only available comprehensive, up-to-date, quantitative information about the Iranian immigrant family comes from the 2006-2008 American Community Survey reports, which provide demographic information about the size, structure, living arrangements, and socioeconomic status of Iranian families and households in the United States. To have a better understanding about the diversity and transformation of Iranian families in exile during the past three decades, the 2006–2008 ACS data have been augmented by data collected from Iranian immigrants in two separate studies, in 1993–1995 and 2003–2005, in Texas. The 2006–2008 ACS data reveal valuable quantitative information about the size, composition, and household structure of Iranian families in the United States. The data collected from Iranians in Texas capture reasons for migration, children's level of Persian fluency in reading and writing, various family problems they have experienced since their arrival, Iranian parents' concerns about their children's upbringing in the United States, and the views of first-generation Iranian men and women about American families and society. Merged together, the results of these two data sets suggest that the Iranian family in exile is a diverse institution that has been transformed and is far from both the ideal Iranian family and Americans' perceptions of a Middle Eastern immigrant family.

Demographic Characteristics of Iranian Immigrant Families in the United States

Much like other aspects of their lives, the structure and functioning of family life for Iranian immigrants in the United States has changed profoundly in the past three decades. These gradual changes were adaptive responses to a combination of social and political forces in Iran and the United States following the Iranian revolution and the hostage crisis. If we contextualize the development of the Iranian immigrant family historically, it becomes apparent that the Iranian family in exile has constantly been adjusting to the major political events in Iran and the United States and the subsequent demographic shifts in migration history of Iranians since the revolution. These political developments have affected and continue to contribute to Iranian immigrants' family tensions and conflicts. Again, the most important unit of social structure in Iran is the nuclear family. Therefore, Iranians feel obligated most strongly toward family members. After the nuclear family, however, Iranians feel obligated to members of the extended family. According to the U.S. Census Bureau's 2006–2008 American Community Survey reports, there were 154,523 households in the United States that were headed by Iranian nationals. These households seem to be diverse in composition and are made up of various relatives and nonrelatives. A majority of Iranian households in the United States (103,530, or 67 percent) were family households with either

nuclear married couples or extended family members and male and female heads of household with no spouse present.[1] Almost half of all Iranian family households (32.3 percent) included at least one child under the
age of eighteen. Most of these children lived with both of their parents in
married-couple households. However, 2.9 percent of Iranian children under eighteen lived in families headed by women with no husbands present.
In addition to the family households, the Iranian population in the United
States encompassed 50,993 (33 percent) nonfamily households consisting
of either a single head of household (28.1 percent) or a head of household
who cohabited with nonrelatives or an unmarried heterosexual or homosexual partner (4.9 percent).

As described earlier, the socioeconomic characteristics of Iranian families in the United States are very impressive, and many Iranian families in
the United States are affluent enough to make a comfortable life and maintain a good living standard. With a median family income of $86,087, a
figure that was $22,876 more than the median family income of other
families in the United States in 2008, nearly 62 percent of Iranian families lived in owned properties with a median value of $553,800 in predomi-
nantly middle- and upper-middle-class neighborhoods. Remarkable educational achievements, self-employment, and relatively high labor-force
participation of Iranian immigrants seem to be the basic fuel for the high
incomes of Iranian families. As noted previously, 58.5 percent of Iranians
in the United States have bachelor's degrees or higher. This exceptionally
high level of education among Iranians has had a major impact on their
annual incomes. Another remarkable characteristic of Iranian immigrants that has affected their relatively high family incomes is their high
rate of economic activity, particularly as self-employed entrepreneurs and
small-business owners. According to the 2006-2008 American Community Survey results, close to 65 percent of working-age Iranians (sixteen
years and older) were in the labor force. A majority of Iranians (78.4 percent) who were employed worked in the private sector. Another 10.7 percent worked in the public sector, and the remaining 10.5 percent were self-
employed. The total unemployment rate for Iranians in the United States
was only 4 percent.

Participation of women either as self-employed or as wage earners in
various economic sectors and industries is another conspicuous characteristic of Iranian immigrants that has contributed to their high family incomes. The 2006–2008 ACS results indicate that the median earning for
working Iranian women who worked full-time year-round was $47,366.
Slightly more than half (54.8 percent) of Iranian women who were of

working age (sixteen years and older) were in the labor force and contributed substantially to their family incomes. Only 3.6 percent of Iranian women who were in the labor force were unemployed. While 51 percent worked in managerial, professional, and related occupations, 31 percent were employed in sales and office occupations. Another 15 percent worked in service occupations such as personal care, food preparation, and health care support. The relative high occupational rankings of many Iranian women in the United States as immigrants are also associated with their distinctly high levels of education. Half the Iranian women in the United States (50.5 percent) had bachelor's degrees or higher.

The Ideal Iranian Family and the Reality of the Iranian Family in Exile

Despite the diversity of the Iranian family in exile and the outstanding educational, occupational, and financial achievements of first-generation Iranian men and women in the United States, the Iranian immigrant family, by and large, has become very unstable and confronts a series of serious challenges internally and externally. While some of these challenges are the inevitable consequences of migration and contact with a divergent culture that affect almost all immigrant groups, others are unique to Iranian immigrants and seem to be distinctly related to the social and political conditions in Iran, U.S.-Iranian postrevolutionary political circumstances, attitudes and perceptions of American people toward Iranian immigrants, and legal barriers imposed on Iranian immigrants by the U.S. government after the hostage crisis.

For example, both Iranian men and women are marrying at later ages, and marriages have become less stable. Even though marital dissolution in Iranian culture is shunned, the divorce rate and the number of single-parent families among Iranians in the United States have increased substantially. There also has been a sharp rise in cohabitation, premarital sex, intergenerational conflict, family tension, and emotional separation of married couples. As indicated in the 2006–2008 ACS report, 32 percent of Iranian immigrants in the United States were single, and 8 percent were either divorced or single parents.[2]

Many Iranian immigrants—scholars and ordinary citizens alike—agree that the Iranian family in exile has undergone dramatic changes in marriage, family relations, gender roles, parent-child relations, and sexual behavior and is overwhelmed by major conflicts and tensions. Family conflicts of Iranian immigrants are so widespread and serious that the focus of many talk shows and other Iranian exile media are devoted to divorce, marital conflict, difficulties in other types of intimate relationships, and various issues related to socialization of second-generation Iranians. All Iranian exile TV channels have regular live weekly counseling talk show programs produced in Los Angeles in which Iranian marriage and family counselors take phone calls from Iranian viewers all over the United States and advise callers on a variety of family issues. Due to the shortage of Iranian family counselors and the prevalence of family problems for Iranian families, some Iranian counselors either provide phone counseling services or have produced self-help books and CDs for sale. Many more place ads on the Internet and in popular Iranian magazines and regularly organize workshops and lectures on family conflict resolution in other states with large concentrations of Iranians.

In addition to the attention of Iranian exile media and the general concern of Iranian immigrants regarding family problems in the past three decades, various aspects of the Iranian family—particularly changes in gender roles, the labor-force participation and sexual behavior of Iranian immigrant women, and their implications for gender and family relations—have been studied by social scientists. A large number of these studies focus on the psychological adjustment and well-being of Iranian women, acculturation and the extent of cultural retention among young Iranian women, attitudes of Iranian women toward intimate relations (Hanassab 1991), various modes of adaptation of Iranian immigrant families (Jalali 1982), family status of Iranian immigrant women in relation to their husbands before and after migration to the United States (Abyaneh 1989), Iranian women's entrepreneurial endeavors in family-run businesses and in home-operated businesses (Dallalfar 1994, Mobasher 1996), changes in gender roles within the Iranian immigrant family, perceptions of gender roles among Iranian immigrant women in the United States (Mahdi 1999, 2001), adaptive strategies of older Iranian immigrant women to the new cultural environments (McConatha, Stroller, and Oboudiat 2001), emotional well-being of postrevolutionary Iranian immigrant women (Dossa 2004), Iranian women's experience of displacement and cultural resistance in exile (Moghissi 1999), changes and emerging patterns of interaction within the Iranian immigrant family (Mahdi 1999), political activities and transformations of Iranian immigrant or refugee women in exile (Bauer 1991), and socioeconomic integration of Iranian women (Niknia 2002).

Guided primarily by the theoretical assumptions of the assimilationist perspective and a narrow focus on adaptation of the individual family members, particularly women, most of these studies and many more have suggested that the changes and family conflicts occurring within the Iranian family in exile are inevitable outcomes of emigration from a traditional, conservative society such as that of Iran and assimilation into a more open, modern, and liberal society. For example, Mahdi's research (2001) on the perceptions of gender roles among female Iranian immigrants in the United States suggests that Iranian immigrant women have shifted away from traditional Iranian cultural values and are in search of new roles and rights. Mahdi maintains that Iranian women have replaced the traditional views of women's role in Iranian society with a more liberal Western view and have changed their views and attitudes about sex, dating, marriage, divorce, women's rights, child rearing, division of labor, labor-force participation, and the role of religion in guiding family values and sexual behavior. Mahdi concludes that most Iranian immigrant women in the United States believe in gender equality or egalitarianism in both public and private spheres of life. This equality is fueled by feminist ideals as defined in the West, including separation of religion from women's sexual behavior and conventions of exogamous interreligious marriages, gender equality in ownership and financial matters, significance of sexual satisfaction as a crucial element for marital happiness and family stability, and career development and joint economic and financial contribution to the family.

Although Mahdi acknowledges the impact of political forces and reception patterns of the host society as well as political relationships between the home and host societies as contributing factors to family tensions of Iranian immigrants, he does not elaborate on these issues and avoids explaining the link between political forces and the transformation of the Iranian family in exile. In another study about the acculturation of young Iranian women in the United States and their attitudes toward sex roles and intimate relationships, Hanassab (1991) explored the extent to which young Iranian women living in Los Angeles kept their traditional Iranian cultural values. Based on a nonrandom sample of seventy-seven young Iranian women between the ages of seventeen and thirty-two from different religious subgroups in Los Angeles, Hanassab concludes that the exposure of Iranian families to incompatible cultural practices and beliefs of Americans generates tension and confronts Iranians with decisions regarding assimilation to American ways of life, retention of original cultural practices, or both. Her findings indicate that Iranian women who identify more closely with mainstream American culture and are more acculturated hold more liberal attitudes toward sex and intimate relationships. Participants' lengths of stay in the United States increased exposure and contact with the host culture and were found to be positively related to acculturation level.

In general, the literature on the Iranian family in exile suggests that the family tensions experienced by Iranian immigrants are related to the uneven, disharmonious pace of acculturation and the ensuing attitudinal disparity between Iranian couples as well as the labor-force participation of women and transformation of gender roles and power relations within the family. Rooted in this perspective is the assumption that immigrant men and women not only react to the new cultural environment differently but also adopt the new norms and values at different paces and in different degrees. As such, it is assumed that female Iranian immigrants in the United States have adopted the egalitarian attitudes toward gender roles at a much faster pace than Iranian men have. Heavy restrictions and social pressures imposed on women in Iran, they conclude, not only motivate Iranian women to leave but also encourage them to have greater desire to renounce the traditional norms of Iranian society and replace them much more quickly than men do with more liberal attitudes of American society toward dating, sex, marriage, gender roles, and egalitarian family relations.

Therefore, unlike Iranian immigrant men who have remained traditional and have retained the traditional cultural values of marriage and family relations, Iranian women have become very liberal soon after their migration. This is particularly the case for Iranian women who left Iran at younger ages and those who have lived in the United States longer and have had more exposure to and contact with American culture. Along with the faster pace of assimilation, the new, liberal attitudes and behaviors that many Iranian women have incorporated into their lives in the United States are strongly at odds with Iranian cultural norms and contradict those of their Iranian male counterparts who view premarital sex, marriage, and gender roles from a traditional standpoint. The faster pace of acculturation for Iranian women combined with the incompatibility of traditional Iranian cultural values toward sex, marriage, and family with cultural values and norms in mainstream American society lead to a serious acculturation disparity and attitudinal discrepancy between Iranian spouses. Therefore, as Iranian women acculturate and assimilate more to these prevailing norms, the level of cultural collision between these two incompatible sets of norms intensifies and creates more cognitive dissonance and leads to interpersonal tensions in the family, marital instability, and divorce. Furthermore, the acceptability of divorce and liberal divorce laws in contemporary U.S. society encourage and facilitate divorce among unhappy Iranian couples. In conclusion, much of the work on the Iranian family and gender relations in exile emphasizes cultural explanations and change in traditional cultural practices and behaviors of Iranian women as a primary source of family conflict. These studies suggest that family issues and marital discord are consequences of change in traditional gender roles caused by the assimilation of Iranian women into mainstream American culture and their adoption of practices and views such as individualism and egalitarianism that are incompatible with the traditional values of collectivism and subordination common in typical Iranian families.

Despite their significant contributions and empirical findings on the extent of change within the Iranian immigrant family, the cultural approach and assimilation model fail to explain the experience of Iranian immigrant families adequately and suffers both theoretically and methodologically in a number of ways. First, a large number of these studies were conducted by psychologists with a narrow focus on adaptation of individual family members. Most research studies on acculturation and integration of Iranian immigrant women have been based only on very small nonrandom samples. Second, the cultural explanations deemphasize the importance of political forces on transformation of the Iranian family in exile and fail to acknowledge the impact of political crisis in Iran and immigration sanctions imposed on Iranian immigrants in the United States after the hostage crisis on instability and insecurity of Iranian immigrant families. Third, many of these studies completely ignore the larger structural forces of integration. They overlook the heterogeneity of Iranian women and families, undermine the considerable ethnoreligious diversity in the family structure among Iranian immigrants, and disregard the family structure of Iranian immigrants who entered the United States in different waves and periods under different conditions in the host society. As noted earlier, Iranian immigrant women in the United States are a diverse group in terms of level of education, social class, length of residence in the United States, religious and political orientation, family structure, and reasons for immigration.

In addition to their diverse demographic profile and in spite of their general criticism of the American family, including gender roles, sexual freedom, and parenting practices of American couples, Iranian women have different, sometimes conflicting, views of American women and family. Some "traditional" Iranian women are extremely critical of American family and fanatically reject the sexual liberation of women and teenagers and find it harmful to the stability of the family—particularly to children. In their rejection of the "modern," "liberal" values of American families regarding sex and individual freedom, traditional Iranian women proudly claim to have a superior, more humane family values system and strive to maintain some traditional gender practices of Iranian culture in different ways, particularly in their relations with their children.

Other than the small number of traditionalist Iranian immigrant women who are judgmental and strongly critical of American women and their family values, a significant number of Iranian women are ambivalent about sexual freedom and American family relations. Like the traditionalists, although less intense and extreme, these ambivalent Iranian immigrant women are also inclined to find the American family structure and values to be loose and lacking moral restraints and integrity. However, while the traditionalists ethnocentrically discard the entire American family and see the Iranian family as the only alternative, ambivalent Iranian women are more realistic and nonbinary in their attitudes toward gender roles, marriage, and family relations in the United States, and they desperately seek a third, hybridized alternative that is neither completely Iranian nor American but has the "best of the two cultures," as indicated by an Iranian woman in Dallas. Despite their long residence in this country, remarkable educational and professional accomplishments, and positive attitudes toward migration and its liberating social and economic outcomes, ambivalent Iranian immigrant women in general have mixed opinions and feelings about marriage and family affairs, divorce, sexuality and sexual freedom, and the role of women in the United States. As best described by an Iranian woman in Dallas: "Iranian women in the United States live in an inferno and are tormented, torn between individual freedom encouraged by the American culture and familial commitments and expectations cultivated by the Iranian culture." Contrary to what most cultural explanations of Iranian women and family indicate, this statement aptly suggests that Iranian women in the United States in general neither have been fully assimilated to the American way of life nor have remained completely Iranian.

Given the heterogeneous make-up of Iranian immigrant women demographically and attitudinally, the cultural explanation and sexual liberation scenario, in my view, would apply to a very small fraction of Iranian immigrant women. Whether single or married, employed or housewives, having family members here or not, most Iranian women have not completely accepted the American cultural and family values, embraced its sexual norms and practices, or identified with it; nor have they retained

Iranian practices of veiling, gender segregation, and submissive roles under the guardianship of their husbands. Depending on their socioeconomic status and unique individual and family circumstances, most Iranian immigrant women land somewhere between these two cultural poles and face unique paradoxes and challenges for reconciling these two ways of life and integrating into American society.

Migration scholars contend that despite the great variation in culture and pattern of migration among immigrant groups, the majority of immigrant families in the United States experience stress in the process of adjusting to their new culture. There is no doubt that Iranian cultural beliefs and norms about sex, marriage, and family completely diverge from those prevalent in mainstream American society. Also, there is no question that some of the family problems and conflicts that Iranian couples have experienced are rooted in Iranian family ideals that are carried over from Iran and stem from a cultural clash due to an inevitable confrontation with American culture. Nevertheless, other factors have greatly affected the transformation and disintegration of the traditional Iranian family and have led to serious family problems in exile.

Therefore, consistent with the central theme of this book, I believe that in addition to cultural factors and the typical stresses of adaptation, acculturation, and adjustment that almost all immigrant families experience in the United States, the foregoing political forces in Iran and the United States that I alluded to in previous chapters have had a profound impact on the structure and functioning of Iranian families in exile and the prevailing conflicts and tensions within it. For example, immigration policies since the U.S.-Iranian diplomatic breakup following the hostage crisis affected immigration of Iranian families to the United States and reunification of individual Iranians with their families. As such, to gain a broader understanding of the major sources of tension within the Iranian immigrant family in exile, we need to contextualize it historically and examine it against the backdrop of the political events in Iran and the United States and shifting political relations between the two countries since the Iranian revolution and the hostage crisis in 1979. These political forces not only complicated and added more tension to acculturation of Iranian families in their new social context but created a host of new challenges and problems for most Iranian families. The following brief life history provides an example of how marriage and family for many Iranian immigrants in exile were strongly tied to and shaped by powerful inevitable political forces in Iran and the United States.

Politics and the Iranian Immigrant Family: Iranian Revolution, Iran-Iraq
War, the Hostage Crisis, and Obstacles to Family Reunification and Family
Formation in Exile

Shireen's Life History

Shireen was thirty-four years old at the time of our interview, an Iranian-
born woman who moved to the United States in 1998. Shireen was living in Austin, Texas, with her husband. They had been married for five
years and had no children. Shireen's childhood was not that of an average little girl growing up in Iran. During her childhood, Shireen's father
was imprisoned for a period of thirteen years for opposing the shah's government. Shireen was originally raised according to the Islamic faith and
practices. Since the revolution in 1979, however, she has held a strong resentment for those who have distorted and manipulated the Islamic faith
for their own political gains and no longer practices Islamic rituals, customs, and beliefs.

Throughout her life, Shireen and her family have been in constant battle with the Iranian government because of her father's political activities
before and after the revolution. That is why she fled to Europe in 1996 and
then to the United States in 1998. When the political situation in Iran became turbulent and unstable, Shireen fled to Europe. At the time of her escape from Iran, Shireen was working for a European company in Tehran.
Her employers became aware of her life-threatening situation and offered
to help her flee the country. After paying approximately ten thousand dollars and waiting for three months, Shireen obtained a visa from the Dutch
embassy. Shireen was the last of her siblings to flee from Iran. Her sisters
had come to the United States several years before Shireen left Iran and resided in California, where almost 50 percent of Iranian immigrants in the
United States reside.

While living in France Shireen met her husband, Hamed, at a family gathering. Several months after their friendship began, Shireen told
Hamed about her uncertain situation in exile and her difficulties in obtaining a visa to reunite with her sisters in California. When Shireen was
in Europe, the U.S. embassies were rejecting most visa applications for
Iranian nationals and were not issuing visas to Iranian citizens. To help
Shireen obtain a visa and reunite with her family in California, Hamed
offered to marry Shireen and move to the United States as her spouse.
Shireen was reluctant at first and claimed that she was not ready for mar-

riage. After careful consideration, Shireen accepted his offer because she realized that this was the only chance that she had to move to the United States. A month after Hamed's proposal, Shireen obtained a K-1 fiancée visa from the United States and entered the country. She first moved to Los Angeles, California, and then to Austin. She obtained a bachelor's degree in psychology and planned to go to graduate school. Despite missing Iran, Shireen loves living in the United States very much and is extremely satisfied with her life in Texas. Her hardships have only taught her to "appreciate the freedom that the U.S. has offered" her, and she is grateful for that. Nevertheless, she still has many unresolved cultural dilemmas and feels detached from American culture and society.

As best indicated in the brief account of Shireen's life story, the repercussions on Iranian families of the Iranian revolution, the hostage crisis, and bans on Iranians' migration to the United States were immediate and devastating. Together, these political forces not only shook the fundamental structure of the Iranian immigrant family and influenced dynamics of family relations in Iran and the United States at all levels but also delayed and created strong barriers to formation of new families for many single Iranians. These forces either hampered or completely curtailed reunification of the existing family unit for many more married Iranians and made it fragile and insecure, rendering a series of ongoing marriage problems and family crises for almost all Iranian immigrants in the United States. These political forces broke many families apart and deepened the physical separation of many more young Iranians from family members in Iran. They undermined the unity and integrity of the Iranian family system, forced many Iranians to leave in a sequence (beginning with the father-husband) and live in split households for many years, and posed major emotional challenges in family relations and integration of Iranians.

On the one hand, the abrupt, involuntary departure of many Iranian families during and immediately after the revolution—particularly members of religious minorities, political activists, high-ranking officials and elites of the former government and the secret police, and entertainers—ruptured family structure, interrupted family relations, and postponed family reunification for these political exiles and refugees for a long time. On the other hand, at the same time that thousands of Iranian families were leaving Iran to reunite with their family members, post–hostage crisis visa restrictions imposed on Iranians and cancellation of visas issued to Iranians excluded them from entering the United States. The visa restrictions created another setback to the development of the Iranian family in exile, damaged the emotional stability of Iranian family members, and de-layed the possibility of family reunification for thousands of Iranian men with their spouse and children who were either in Iran or another country. In addition to mass migration of Iranian elites and political activists, soon after the revolution, political turmoil, Islamization and domestic policies of the postrevolutionary government, and traumatic cultural changes cou-pled with the devastating economic and social consequences of the Iran-Iraq war drove thousands more families—especially the ones with young, drafting-age sons—out of the country in search of better jobs, political se-curity, freedom, and better social conditions.

While some families left Iran collectively and were able to maintain their unity in one household, others were broken apart and left Iran in a sequence, beginning with the husband-father, and lived in split house-holds for several years before they were reunited. These long-term, invol-untary separations not only fragmented households and interrupted fam-ily harmony but also forced family members to develop new family roles and rules for interaction with family members. Cancellation of Iranian visas after the hostage crisis exacerbated the family problems of Iranian immigrants and posed major emotional challenges in family relations and the social integration of Iranians. The new immigration policies created strong barriers to marriage and the formation of new family households for many single Iranians in exile, extending the physical separation of many more young Iranians from family members in Iran and undermin-ing the unity and integrity of the Iranian family system. Adapting to these previously unknown split households that were thousands of miles apart under harsh social and political conditions was very challenging, with conflictual personal and family outcomes for most Iranian immigrants.

As indicated by Purkayastha (2002), family life for most nonwhite groups in the United States has been influenced by immigration and natu-ralization laws. In her view, periodic immigration bans as well as a host of other laws, such as country quotas on family reunification and tempo-rary work permits for skilled workers with few rights or supports for their families, have restricted immigrants' ability to marry, create families, or become reunited with their families. These laws have also curtailed immi-grants' access to the social resources necessary to maintain families. Pur-kayastha's perspective on immigration laws and family life for migrants is best manifested in the case of Iranian immigrants in the United States. Before the hostage crisis, Iranians with valid multiple U.S. visas who had left their native country legally could return to Iran and come back without requesting new entry visas from American consulates abroad. After the hostage crisis and cancellation of all visas, the scenario changed and all Iranians, including those who previously held multiple entry visas, were required to have new entry visas upon their return to the United States. Single Iranians left in the United States could either return to Iran and face the same social and political conditions—including the military draft for men—that were driving many Iranians to exile, remain bachelors, marry other single Iranians in the United States, marry non-Iranian nationals in the United States, or marry Iranian "picture brides" living either in Iran or another country through family arrangements and networks of friends.

Each of these options adopted by Iranians gave rise to distinct family structures and dynamics in exile, each with its unique tensions and weaknesses. One option adopted by a large number of single Iranian men whose visa status was threatened by the Iranian hostage crisis was marriage with U.S. citizens. Although some of these interethnic marriages were genuine and based on love and long-term mutual commitment, others were fake business marriages that occurred with complete strangers in return for several thousand dollars and were arranged through networks of friends and relatives. These marriages often consisted of several encounters between the couples mainly for the purpose of rehearsing the immigration interview process and were terminated shortly after the green card was issued. Many others were unions either between acquaintances in college and workplaces or dating couples and involved more trust as well as personal knowledge and emotional attachment. The Iranian community in Dallas where I lived and conducted my fieldwork was filled with striking stories about faked marriages, some with unintentional, unpleasant consequences. The incidence of faked matrimonies among Iranians that were primarily for visa adjustment from temporary to permanent residency was so prevalent that immigration officers suspected all marriages between Iranians and U.S. citizens and regarded them as a sham. In an interview during my fieldwork in 1994, when asked about the perception of immigration officers regarding Iranians who apply for green cards through marriage, a high-ranking member of the immigration services in Dallas replied: "We conduct interviews with Iranians and review their application with the assumption that this is a fraudulent marriage." The widespread, stereotypical perception of faked marriages among Iranians, notwithstanding its legitimate ground, had humiliating and dehumanizing consequences for Iranian applicants and their spouses. To verify the authenticity of a marriage between an Iranian and a U.S. citizen and to ensure that the couple lived together, immigration officers separated the couple into two rooms and asked degrading, detailed questions about their private marital life, including sexual behaviors and sleeping patterns.

Between 1986 and 1988, a combination of political factors in Iran and the United States, including the end of the Iran-Iraq war, the Immigration Reform and Control Act, and the major changes in Iranian laws regarding Iranian immigrants, removed all the migration barriers for Iranian men and facilitated temporary visits for Iranians with their family members in Iran, as well as bride selection for many single Iranian men who returned to Iran and the formation of new families through marriage. First, the IRCA and the legalization process and eventual U.S. citizenship provided an opportunity for thousands of Iranians to obtain permanent residency, travel outside of the United States, marry in Iran, and file petitions to bring their spouses, siblings, and parents to the United States over several years. Another important consequence of the IRCA of 1986 that ultimately altered the demographic composition of the Iranian community in the United States has been the increase in the number of Iranians who have become naturalized citizens of the United States. This increase in the naturalization trend in turn increased the number of new immigrants who entered the United States for family reunification purposes. This has been especially the case for many Iranian women who entered the United States as the wives of naturalized Iranians. Second, changes in the policies for return migrants implemented by the Iranian government at the end of the Iran-Iraq war meant that a significant number of single Iranian men who had either escaped the war and left Iran or refused to visit their families due to fear of being drafted were able to return to Iran freely and marry, file petitions for their wives, and bring them to the United States.

Contrary to obstacles to family formation during the 1980s, in the 1990s the Iranian community in the United States went through the formation and growth of a type of Iranian family in exile composed of newly arrived brides from Iran, often called imported brides (*aroos varedati*) by some Iranians. The increase in migrant women from Iran reflects this growth. Beginning in 1992 the number of Iranian women who have been admitted to the United States has continually exceeded that of men. Based on Department of Homeland Security reports, between 1992 and 2002, nearly 56,410 Iranian women were admitted to the United States. The number of Iranian men during the same period was 47,086.[3] Many of these marriages were arranged by family members and friends during one or several short consecutive visits to Iran. In some cases, the legal immigration sponsorship process for reuniting with their spouses took several years. These were mainly the cases for non–U.S. citizen Iranian men who had yet to be naturalized.[4] These two political reforms not only reconnected and linked the community of Iranian immigrants who were living in exile for a long time to their home society but also facilitated family reunification and formation of new Iranian families in exile.

In summary, the attainment of permanent residency and eventual citizenship through the IRCA of 1986, coupled with the removal of such barriers as Iranian military conscription, changed the patterns of Iranian migration to the United States. Moreover, the combined effect of these political and legal forces altered the demographic composition of Iranian communities in the United States and affected the structure and dynamics of the Iranian family in exile in a number of ways. First, as indicated earlier, after 1988 there was a large increase in the number of Iranian women in the United States. Many of them were sisters and mothers of Iranians who had become U.S. citizens and entered under the family-sponsored preferences category. Many more, however, were wives and fiancées of Iranian men. The massive flow of Iranian women to the United States—some directly from Iran and others from other countries—changed the gender distribution of Iranian immigrants admitted to the United States for the first time and added a new type of family with its unique problems to the pool of Iranian families in exile.

The second demographic consequence of the IRCA of 1986 and legalization of thousands of Iranians was an acceleration in the immigration of older Iranian men and women to the United States as permanent-resident parents of naturalized Iranian immigrants for the purpose of reunification with their sons and daughters. As indicated in the immigration reports, between 1980 and 1989, the total number of Iranians ages sixty or older who entered the United States was 1,354. Between 1990 and 1999, this number jumped to 14,963. The "oldest old"—those ages eighty and older—increased from 98 to 1,925 during the same period.[5] Acceleration of the Iranian elderly population in the United States added yet a new host of tensions to the existing family issues of Iranian immigrants. Given the increasing rate of naturalization among Iranian immigrants, there are likely to be more elderly Iranians coming to the United States in the future. As rightly indicated by McConatha, Stroller, and Oboudiat (2001), older Iranian immigrants suffer more from the transitional stress and identity issues because during the recent history of Iran they experienced several rapid and radical social transformations. During the years prior to the revolution they experienced the fundamental social transformation of Iran from a traditional into a modern "Western"-style country. Following the revolution, however, the country was returned to a more traditional religious society.

Double Marginality, Anomie, and Family Conflict

Despite all the changes and strains in the past thirty years and regardless of their source, the Iranian immigrant family remains the cornerstone of the Iranian community and continues to be the most important agent of socialization for second-generation Iranians in exile. Nevertheless, as indicated before, an amalgamation of cultural and political forces has reconfigured the Iranian immigrant family and made it far from the ideal "traditional" Iranian family. Even though many Iranian families, particularly the ones with teenage children, acknowledge that the Iranian family in exile has been transformed and realize that some major norms and values of the Iranian family are impractical and inconsistent with realities of family life in the United States, they strive vigorously to retain most of its core values and refuse vehemently to replace them completely with family norms of Americans. At the same time, as revealed in the following comments, in spite of their extremely distorted, negative perceptions of the American family, in their vain attempt to reduce family tensions and create more resilient families in exile, Iranian immigrants selectively and warily incorporate some family practices of Americans into the structure of their marital and parental relationships.

After many years of trial and error, Iranians have failed to find the hybrid, ideal, exilic family with a balanced injection of both Iranian and American practices into its cultural tissue, and they continue to face the same challenges and suffer from the same tensions. Once again, in sharp contrast to the assimilationist scholars and consistent with my discussion in previous chapters, in my view this failure and the persistence of the prevailing conflicts in Iranian immigrant families are primarily anomic outcomes and responses to a set of external social and political forces rather than the result of cultural incompatibility between their traditional family patterns and unsuccessful adjustment to the new host culture. There is a fundamental difference between incompatibility between two cultural systems and detachment or retreat from both of them. The point that many scholars have overlooked about the Iranian family in exile is that Iranian immigrants—even those who have lived in the United States for a long time—neither completely endorse nor entirely shun either cultural system. As previously noted, the prevailing anti-Iranian and anti-Muslim attitudes of many Americans after the hostage crisis made many Iranians ambivalent about American society and people but also alienated them from American culture and created a cultural backlash and resistance against their fundamental values, including family values.

At the same time, Islamization of Iranian society and the postrevolutionary family policies of the Iranian government and treatment of women in Iran—not assimilation to American culture and gender roles—turned so many Iranian immigrant women away from the traditional family values of Iranian culture. In other words, the deviation of most Iranian women from the traditional family norms and gender roles of Iranian culture seems to be as much a reaction to the treatment of women in Iran and the ideal postrevolutionary Islamic family in Iran, if not more so, than their adoption of the liberal values of American society. Quite like second-generation Iranians, albeit at a different level and on a more complex scale, to cope with the predicament of double anomie or double cultural loss, most Iranian women are constantly searching for novel ways to create a third alternative model of marriage, family relations, and gender roles. In their resistance against the traditional Iranian family practices on the one hand and reaction to cultural beliefs and practices of Americans on the other, Iranian women are idealizing a marital relationship and family structure that represents a compromise between the core opposing values of individualism, attainment of personal gains, sexual satisfaction, and career advancement encouraged by American culture with collectivism, making sacrifices for their children and other family members, and loyalty and commitment to family needs embedded in and cultivated by the Iranian culture. Whether they succeed in creating this hybrid family system in exile remains to be seen.

Conclusion

Despite the tough immigration control after 9/11 and the continuing perception and treatment of Iranians as a suspect group, Iranians are still entering the United States in surprising numbers. According to statistics compiled by the U.S. Department of Homeland Security in 2008, between 2002 and 2008 nearly 82,770 Iranians obtained legal permanent resident status, and another 45,653 nonimmigrant residents entered the United States from Iran. As in previous decades, most of the post-9/11 Iranians who entered the United States came as immediate relatives of U.S. citizens or as students and tourists. A lucky few entered the United States, winning the green-card lottery. Besides the immigrants and nonimmigrants, during the same period 21,466 Iranian nationals arrived in the United States as refugees, and another 2,011 individuals from Iran were granted political asylum. With the rise of antigovernment sentiments inspired by protests in Iran over the contested reelection of Mahmoud Ahmadinejad in July 2009 and the escalation of political conflict between conservatives and reformists in Iran, it is likely that more Iranians will leave the country for political reasons in the future. Irrespective of the extent of Iranians' immigration in the coming years, as I have tried to demonstrate in this book, various political events in Iran and the United States over the past few decades—particularly the 1979 hostage crisis and the 9/11 terrorist attacks—have strongly affected and continue to have an impact on the lives of Iranians in diaspora. Given the continuation of Iranian-U.S. political tension over Iran's nuclear program and U.S. economic sanctions against Iran, it seems unlikely that the immigration policies and the overall level of prejudice and discrimination against Iranians will be altered in the foreseeable future. Nevertheless, in view of the restrictions, the unfair treatment of some Iranian nationals, and the scale of political and social pressures on Iranian nationals after 9/11, the continuing increase in Iranians' participation in U.S. politics for civil rights protection and political empowerment is promising and indicative that Iranians are learning to live in the United States as Iranian Americans rather than just as Iranians in America.

Soon after 9/11, while condemning the terrorist attacks, Iranians across the United States created a number of nonprofit, grassroots, civil liberties and educational organizations such as the National Iranian American Council (NIAC), Persian Watch Center, Iranian American Political Action Committee (IAPAC), National Legal Sanctuary for Community Advancement (NLSCA), Iranian-American Anti-Discrimination Council (IAADC), and Public Affairs Alliance of Iranian Americans (PAAIA). While some of these organizations focus exclusively on the Iranian American community and Iranian expatriates in exile, others concentrate on both Iran and Iranian immigrant communities outside Iran. Overall, the common goal of these organizations is to advance the political interests of the Iranian American community by reaching out to Iranians and protecting their legal civil rights through education and dissemination of information about hate crimes and discrimination. For example, in June 2005, in response to the rise in FBI surveillance of families and students, a coalition of Iranian and American organizations including the NLSCA, IAPAC, IABA, National Lawyers Guild, Equal Employment Opportunity Commission, Amnesty International, and the American Civil Liberties Union (ACLU) launched a "Know your rights" campaign in order to address concerns of the Iranian community and to create a safety net for Iranian Americans in the face of various forms of discrimination. One resource offered in this campaign was a pamphlet in Persian that contained detailed information about what Iranians should do if questioned by police, FBI, customs, or immigration officers.

In addition to political socialization of Iranians regarding their legal and civil rights as U.S. citizens, these organizations have been trying to educate policy makers in Washington, D.C., about Iran. The organizations have sponsored numerous public forums in which members of Congress, immigration officers, and legal advocates from various Iranian associations met to provide an avenue for Iranians to discuss their concerns over the immigration process with members of Congress and government officials in their community. Also, they have organized meetings with various U.S. government agencies and officials to address the troubling legal issues confronting Iranian Americans including FBI background checks, delays in processing immigration cases, and deportation and removal proceedings, as well as issues surrounding the NSEERS (National Security Entry Exit Registration System) special registration program. For example, on September 1, 2004, the IAPAC organized a forum and hosted Congressman Marty Meehan from the House Judiciary Committee and U.S. citizenship and immigration officers together with leading Iranian American legal advocates from the Iranian American Bar Association and the National Legal Sanctuary for Community Advancement to answer Iranians' general concerns about immigration issues (B. Mahdi 2005).

Another major collective objective of these organizations has been political empowerment by encouraging Iranians to actively participate in political processes and to vote and lobby against federal policies such as the Patriot Act, the Enhanced Border Security and Visa Entry Reform Act of 2002, and House Resolution 3525. When in 2002 the U.S. Congress passed H.R. 3525, an antiterrorism law that banned nonimmigrant citizens of Iran and six other countries from entering the United States, the IAADC started a massive campaign and collected thousands of signatures from Iranian Americans objecting to the law on the grounds that no Iranian citizen had ever been involved in a terrorist attack on the United States. In their appeal, the petitioners asked the U.S. government to at least amend the law and either exempt Iranian nationals or allow close relatives of Iranian American citizens to enter the United States and to refrain from categorically prohibiting them from visiting their relatives in the United States (McGill 2002).

The growing political influence of Iranians after 9/11 has manifested in their election or appointment to various political positions. Until 9/11, despite their wealth, high levels of education, and professional achievements in business, law, medicine, engineering, and academia, only a handful of Iranian Americans were elected to public office, none of them on Capitol Hill. After 9/11, however, the number of Iranian Americans or individuals of Iranian descent who have been elected for various political offices in the United States has steadily increased. These positions include U.S. House of Representatives member, county superior court judge, district attorney, mayor, city council member, and local board of supervisors member.[1] For instance, in Beverly Hills, California, three of the six candidates running for city council and mayor in 2007 were born in Iran. To make voting more accessible to Iranians in Beverly Hills, the entire city's absentee and sample ballots were translated to Persian (Barboza 2007).

This remarkable political and ethnic mobilization among Iranian immigrants since 9/11 has been largely undertaken by second-generation Iranians. The sociology of immigration has established that the first-generation immigrants are torn between old loyalties and new realities and are preoccupied with the home country as a primary source of identity. It befalls the second generation to carry forward the ethnic incorporation process. According to Portes and Rumbaut (2006), the political concerns and orientation of first-generation immigrants are affected by a complex combination of factors pertaining to their places of origin as well as their points of destination.

Beyond events in the sending and receiving countries, immigrant politics are affected by immigrants' past political socialization, their commitment to return, and the national situations that they have left behind. Depending on the nature of interaction among these forces, Portes and Rumbaut maintain, immigrants may choose from several sets of political activities. They may passionately commit themselves to political causes at home, or they may concentrate on establishing new lives in their new homes. As described earlier, for a large number of Iranians, immigration to the United States was political in the sense of escaping from the revolutionary government and the postrevolutionary socioeconomic and political conditions in Iran. While some of them wanted to return, others never really intended to return. Iranian political activists, religious minorities, and members of various political organizations in Iran and in exile before and after the revolution are notable in the latter respect. Besides political migrants, a significant segment of Iranian immigrants who entered the United States before, during, and immediately after the revolution was comprised of middle- and upper-middle-class students, professionals, intellectuals, artists, skilled artisans, and entrepreneurs from big cities who intended to return, at least initially.

Overall, most Iranians have settled in the United States, although for most of them this journey was temporary. Given the political nature of Iranian immigration and the sociodemographic characteristics of Iranian immigrants, it is not surprising to find that most of them who were born in Iran are strongly committed to politics in Iran. This overriding preoccupation with Iran among first-generation Iranians helps explain the political impotence and docility of Iranian immigrants as a group for political mobilization during the hostage crisis. The passive posture of Iranian immigrants during the hostage crisis was also due to sharp political divisions within the Iranian community, lack of a united political voice, and lack of legal rights as U.S. citizens at the time of the crisis. Most newly arriving

Iranians focused on cultural adjustment and were otherwise preoccupied with the trauma of revolution and war at home. Also, they suffered from limited knowledge of the host culture and its political structure.

While first-generation Iranians remained inattentive and distant from politics in their newly adopted country, second-generation Iranians have been gradually adapting to American political institutions and are trying to enter the mainstream of politics in the United States. Therefore, unlike their predecessors who passively endured all the discrimination and restrictions imposed on them during the hostage crisis, a growing number of second-generation Iranian Americans have taken active roles in encountering the political culture of the United States in the aftermath of the 9/11 terrorist attacks. They have not only been more politically active and vocal in challenging new immigration sanctions against Iranians and protecting the civil rights of naturalized Iranians in the United States but also in reclaiming, retaining, and redefining the Iranian ethnicity that has been under suspicion and, at times, attack for the past thirty years.

As long as Iran is perceived as a node in the "axis of evil" or a "state sponsor of terrorism" and as long as U.S.-Iranian bilateral relations and the conflict over Iran's nuclear program continues, Iranian immigrants in the United States remain socially and politically vulnerable and will continue to be treated in a way somewhat similar to Americans of German or Japanese citizenship during World War II. That is, they will have diminished prospects for full integration. Indeed, it is possible that U.S-Iranian political conflict will escalate and lead to greater anti-Iranian sentiments among American political leaders, producing new forms of "trickle down" overt and covert discrimination and prejudice against Iranian nationals. The only way that Iranian immigrants can challenge the existing discriminatory practices against them and curtail the potential adverse consequences of U.S.-Iranian conflict in the future is political empowerment through more active organization that would lead to visibility and weight at all levels of American society. This political empowerment can best be accomplished by second-generation Iranian Americans because they have a much deeper sense of attachment to and understanding of American society and culture and a greater ease with American English, and they have been politically socialized in the United States, are very resourceful professionally and legally, and are endowed with remarkable human capital. At the same time, because of their inherent attachment to their ethnic roots and culture they can maintain Persian or Iranian identity as a central part of their political incorporation.

Appendix Research Methodology

Fieldwork and Participant Observation

To understand the structure, characteristics, and dynamics of the Iranian community as well as Iranians' perceptions of the 1978–1979 revolution, experiences of living in the United States, views on ethnic identity, and attitudes toward American society and people, I conducted long-term fieldwork during two periods, 1993–1995 and 2003–2005. Each fieldwork period persisted for two years and was supplemented by multiple community surveys and numerous face-to-face interviews. The study population during the first period was limited to the Iranian community in Dallas; during the second period I conducted fieldwork in the three largest Iranian communities in Texas—Houston, Dallas, and Austin.

The eight-year gap between the two fieldwork periods enabled me to document the major demographic and structural changes that occurred in the Iranian community in Dallas since I left the field in 1995. Similarly, participant observation in three Iranian communities provided an excellent comparative perspective and offered a great opportunity to observe the major similarities and differences among these communities. Although all the notes collected during both fieldwork periods were integrated together throughout this entire manuscript, the bulk of the data for Chapter 1 and a great part of the information presented in Chapter 3 were collected during the first and second fieldwork periods, respectively.

Despite the differences in fieldwork intervals and field locations, the challenges of data collection remained the same throughout the entire project. During both fieldwork periods and in all three communities I confronted very similar methodological challenges and issues that influenced and shaped the stages, processes, and methods of data collection for the entire project. The main methodological issue I encountered during the fieldwork was the unavailability of any accurate, official or unofficial, complete list of Iranians or Iranian households in any of the three communities that would allow for a random sample to be drawn. Several local community leaders, sponsors of concerts and other community events, ethnic grocery store owners, and publishers of Iranian magazines, newspapers, and business directories had either mailing or email lists of up to a few thousand first- and second-generation Iranian Americans in Texas, but none were reliable and comprehensive enough for sampling purposes.

The second methodological concern that I confronted during the fieldwork was Iranians' sensitivity, suspicions, cynicism, and unwillingness to be questioned and observed by any researcher. This issue is not unique to Iranians in Texas and has been reported by other scholars who have worked with Iranian immigrants in the United States. To secure Iranians' trust and gain their support and cooperation for participation in my project, I relied on my extensive network of Iranian friends, business owners, students, and community leaders and asked them to invite me to their gatherings so I could introduce myself to more Iranians and publicize my research intentions. For the first four months during each project period, I attended twenty-eight family and friend gatherings and participated in twenty-two community events in Dallas, Houston, and Austin. Participating in these gatherings and events not only provided an opportunity to get acquainted with more Iranians from different ethnoreligious and socioeconomic backgrounds but also offered me ample time to establish my identity as an anthropologist and publicize the purpose and main motive of my research project. As I met more Iranians, expanded my network, and explained who I was and what my research intentions were, the topic of my research caught the attention of many more Iranians, and I received more support from Iranians. For a few months after I started each project period, I heard from friends and other members of the community that my research topic and survey questionnaires had become a discussion topic on many occasions in different Iranian gatherings. This was even truer after I became involved in two brief local Iranian radio broadcasts on the topic and purpose of my research during the first project period in 1994.

In general, social networking with Iranians during the preliminary phase of the research combined with my fluency in the Persian language, my thorough understanding of Iranian culture as an Iranian national, and my membership and involvement with Iranian communities for several years in Dallas and Houston paved the way for my entrance into the community, facilitated data collection during the subsequent phases of research, and allowed me to maintain rapport with Iranians throughout the fieldwork.

Ethnographic participant observation was the backbone of both research project periods, providing the most essential and valuable information for this book. During both fieldwork periods I frequented local Iranian restaurants and grocery stores to collect ethnic publications and handouts about community events, and I attended wedding and funeral ceremonies, Persian concerts, poetry reading nights, the NoRuz (New Year) and other national celebrations, Iranian film festivals, Iranian plays and lectures, art festivals, and religious ceremonies and gatherings.

While participating in community events, I was primarily eager to explore the various ways in which Iranian immigrants identify and represent their ethnic origin, maintain their ethnic boundaries with Americans and other immigrant groups, and retain and perpetuate their cultural heritage. I was also interested in discovering how Iranians view American society and people and what mechanisms they adopt, particularly after the 9/11 attack, to cope with the stigma of being Iranian. As an anthropologist, the insights I gained through participant observation enhanced my understanding of the Iranian community and the major institutional problems most Iranians face in exile and helped to reveal how Iranians view themselves, their co-ethnics, and Americans. Furthermore, participating in religious, cultural, political, and social events took me behind the façade of the Iranian community and exposed me to new layers of Iranians' private and public life that had remained hidden from my eyes. Through fieldwork I became aware of the extent of political conflict, religious rivalry, ethnic and cultural chauvinism, cultural resistance, family tension, intergenerational discord, and collective ambivalence among Iranian immigrants. Moreover, it gave me an opportunity to put the whole migration experience of Iranians into perspective and understand the deep collective meanings that Iranian immigrants attach to exile, home, nationality, revolution, and ethnic identity.

Community Survey Questionnaire

Given the unavailability of any official or unofficial exhaustive list of Iranian households in Texas and the impossibility of compiling such a list, the best way to survey Iranians and answer the research questions was to rely on snowball sampling and mass distribution of questionnaires throughout the Iranian communities in Dallas, Houston, and Austin. During the first four months of the first project period in 1994 I distributed 3,500 questionnaires in the Iranian community in Dallas. Similarly, during the first nine months of the second project period (September 2003–May 2004), I distributed 6,000 questionnaires in Dallas, Houston, and Austin. The most effective strategy for reaching as many Iranians as possible was to distribute the surveys through the three widely circulated Iranian newspapers and magazines in Texas: *Asheghaneh, Parasto,* and *Shahrvand.* After discussing limitations of and barriers to my data collection with the editors of these local magazines and newspapers, they agreed to insert a copy of my questionnaire with a self-addressed return envelope inside each of the 2,500 to 5,000 publications they would circulate throughout Texas and across the country for two consecutive months free of charge. Due to financial limitations, I was unable to include a stamp for the return postage. This probably affected the response rate of my questionnaire.

Since these publications were delivered free of charge, there was good reason to believe that to keep up with community events and news, a large number of Iranian households received them. Those who did not receive them through the mail could pick up free copies at any one of the Iranian restaurants and ethnic grocery stores in cities where they were distributed. Therefore, to include those Iranian households that were excluded from the mailing lists, additional single copies of the questionnaire were inserted inside the magazines that were left in Iranian restaurants and grocery stores. For those Iranians who did not read the magazine but who visited the restaurants and grocery stores and those who requested second copies for a family member or friend, additional surveys with self-addressed return envelopes were put near the cash registers at the ethnic grocery stores. Finally, to include those Iranians who did not visit the ethnic restaurants and grocery stores due to distance but attended community events, I personally distributed questionnaires at major popular community events including the annual Iranian film festival, New Year celebration, and Iranian concerts.

Undoubtedly, mailing through the magazine was the most efficient strategy with the highest response rate. Mailing the questionnaire allowed me to have access to a wider geographic range at minimal cost. With such sensitive questions as reason for migration and immigration status, the mail questionnaire elicited a higher response rate due to strict confidentiality.

In addition to mass distribution of the surveys through local magazines, Iranian restaurants, grocery stores, and personal delivery, I utilized snowball sampling technique as the final strategy for including more Iranians in the sample.

After making initial contact with Iranians in formal and informal settings who showed interest in the study, I asked each of them to either introduce me to their friends or family members or take five surveys and give them to other Iranians they knew who might be interested in participating in this study. The new Iranians I met through these initial contacts, in turn, were asked to identify and give additional references for other Iranians who were interested for inclusion in the sample. The process continued until a sufficient number of surveys was collected.

Despite my sincere guarantee of the absolute scientific aim of the study and anonymity of respondents, many Iranians refused to participate in the study. With the exception of two Iranian men who confronted me at an Iranian concert in Houston and after questioning me about my research intentions accused me of collecting information for the Iranian government, most Iranians acted very professionally toward me, showed respect for me as a professor and an anthropologist, and showed enthusiasm for participating in the project. While some volunteered to be interviewed, others asked for my mailing address and sent me very long stories and personal accounts about their journeys to America and experience as Iranians. In general, the overall cooperation and support of Iranian respondents in Texas for this project exceeded my expectations.

The number of questionnaires that were completed during the first and the second project periods were 485 and 507, respectively. Both questionnaires were self-administered by respondents and were printed in Farsi with very simple and straightforward questions that could be comprehended by everyone. After an extensive review of the methodological issues in survey research, all the major factors such as questionnaire format, cover letter, method of mailing, adequate spacing, typography, color, and length were considered in designing both questionnaires.

To identify myself and to explain the purpose and the significance of the study to the respondents, I provided a brief typed semiformal introductory letter telling respondents that I am an academician and my intentions for conducting this research were purely intellectual. At the end, respondents were told that the findings of this research would be published in professional social science journals and local Iranian magazines. Respondents were also advised to either contact me directly or my department in case of any questions. To introduce the sponsor of the study to the respondents, I provided my department's telephone number and mailing address. My academic affiliation and my teaching career not only affected the response rate, but it also convinced the respondents of the legitimacy and value of the study. It persuaded them to participate in the survey. To assure the anonymity of the respondents, following the sponsorship section, this was printed in bold letters: "Please do not write your name and telephone number."

To identify the flaws in the questionnaire, the first drafts were pretested. The respondents who pretested the questionnaire were told to analyze all aspects of the questionnaire such as question wording, question order, redundant questions, missing questions, inappropriate, inadequate, redundant, or confusing response categories, and any other aspects of the questionnaire that they found inadequate. Pretesting proved to be of importance in the research process. Some of the questions were slightly modified and reworded (the same procedures were used for the second-generation survey discussed in the next section).

The final draft of the questionnaire for the first project contained twenty-eight questions and covered various demographic characteristics, migration histories, economic activities, and sociocultural characteristics of Iranians in Dallas. It also consisted of questions regarding the views of participants toward other Iranians and the Iranian community in Dallas and the nature of major problems the respondents experienced since arrival.

The questionnaire for the second fieldwork period, however, was much longer and included sixty closed-ended and three open-ended questions. The three open-ended questions provided valuable information about the respondent's perceptions of Iranian nationals and the Iranian community in Texas and the United States as well as his or her attitudes toward Americans and their society. Much like the first questionnaire, this one consisted of major pre- and postmigration demographic questions related to education, purpose for migration, religious orientation, income, family and marital status, occupation, immigration and citizenship status, and home ownership. Unlike the first questionnaire, however, in this questionnaire in addition to the demographic questions I asked questions about the respondent's subjective feelings and experiences regarding racism and prejudice before and after 9/11, post-9/11 attitudinal and behavioral changes in the community, political participation, Iranian ethnic identity, relationship with second-generation Iranians, interaction with other Iranians and the Iranian community, and American culture, people, and society.

My objectives in conducting these two community surveys were to collect some demographic facts about Iranians and their communities in Texas and assess their social and economic characteristics as a group; to understand how Iranians viewed themselves, their ethnic community, and their new host society; and to find out how political forces including the 9/11 attack and Iranian-U.S. political conflicts since the 1979 Iranian revolution had affected Iranians individually and collectively. The data gathered through the surveys were essential in understanding the class structure within the Iranian immigrant group and its impact on the group's level of social and economic integration; the impact of such class resources as premigration characteristics, human capital, and education of Iranians on their current perceptions of American society and people and the structure of Iranian immigrant family, and major concerns and worries of Iranian parents about their second-generation, American-born children.

Personal and Face-to-Face Interviews

While the questionnaires enabled me to collect objective aggregate demographic data, the in-depth, open-ended, face-to-face and telephone interviews provided an excellent opportunity to uncover and understand the subjective dimensions of family life and marriage, intergenerational conflict, interethnic and intra-ethnic relations, religious and national identity, ethnic solidarity, and personal dilemmas—social issues for Iranian immigrants in exile. For both project periods I interviewed a total of eighty-two first-generation Iranian immigrant men and women in Dallas, Houston, and Austin. Almost 50 percent of the interviews were conducted in Dallas. To find potential candidates for the personal interviews and to expedite the interviewing process, I utilized the same snowball sampling technique described above, which had proven to be very effective.

I started my interviews with a few Iranians who had agreed to be interviewed and proceeded to other interviews based on referrals until I conducted a significant number of interviews. In these interviews, I decided to take notes instead of tape-recording because most respondents were reluctant to be taped. Interviews lasted from forty-five minutes to two hours, depending on the level of cooperation and receptiveness of the interviewee. All the interviews were open-ended and covered topics from occupation, family status, and other premigration demographic characteristics to reasons for migration, process of becoming a permanent resident and a citizen, current socioeconomic characteristics, and overall feelings and attitudes about living in the United States and Iran. With the exception of one, all the interviews were conducted entirely in Farsi. Only in twelve cases did I have the opportunity to interview married couples together. Twenty-two of the eighty-two interviews took place over the phone, and the remaining sixty were conducted face to face either at the interviewees' homes or business locations or in Iranian restaurants and local coffee shops. Fifteen of the twenty-two respondents who were interviewed over the phone were women. The reasons that many women chose to be interviewed over the phone were a desire for anonymity and the uneasiness experienced by some married women to be interviewed by a strange man.

To yield more precise results in capturing the experience of Iranians in exile, I ensured that Iranians with different social classes, professions, levels of education, arrival times, family status, and lengths of residence were interviewed. This quota sampling technique allowed me to reconstruct the story of Iranian immigrants based on the recurring themes articulated by Iranian men and women from various social backgrounds and to highlight the unifying subject matter such as discrimination that are part of their collective memory.

The Second-Generation Survey and Personal Interviews

In addition to the eighty-two interviews and the two Farsi surveys that were designed for first-generation Iranians, using the same snowball sampling method, I conducted fifteen open-ended personal interviews and collected 105 surveys from the second-generation Iranian Americans in Texas. I also conducted two focus group discussions with twenty-five second-generation graduate and undergraduate Iranian students at the University of Houston. Despite the complete fluency in speaking and understanding basic Farsi by many second-generations in the study, most of them felt more connected to the English language for expressing their ideas and preferred to conduct the interviews in English. Occasionally some respondents spoke in a mixed English-Farsi fashion, as is often the case with second-generation Iranian Americans in their interactions with their parents and other first-generation Iranians. Given that most second-generation Iranian Americans have no or very little competency in writing and reading Farsi, the entire survey was also designed in English. My main objectives for surveying and interviewing second-generation Iranian Americans were to elucidate their general characteristics, to elicit information on the processes by which they reconcile cultural contradictions and live in a hybrid Iranian American culture, and to understand how they see themselves and what ethnic labels they use for ethnic identification.

Unlike their parents, the second-generation Iranian Americans were much more receptive to my project and had no fear of disclosing their identity or feelings and attitudes about their parents and family relations. Although the interviews and the survey contained many personal and sensitive questions about their private lives, including sexual practices, drug use, and alcohol consumption, most respondents answered the questions very openly. In addition to the demographic and sensitive personal questions, the English survey incorporated a series of questions regarding the respondents' level of involvement with the Iranian community, perceptions of first-generation Iranians and the Iranian community in exile, beliefs about second-generation Iranian Americans and major problems they confronted in relationship with their parents, perceptions of American people and society, extent of participation in community events, ethnic identity crisis, and challenges of blending the Iranian and American cultures together.

The personal interviews and focus-group discussions covered the same topics. All the interviews were taped and then transcribed. Two out of the three life stories presented at the beginning of Chapter 4 were drawn from the face-to-face interviews. I chose these two because they each represented an ideal type within the typology of second-generations outlined in the chapter that are most commonly found in the Iranian community. The first narrative, written by Jairan self-reflectively, represents the third ideal type within the typology, exemplifying the majority of second-generation Iranians in the United States. Using her real name and her own voice, Jairan vividly and skillfully depicts the details of her public and private life from the time she was born in Ireland until now and expresses the intricate challenges and contradictions of a transnational life in her own words, from her own perspective, and based on her own feelings.

Data Analysis

Data analysis for this study was carried out in two phases. During the first phase of data analysis I used the SPSS computer software to summarize responses to questionnaires.

Given the dispersion of Iranians throughout Dallas, Houston, and Austin, lack of a clustered Iranian neighborhood or ethnic enclave, and unavailability of a complete listing of all Iranians in these cities for creation of an adequate sampling frame, a nonprobability sample was the most appropriate technique for data collection during both research project periods. However, since I utilized various techniques to collect as many questionnaires as possible, I feel confident about the results of the community surveys to be representative of the universe of Iranian immigrants in Texas. During the second phase of data analysis I summarized all the field notes, transcribed the interviews, translated the comments made by first-generations from English to Farsi, and coded responses to the open-ended questions. In doing so, I looked to see how widely similar incidents or responses occurred through a number of different situations. Then, I classified the data into separate categories and typologies such as the three images of the United States and American people in the minds of Iranians in Chapter 3 and three types of second-generations and ethnic identities outlined in Chapter 4.

As indicated in the preface, despite structural differences between Iranian communities and some major demographic differences between first- and second-generation Iranian Americans in Texas and other states in the country, most Iranians in the United States have confronted the same challenges and experienced the same frustrations caused by Iranian-U.S political tensions. As such, I strongly believe that generalizations about Iranians' ethnic identity concealment, attitudes toward American society and people, family struggles, intergenerational conflicts, disappointments with their communities, mixed feelings about living in the United States, disappointments with the outcomes of the revolution, and ambivalence about Iran and the Iranian community outlined in the book would apply to a majority of Iranian immigrants. Similarly, the data presented in Chapter 4 on second-generation Iranian Americans and the challenges they confront in their relations with their parents as well as in being both Iranian and American can be applied to most second-generation Iranian Americans whose parents both are Iranian.

Note on the Term "Iranian"

Iran today has a population of about 72 million, representing several ethnic, religious, and linguistic groups. Most inhabitants of Iran speak Persian, the official language of Iran. There are, however, people who speak Arabic, Turkish, Kurdish, Baluchi, and a variety of Iranian languages and dialects. The most powerful force that unifies Iranian citizens from diverse backgrounds is the Islamic faith. Over 98 percent of the population of Iran is Muslim. Armenian Christians who came to Iran from Armenia in the seventeenth century, Assyrian Christians, Jews, Baha'is whose faith originated in Iran in the second half of the nineteenth century, and Zoroastrians whose religion was followed by a majority of Iranians before Islamization of the country in the seventh century are among the non-Muslim minority groups in Iran that have maintained their separate religious identities despite some common characteristics that they share with the dominant Persian-speaking Muslim culture. This ethnic, linguistic, and religious diversity, characteristic of Iran since a long time ago, is also represented by Iranian immigrants who are residing in Dallas.

Thus, unlike many immigrant minorities whose ethnic identity coincides with their national origin, the Iranian immigrant group is ethnically diverse and contains many subgroups. The presence of ethnic groups within an immigrant group is referred to as internal ethnicity (Bozorgmehr 1992). While I am aware of the internal ethnicity among Iranian immigrants, in this study I have used the term "Iranian" in its broadest sense as a national designation, not an ethnic one, mainly because of the lack of sufficient and reliable data regarding the proportions of the various religious and linguistic groups among Iranians in Dallas. Therefore, operationally, an Iranian is defined as any individual who originated within the borders of the modern nation-state of Iran. This would include Zoroastrians, Jews, Muslim, Armenians, Assyrians, and Baha'is as well as Turks, Kurds, and Baluchi.

A Note on Anonymity

To protect the privacy and anonymity of the respondents, the Iranians in the life histories are identified by pseudonyms.

Notes

Introduction

1. There are no reliable statistics on the exact number of Iranians in diaspora, but scholarly reports and journalistic accounts estimate that between two million and four million Iranians have left Iran since the revolution. It is believed that after Turkey, with its large number of Iranian refugees, the United States has the largest Iranian population in exile. Although according to the 2006–2008 American Community Survey results published by the U.S. Census Bureau, 422,664 persons with an Iranian ancestry live in the United States, the actual number is believed to be at least three to four times larger. The 2000 U.S. Census estimated the total number of persons of Iranian ancestry at about 338,266. This number indicates a 53.2 percent growth rate since the 1990 U.S Census.

2. *Houston Post*, 1980, "Few Iranian Students Deported, INS Chief Tells Senate Panel," April 3.

3. H. George Gallup, 1972–1977, *The Gallup Poll, Public Opinion 1972–1977*, volume 2, 1976–1977 (Scholarly Resources).

4. George Gallup Jr. 1989. *The Gallup Poll 1989* (Wilmington, Delaware: Scholarly Resources).

5. Pew Research Center for the People and the Press 2006, "Iran a Growing Danger, Bush Gaining on Spy Issue," February 7. http://people-press.org/report/269/iran-a-growing-danger-bush-gaining-on-spy-issue.

6. Jim Lobe 2006. "Polls: Anti-Iran Propaganda Working," February 10. http://www.antiwar.com/lobe/?articleid=8526.

7. Polling Report. N.d. "Iran." http://www.pollingreport.com/iran.htm. Dana Blanton 2006. "FOX News Poll: Trust Iran? No. Talk with Iran? Yes." *Fox News*, June 21. http://www.foxnews.com/story/0,2933,200415,00.html.

8. Some of the Iranian television channels in exile air weekly programs in which Islamic teachings and beliefs are openly mocked and scorned. Also, in Houston, where part of the fieldwork for this project was conducted, pamphlets in which return to a "pre-Islamic Free Iran" were promoted were regularly circulated in some Iranian grocery stores. According to Iranian Christian International estimates, by 2002 there were more than sixty thousand Iranian Christians worldwide. Half of these were Muslim converts and

the other half from various religious minorities. Iranian Christians International, n.d., "Iranian Christians: Who Are They?" http://www.iranchristians.org/whoarethey2.shtml.

9. For a better understanding of the emerging field of Iranian American studies and substantive areas of research on Iranians read Mehdi Bozorgmehr's "From Iranian Studies to Studies of Iranians in the United States" (1998).

Chapter 1

1. Bazaar is a permanent merchandising area or street of shops where goods and services are exchanged or sold.

2. A chador is a full-length semicircle garment open down the front that is thrown over the head and held closed in front. Iranian women are not expected to wear chadors, but many do wear them in public as a form of Islamic hijab or covering. The chador has no hand openings or closures and is held by the hands or by wrapping the ends around the waist.

3. In 1953 the CIA overthrew the government of the popular Prime Minister Mossadeqh at the request of, and with support from, the British government. The coup d'etat was called Operation Ajax, and it brought Mohammad Reza Pahlavi back to power and enabled him to rule Iran for twenty-six years, until he was overthrown in 1979. For an excellent coverage of the coup, its roots, and the consequences read Stephen Kinzer's *All the Shah's Men: An American Coup and the Roots of Middle East Terror* (2008).

4. Immigration from Iran and to the United States during the first half of the twentieth century was negligible and too small to warrant a separate breakdown in immigration statistics; Iranian nationals were listed with other Asian immigrants in a merged category.

5. By 1977 the shah had gathered weapons at a level that equaled that of a major power preparing for war. According to Mackey (1996), conventional military forces and the internal security apparatus consumed more than 40 percent of the Iranian budget ($9.4 billion).

6. To move Iran toward a secular society fashioned on the Western model, the shah's father initiated an attack on traditional Islam and on Muslim clerics. In his view Islam and Islamic institutions were incompatible with modernity and progress. Therefore, he minimized the power of the Islamic clergy and imposed ancient cultural and linguistic features on the country. Moreover, he suppressed Islam and resurrected the pre-Islamic civilization of ancient Persia (from the Achamaned to Sassanid periods). In his effort to connect Iran with pre-Islamic Persian civilization, Reza Shah emphasized the Persian identity as distinct from Arabs and Muslims. Drawing inspiration from pre-Islamic Persian history, Reza Shah promoted construction of new government buildings inspired by Achamaned architecture and initiated a language purification process by which ancient Persian words replaced Arabic. He also changed the name of the country from Persia to Iran and replaced the Islamic calendar with a modernized form of the ancient Zoroastrian calendar in which the names of the months were Persian. In addition to his attempts at redefining Iranian history and purifying the Persian language, Reza Shah started major reforms in law, education, land ownership, and the status of women. To minimize the power of Islamic religious leaders, Reza Shah reduced the influence of Islamic law in criminal jurisprudence and banned clerics from interpreting the law under the Islamic tradition and from judicial roles. Judges were to acquire secular university education.

Compulsory modern education, technical expertise, and state bureaucracy threatened the financial status of the clerics by denying their control of revenues from the holy Muslim shrines and sanctuaries. Farr 1999, Keddie 2006, Mackey 1996.

7. It is estimated that as many as fifty thousand Americans were living in Iran before the revolution. Some of the American military technicians received an average annual salary of $120,000 a year; Mackey 1996. Such high dollar salaries combined with employee perks provided a very comfortable life with big houses and luxury apartments, servants, and chauffeurs for almost all Americans in Iran. The little suburbia of north Tehran where most Americans lived offered Hollywood films, fast-food restaurants serving pizza and hamburgers, and shops selling only American-produced goods priced in dollars. After the revolution and the takeover of the American embassy in Tehran the American community totaled perhaps two thousand; *Houston Post*, December 31, 1979. Many of the Americans who stayed in Iran after the revolution were women married to Iranians they met at college in the United States.

8. Overall, during the rapid modernization of Iran in the 1960s an average of 5,116 government officials, temporary visitors for business and pleasure, students, international representatives, exchange visitors, and intracompany transferees along with their spouses and children visited the United States. This number increased eightfold to 43,310 between 1970 and when the shah was deposed from power in 1978. U.S. INS, Annual Reports 1970–1977.

9. Ibid.

10. CISNU had grown out of a number of Iranian student circles in Europe during the 1950s. The U.S. chapter joined the confederation when the second congress of the European confederation met in Paris in January 1962 and formed the World Confederation. In 1965 CISNU began to publish *Shanzdahom-e azar* (the 16th of Azar) as its official monthly organization newsletter and *Nameh-ye Paris* as a cultural quarterly. By 1972 CIS had as many as five thousand active student members in eighty-five chapters all over the world. Matin-Asgari 2001.

11. On one occasion six college students from the Iranian Student Association and the Revolutionary Student Brigade chained themselves inside the Statue of Liberty for more than five hours to protest the imprisonment of a group of Iranian political activists who were tortured and held without trial in Iran. On another occasion ninety-three Iranian students were arrested in demonstrations that turned violent in downtown Houston in 1976. After eight days of a hunger strike in jail they were freed on bond. "Statue of Liberty Site of Iran-Linked Protest," *Houston Post*, February 16, 1977; "Dismissing Charges against 93 Iranians Now Appears Likely," *Houston Post*, December 8, 1977.

12. "When Persians Collide," *Newsweek*, November 28, 1977.

13. For a full account of the CIS and its history of political activities in exile read Matin-Asgari's *Iranian Student Opposition to the Shah* (2001).

14. Reserve Officers Training Corps (ROTC) is a body of students at some colleges and universities who are given training toward becoming officers in the armed forces.

15. Most scholars divide the trends and migration history of Iranian immigrants to the United States into two phases—before and after the revolution. I believe the Iranian revolution was a decisive point in emigration of thousands of Iranians from Iran, but such a high volume of entry into the United States between 1977 and 1979 calls for a discrete

analysis. Therefore, I have divided the Iranian migration trends to the United States into three chronological phases: the prerevolutionary period (1950–1976), the revolutionary period (1977–1979), and the postrevolutionary period (1979–present), each with distinct characteristics. Pinpointing the defining moments and the breaking points for the flight of thousands of men and women out of Iran is very difficult. Even though the anti-shah riots in Iran started in the summer of 1978, gained momentum in fall of 1978, and continued until the shah left Iran in January 1979, public discontent and the outbreak of opposition to the shah's dictatorship in Iran and abroad began in 1977. Keddie 2006. Therefore, despite the sudden, dramatic changes and the unprecedented social and psychological consequences of the Iranian revolution that forced many Iranians to leave their country, the exodus of thousands of individuals and families from Iran was a gradual and continuous process that reached its peak shortly before and during the revolutionary turmoil. Nevertheless, the time between the outbreak of domestic and international public discontent in 1977 and several months after the establishment of the provisional government in spring 1979 (followed by massive anti-shah and in some cases bloody demonstrations in 1978) seems to have been a watershed in the history of the Iranian exodus.

16. For example, before April 1980 an estimated one-half of Iran's seventy thousand Jews had left Iran for either Israel or the United States. Allen and Turner 1988.

17. According to Nikki Keddie, one of the most prominent scholars of Iranian history and culture, the Iranian Revolution had several distinct features. Keddie argues (2006) that regardless of its roots, a distinctive character of the Iranian revolution of 1978–1979 was the prominent role of clerics and their monopoly of power after the downfall of the shah.

18. Immediately after the hostage crisis the number of visas issued to Iranians dropped radically, from 63,813 in 1979 to 13,332 in 1980 and 16,926 in 1981. Starting in 1984 an inverse movement in the trends and volume of immigrants and nonimmigrants from Iran to the United States occurred. U.S. INS Statistical Yearbooks 1978–1986.

19. Between June 1983 and September 1986 Iranians in the United States had the highest number (10,728) of asylum cases approved (Bozorgmehr and Sabagh 1988). Based on the Department of Homeland Security's Office of Immigration Statistics 2008 report, in 2006, 2007, and 2008, with an estimated 2,792, 5,481, and 5,270 refugees, respectively, Iran was among the top four countries that were principal sources of refugees arriving in the United States.

20. The other three consulates were in New York, Chicago, and San Francisco. In response to the provisional government's call for a referendum, the Iranian embassy in Washington, D.C., and its four consular offices administered ten voting sites across the United States.

21. According to Hakimzadeh (2006), in the 1977–1978 academic year 36,220 Iranian students were studying in U.S. institutes of higher education. This number increased to 45,340 and peaked to 51,310 in the 1978–1979 and 1979–1980 academic years, respectively.

22. "Visa Checks to Begin Today—Local Iranian Students Must Submit to 10-Minute Interviews," *Houston Post*, November 15, 1979.

23. In 1979 Iranian enrollment at Texas Southern University in Houston peaked at about 950. Other Houston colleges and universities with high Iranian enrollment included the University of Houston with 250, Houston–Downtown College with 115, San Jacinto

Junior College with 262, and Galveston College with 75 Iranian students. Another 128 Iranian military officers were in Air Force or Navy flight training at Laughlin Air Force Base (AFB) in Del Rio, Shepherd AFB in Wichita Falls, Reese AFB in Lubbock, Kelly AFB in San Antonio, and Corpus Christi Naval Air Station in Texas. *Houston Post,* November 9, 1979.

24. The earliest date for Iranian migration to Texas is unknown. However, the results of my interviews and the community survey on the migration history of Iranians to Texas parallels that of the national level reported by the INS. As anticipated, the findings of the community survey revealed a noticeable growth in the number of Iranian immigrants in Dallas and Houston shortly before the Iranian revolution in 1978. The bulk of the present Iranian population in the two largest Iranian communities in Texas is composed of individuals who arrived from 1977 through 1980, when the migration of Iranians to the United States was at its peak.

25. Based on the available data, in the period 1960–1977, of the 376,844 nonimmigrants entering the United States, 82,288 or 21 percent were students who adjusted their status to permanent residents mostly by marrying U.S. citizens; Bozorgmehr and Sabagh 1988, Lorentz and Wertime 1980. In contrast, tourism and occupational preferences have played a small part in the admission of Iranians to the United States during this period. According to Lorentz and Wertime (1980), of all the Iranian immigrants who came to the United States between 1958 and 1976, only 9 percent were admitted specifically on the basis of demand for their occupational skills. This does not mean that Iranian immigrants are predominantly unskilled or poorly educated. On the contrary, Bozorgmehr and Sabagh (1988) find that Iranian immigrants, as a group, have a high level of educational achievement. As indicated by Lorentz and Wertime (1980), about 54 percent of Iranian immigrants in the United States between 1958 and 1976 who had occupations fell into the professional and technical categories.

26. Except for a handful of Persian rug galleries, small retail shops, and ordinary nonethnic restaurants scattered throughout the city, there were no other Iranian-owned enterprises in Dallas. It was not until 1983–1984 that the first Iranian grocery store and a few small restaurants that served Persian food only on weekends were established. Prior to that, most Iranians purchased their ethnic food items from a Lebanese grocery store in central Dallas that was sold to an Iranian in 1985.

27. "Americans Take to the Streets to Vent Wrath over Events," *Houston Post,* November 10, 1979; "Nationwide, Americans Vent Anger with Rallies," *Houston Post,* November 11, 1979.

28. "Action Lauded Here; Some from Mid-East Report Harassment," *Houston Post,* November 12, 1979.

29. About 350 University of Texas students held a rally in Austin to demand the release of the American hostages and revocation of visa rights for Iranian students in the United States. In another demonstration sponsored by Students for Safety of Americans Abroad, about 450 people gathered at the University of Texas in Austin to protest. At North Texas State University, with an Iranian student population of 386, a group of American students gathered around the library with posters and sang "God Bless America." About 100 demonstrators from the University of Akron organized a demonstration and chanted "Drink your oil and eat your sand." Another 500 students from the University of

Minnesota shouted "Khomeini is a murderer." In a demonstration organized by students at the University of South Carolina protestors shouted "Iranians go home." Three Michigan State University students were arrested for painting anti-Iranian slogans on a pedestrian bridge. "Americans Take to the Streets," *Houston Post*.

30. "Americans Take to the Streets" and "Iranian Students' Claims Taunted at TSU Rally," *Houston Post*, November 10, 1979.

31. Ibid.

32. "Protesters Demand Iranian Students Leave United States" and "Action Lauded Here," *Houston Post*, November 12, 1979.

33. "700 Iranian Students to Face Deportation Proceedings," *Houston Post*, November 21, 1979.

34. "Americans Take to the Streets" and "Iranian Students' Claims Taunted," *Houston Post*, November 10, 1979.

35. Ibid.

36. "Local Processing of Students Halted by Immigration Officers," *Houston Post*, December 13, 1979.

37. "YAF Chairman Urges Iran Blockade," *Houston Post*, December 7, 1979.

38. "Hostages in Iran—Congressmen's Reactions Vary from 'Act of War' to Caution" and "Protests Spread across Nation in Ire over Embassy Occupation," *Houston Post*, November 9, 1979.

39. Ibid.

40. "Iranian Pilot Trainees Caught in Middle of No-Win Situation," *Houston Post*, January 21, 1980.

41. "Louisiana House Votes to Ban Iran Students," *Houston Post*, May 27, 1980.

42. In a press conference Houston's mayor said, "I think it's time that the Iranian students recognize the fact that a lot of Houstonians have had about enough of them. We are trying to be as patient as we can, but our patience is running out." Bill Clements, Texas governor during the hostage crisis, in his weekly news conference suggested that Iranians in Texas stay "out of sight and out of mind." Eventually some universities, including Texas Southern University in Houston, banned political activities and demonstrations of Iranian students. "Iranian Students' Claims Taunted" and "Brief Items Relating to the Iran Crisis," *Houston Post*, November 10, 1979.

43. "Visa Checks to Begin Today," *Houston Post*, November 15, 1979.

44. "68 Iranians Here Found in Violation of Visas" and "400 Iranian Students May Face Deportation," *Houston Post*, November 17, 1979.

45. "Few Iranian Students Deported, INS Chief Tells Senate Panel," *Houston Post*, April 3, 1980.

46. "7,592 Iranians Admitted to U.S. since Crackdown," *Houston Post*, January 16, 1980.

47. "Few Iranian Students Deported," *Houston Post*, April 3, 1980.

48. Ibid.

49. Ibid.

50. "Iranian Student at TSU Faces Some Unanswerable Questions," *Houston Post*, December 4, 1979.

51. "Federal Judge Orders Halt to Deporting of Iranians," *Houston Post*, December 12, 1979.

52. "Federal Judge Orders Halt to Deporting of Iranians" and "Iranian Students Win. UH Professor Praises U.S. Court Ruling," *Houston Post*, December 12, 1979.

53. "Court Allows Checks of Iranian Students," *Houston Post*, December 15, 1979.

54. "U.S. Seeks Stay of Judge's Ban," "Local Processing of Students Halted by Immigration Officers," and "S.A. Demonstration Tentatively Slated," *Houston Post*, December 13, 1979.

55. "U.S. Seeks Stay of Judge's Ban," *Houston Post*, December 13, 1979; "Court Allows Checks of Iranian Students," *Houston Post*, December 15, 1979.

56. "Court of Appeals Urged to Uphold Deportation Plan," *Houston Post*, December 21, 1979; "Court Upholds Right to Check Iranians' Visas," *Houston Post*, December 28, 1979; "Iranians Ask Full Court Review of Visa Order," *Houston Post*, December 29, 1979.

57. "Iranian Consulate Here Closed Indefinitely," *Houston Post*, November 16, 1979.

58. "Iran Consulate in City Closed," *Houston Post*, April 8, 1980.

59. "Iranian Pilot Trainees Caught in Middle," *Houston Post*, January 21, 1980.

60. "No Decisions Made to Stop Training Military Students; Program Undergoing Review," *Houston Post*, November 16, 1979.

61. "U.S. Announces New Visa Policy to Pressure Iran," *Houston Post*, April 13, 1980.

62. "Iranian Students Have Problems Cashing Checks, Officials Report," *Houston Post*, December 6, 1979; "2 Iranian Banks Get Approval to Bring in Funds," *Houston Post*, December 18, 1979.

63. "Visa Decision Won't Immediately Affect Iranian Students in U.S.," *Houston Post*, April 9, 1980.

64. A memo issued by the FBI in November warned INS officers that about fifty Iranian students were attempting to enter the United States to engage in terrorist activities and were bringing with them supplies, film, and other propaganda material. "Agents Say Search Policy for Iranians Lax," *Houston Post*, March 27, 1980.

65. "American Flags Show Support for Hostages," *Houston Post*, December 19, 1979.

66. "Showing the Colors for Unity . . . and Discord," *Houston Post*, December 19, 1979.

67. A few years after the revolution and the hostage crisis there was a drastic downward trend in the migration of Iranian immigrants and nonimmigrants to the United States. Starting in 1984, however, an inverse movement in the trend of nonimmigrants occurred. The number of nonimmigrants increased from 22,955 in 1983 to 44,629 in 1984 and 57,831 in 1985. The only plausible explanation for this increase is that many Iranians resided in other countries for a few years before they were able to migrate to the United States. U.S. INS, Statistical Yearbooks 1978–1986.

68. Between 1990 and 2000 as many as 133,389 Iranians were naturalized citizens. U.S. DHS, Statistical Yearbook of the Immigration and Naturalization Service 1986–2008.

69. Ibid.

70. For a comprehensive chronological list of major initiatives taken by the U.S. government after 9/11 read Mehdi Bozorgmehr and Anny Bakalian's "Government Initiatives after the September 11th Attack on America" (2005). Another excellent article that

discusses the impact of profiling and discrimination against Iranians after the hostage crisis and 9/11 on Iranians' identity is Sara Mahdavi's "Held Hostage: Identity Citizenship of Iranian Americans" (2006).

71. Pacific News Service, August 19, 2004; National Iranian American Council, http://www.niacouncil.org.

Chapter 2

1. George H. Gallup. 1980. *Gallup Poll, Public Opinion 1980*. Wilmington, Delaware: Scholarly Resources.

2. A complete review of the survey results is provided in "Political Attitudes and Patterns of Political Participation of Iranian Americans in California" by Dariush Zahedi, Institute of Government Studies, University of California, Berkeley, 2008. http://repositories.cdlib.org/igs/WP2008-1.

3. The study, "Californians Surveyed in 12 Languages on Impact of 9/11," was conducted by Bendixen and Associates; the findings were released September 4, 2002, by New California Media and the University of Southern California-Annenberg's School for Justice and Journalism. Further information is posted at http://news.newamericamedia.org/news.

4. http://www.youtube.com/watch?v=ADU1lhEb1Xo.

5. Emile Durkheim used the term in his 1897 book *Suicide*, reprinted in 1997 by Free Press.

6. Barth 1969, Cornell and Hartmann 1998, Nagel 1994.

7. There is no reliable information for the number of Iranian Christians with Islamic family backgrounds inside and outside of Iran. However, Iranian Christians International (ICI) claims that since 1979 the number of Iranians with Muslim families and backgrounds has increased from 300 to an estimated 70,000.

8. For an interesting analysis of ethnic identity preservation among Iranian ethnoreligious subgroups in Los Angeles read Mehdi Bozorgmehr's 1982 dissertation, "Internal Ethnicity: Armenian, Bahai, Jewish, and Muslim Iranians in Los Angeles."

Chapter 3

1. The American Community Survey 2006–2008 report provides data for all Iranians and Iranian women sixteen and older in the labor force. The employment rate for Iranian men was calculated and inferred from table S0201, Selected Population Profile in the United States for Iranians. According to the 2006-2008 ACS reports published by the U.S. Census Bureau, 176,824 of the 340,124 Iranians were comprised of men and the remaining 163,300 were women age sixteen and older. Nearly 70 percent (122,206) of Iranian men and nearly 55 percent (89,488) of Iranian women ages sixteen and older were employed in the civilian labor force in 2008.

2. The U.S. Census Bureau defines a household as all the people who occupy a housing unit as their usual place of residence and a family as a group of two or more people who reside together and who are related by birth, marriage, or adoption.

3. Cultural and identificational assimilation are two stages of assimilation developed by Milton Gordon, author of *Assimilation in American Life* (1964), in which he distinguishes an array of possible assimilation outcomes. Cultural assimilation refers to accepting

and practicing the culture of the host society or the majority, and identification assimilation refers to a situation of the members of both the immigrant minority group and the host society sharing the view that they are part of the same group. According to Gordon, identificational assimilation is a two-way process and involves recognition of minority group members by members of the host society. Only when immigrant minority groups no longer have mental ties or identify with their country of origin or ethnic community and are no longer perceived by members of the host society as foreigners do prejudice and discrimination against minority groups disappear.

Chapter 4

1. The Zoroastrian faith was the state religion of the Persian Empire until the seventh century AD. With the spread of Islam to Iran, most Zoroastrians converted to the new faith. Worldwide, the Zoroastrian population numbers about 125,000, including 80,000 in India, 30,000 in Iran, and more than 3,000 in the United States. Kelley, Friedlander, and Colby 1993.

2. Barth 1969, Cornell and Hartmann 1998, Nagel 1994.

3. Kibria 2000, Suarez-Orozco and Qin 2006.

Chapter 5

1. According to the U.S. Census Bureau, a family includes a householder and one or more people living in the same household who are related to the householder by birth, marriage, or adoption. All people in a household who are related to the householder are regarded as members of his or her family. A family household may contain people not related to the householder, but those people are not included as part of the householder's family in census tabulations. Thus, the number of family households is equal to the number of families, but family households may include more members than do families. A household can contain only one family for purposes of census tabulations. Not all households contain families, since a household may comprise a group of unrelated people or one person living alone.

2. According to the 2000 U.S. Census, 5.2 percent of Iranians in the United States in 1999 cohabited with unmarried heterosexual or homosexual partners in nonfamily households.

3. Department of Homeland Security, Statistical Yearbook of the Immigration and Naturalization Service 1986–2002.

4. During my fieldwork in Dallas, I interviewed two young non–U.S. citizen men who were reunited with their families in the United States after six years. During this time, they had become fathers and were supporting two households, one in Iran and another one in the United States.

5. Department of Homeland Security, Statistical Yearbook of the Immigration and Naturalization Service 1986-2002.

Conclusion

1. For a complete list of all the Iranian candidates since 2004 see the IAPAC's website at http://www.iranianamericanpac.org/candidates/iapac.shtml.

Bibliography

Abrahamian, Ervand. 1982. *Iran between Two Revolutions*. Princeton, New Jersey: Princeton University Press.

Abyaneh, Parvin. 1989. "Immigrants and Patriarchy: The Case of Iranian Families." *Women's Studies* 17: 67–69.

Alexander, J., R. Eyerman, B. Giesen, N. Semelser, and P. Sztompka. 2004. *Cultural Trauma and Collective Identity*. Los Angeles: University of California Press.

Allen, James P., and Eugene James Turner. 1988. "Iranian Ancestry." In *An Atlas of America's Ethnic Diversity*, edited by James Allen and Eugene Turner, 138–139. New York: Macmillan.

Allport, W. Gordon. 1954. *The Nature of Prejudice*. New York: Addison-Wesley.

Ansari, M. 1988. *Iranian Immigrants in the United States: A Case of Dual Marginality*. New York: Associated Faculty Press.

———. 1992. *The Making of the Iranian Community in America*. New York: Pardis Press.

Askari, Hossein, John T. Cummings, and Mehmet Izbudak. 1977. "Iran's Migration of Skilled Labor to the United States." *Iranian Studies* 10:3–39.

Bakalian, Anny, and Medhi Bozorgmehr. 2009. *Backlash 9/11. Middle Eastern and Muslim Americans Respond*. Berkeley: University of California Press.

Barati-Marnani, A. 1981. "Assimilation of Iranian Immigrants in Southern California." Ph.D. dissertation, United States International University, San Diego.

Barboza, Tony. 2007. "For Some, Beverly Hills Ballots Went Too Farsi." *Los Angeles Times*, March 4.

Barth, F. 1969. *Ethnic Groups and Boundaries*. Boston: Little, Brown.

Bauer, Janet. 1991. "A Long Way Home: Islam in the Adaptation of Iranian Women Refugees in Turkey and West Germany." In *Iranian Refugees and Exiles since Khomeini*, edited by Asghar Fathi, 77–101. Costa Mesa, California: Mazda.

———. 1993. "Ma'ssoum's Tale: The Personal and Political Transformation of a Young Iranian Feminist and Her Ethnographer." *Feminist Studies* 19, no. 3 (Fall): 519–549.

Blair, B. 1991. "Personal Name Changes among Iranian Immigrants in the USA." In *Iranian Refugees and Exiles since Khomeini*, edited by A. Fathi, 145–160. Costa Mesa, California: Mazda.

Bogardus, Emory S. 1926. "Social Distance in the City." *Proceedings and Publications of the American Sociological Society* 20:40–46.

———. 1933. "A Social Distance Scale." *Sociology and Social Research* 17:265–271.

Bozorgmehr, Mehdi. 1992. "Internal Ethnicity: Armenian, Bahai, Jewish, and Muslim Iranians in Los Angeles." Ph.D. dissertation. Ann Arbor, Michigan: University Microfilms International Dissertation Services.

———. 1998. "From Iranian Studies to Studies of Iranians in the United States." *Iranian Studies* 31:5–30.

———. 2000. "Does Host Hostility Create Ethnic Solidarity? The Experience of Iranians in the United States." *Bulletin of the Royal Institute for Inter-Faith Studies* 2 (1): 159–178.

———. 2007. "Iran." In *The New Americans: A Guide to Immigration since 1965*, edited by Mary C. Waters and Reed Ueda, 469–478. Cambridge: Harvard University Press.

Bozorgmehr, Mehdi, and Anny Bakalian. 2005. "Government Initiatives after the September 11, 2001, Attack on the United States." In *Encyclopedia of Racism in the United States*, edited by Pyong Gap Min, 245–249. Westport, Connecticut: Greenwood Press.

Bozorgmehr, Mehdi, and Georges Sabagh. 1988. "High Status Immigrants: A Statistical Profile of Iranians in the United States." *Iranian Studies* 21 (3–4): 5–36.

Campbell, Jane. 1997. "Portrayal of Iranians in U.S. Motion Pictures. In *The U.S. Media and the Middle East: Image and Perception*, edited by Yahya R. Kamalipour, 177–186. Westport, Connecticut: Praeger.

Carswell, R., and R. Davis. 1985. "The Economic and Financial Pressures: Freeze and Sanctions." In *American Hostages in Iran: The Conduct of a Crisis*, edited by Warren Christopher and Paul H. Kreisberg, 173–200. New Haven, Connecticut: Yale University Press.

Carter, Jimmy. 1995. *Keeping Faith: Memoirs of a President*. Fayetteville: University of Arkansas Press.

Chaichian, Mohammad. 1997. "First Generation Iranian Immigrants and the Question of Cultural Identity: The Case of Iowa." *International Migration Review* 31:612–627.

Christopher, Warren, and Paul H. Kreisberg, editors. 1985. *American Hostages in Iran: The Conduct of a Crisis*. New Haven: Yale University Press.

Cornell, Stephen, and Douglas Hartmann. 1998. *Ethnicity and Race. Making Identities in a Changing World*. Thousand Oaks, California: Pine Forge Press.

Dallalfar, Arlenee. 1989. "Iranian Immigrant Women in Los Angeles: The Reconstruction of Work, Ethnicity, and Community." Ann Arbor, Michigan: University Microfilms International Dissertation Services.

———. 1994. "Iranian Women as Immigrant Entrepreneurs." *Gender and Society* 8 (4): 541–561.

Dossa, Parin. 2004. *Politics and Poetics of Migration: Narratives of Iranian Women from the Diaspora*. Toronto: Canadian Scholars' Press.

Durkheim, Emile. 1951. *Suicide: A Study in Sociology.* Translated by John A. Spaulding and
   George Simpson. London: Free Press of Glencoe, Collier-Macmillan.

Eyerman, Ron. 2001. *Slavery and the Formation of African American Identity.* Cambridge,
   England: Cambridge University Press.

Farr, Grant. 1999. *Modern Iran.* Boston: McGraw-Hill.

Fathi, Asghar, editor. *Iranian Refugees and Exiles since Khomeini.* Costa Mesa, California:
   Mazda.

Feagin, Joe R., and Clairece Booher Feagin. 1999. *Racial and Ethnic Relations.* Upper
   Saddle River, New Jersey: Prentice Hall.

Fischer, Michael M., and Mehdi Abedi. 1990. *Debating Muslims: Cultural Dialogues in
   Postmodernity and Tradition.* Madison: University of Wisconsin Press.

Gaffarian, Shireen. 1987. "The Acculturation of Iranians in the United States." *Journal of
   Social Psychology* 127 (6): 565–571.

Gerges, Fawaz. 1997. "Islam and Muslims in the Mind of America: Influences on the
   Making of U.S. policy." *Journal of Palestine Studies* 26 (2): 68–80.

Goffman, Erving. 1963. *Stigma: Notes on the Management of Spoiled Identity.* New York:
   Simon and Schuster.

Gordon, Milton. 1964. *Assimilation in American Life: The Role of Race, Religion, and
   National Origins.* New York: Oxford University Press.

Hakimzadeh, Shirin. 2006. "Iran: A Vast Diaspora Abroad and Millions of
   Refugees at Home." *Migration Information Source,* September. http://www.
   migrationinformation.org/profiles/print.cfm?ID=424.

Hanassab, Shideh. 1991. "Acculturation and Young Iranian Women: Attitudes toward
   Sex Roles and Intimate Relationships." *Journal of Multicultural Counseling and
   Development* 19:11–21.

———. 1998. "Sexuality, Dating, and Double Standards: Young Iranian Immigrants in
   Los Angeles." *Iranian Studies* 31:26.

Hanassab, Shideh, and Romeria Tidwell. 1993. "Change in the Premarital Behavior
   and Sexual Attitudes of Young Iranian Women: From Tehran to Los Angeles."
   Counseling Psychology Quarterly 6 (4): 281–291.

Harris, Marvin. 1995. *Cultural Anthropology.* Fourth edition. New York: HarperCollins
   College.

Hoffman, Diane M. 1989. "Language and Culture Acquisition among Iranians in the
   United States." *Anthropology and Education Quarterly* 20 (2): 118–132.

———. 1990. "Beyond Conflict: Culture, Self, and Intercultural Learning among
   Iranians in the U.S." *International Journal of Intercultural Relations* 14:275–299.

Hojat, Mohammadreza, Reza Shapurian, Danesh Foroughi, Habib Nayerahmadi, Mitra
   Farzaneh, Mahmood Shafieyan, and Mohin Parsi. 2000. "Gender Differences in
   Traditional Attitudes toward Marriage and the Family." *Journal of Family Issues* 21
   (4): 419–434.

Iranian Christians International. N.d. http://www.iranchristians.org.

Iranian Studies Group at MIT. 2005. http://isgmit.org.

Jalali, Behnaz. 1982. "Iranian Families." In *Ethnicity and Family Therapy,* edited by M.
   McGoldrick, J. Pearce, and J. Giordano, 289–309, New York: Gulford.

Jones, Melinda. 2002. *Social Psychology of Prejudice*. Upper Saddle River, New Jersey: Prentice Hall.

Karim, M. Persis. 2008. "Charting the Past and Present: Iranian Immigrant and Ethnic Experience through Poetry." *MELUS* 33, no. 2, Iranian American Literature (Summer): 111–127.

Katouzian, Homa. 1981. *The Political Economy of Modern Iran*. New York: New York University Press.

Keddie, Nikki R. 2006. *Modern Iran: Roots and Results of Revolution*. New Haven, Connecticut: Yale University Press.

Kelley, R., Jonathan Friedlander, and Anita Colby. 1993. *Irangeles: Iranians in Los Angeles*. Los Angeles: University of California Press.

Keshishian, Flora. 2000. "Acculturation, Communication, and the U.S. Mass Media: The Experience of an Iranian Immigrant." *Howard Journal of Communication* 11:93–106.

Kibria, Nazli. 2000. "Race, Ethnic Options, and Ethnic Binds: Identity Negotiations of Second-Generation Chinese and Korean Americans," *Sociological Perspectives* 43 (1): 77–95.

Kinzer, Stephen. 2008. *All the Shah's Men: An American Coup and the Roots of Middle East Terror*. New York: Wiley and Sons.

Lapinski, S. John, Pia Peltola, Greg Shaw, Alan Yang. 1997. "Trends: Immigrants and Immigration." *Public Opinion Quarterly* 61 (2): 356–383.

Levit, Peggy, and Nina Glick Schiller. 2004. "Conceptualizing Simultaneity: A Transnational Social Field Perspective on Society." *International Migration Review* 3 (1): 1002–1039.

Light, Ivan H., and Stavros Karageorgis. 1993b. "The Ethnic Economy." In *Handbook of Economic Sociology*, edited by Neil Smelser and Richard Swedberg, 1–78. New York: Russell Sage Foundation.

Light, Ivan H., Georges Sabagh, Mehdi Bozorgmehr, and Claudia Der-Martirosian. 1993. "Internal Ethnicity in the Ethnic Economy." *Ethnic and Racial Studies* 16 (4): 581–597.

———. 1994. "Beyond the Ethnic Enclave Economy." *Social Problems* 41 (1): 65–80.

Lorentz, John, and John T. Wertime. 1980. "Iranians." In *Harvard Encyclopedia of American Ethnic Groups*, edited by Stephen Thernstrom, 521–524. Cambridge: Harvard University Press.

Lyman, Stanford, and William Douglas. 1973. "Ethnicity: Strategies of Collective and Individual Impression Management." *Social Research* 40 (2): 345–365.

Mackey, Sandra. 1996. *The Iranians: Persia, Islam, and the Soul of a Nation*. New York: Penguin Putnam.

Mahdavi, Sara. 2006. "Held Hostage: Identity Citizenship of Iranian Americans." *Texas Journal on Civil Liberties and Civil Rights* 11 (2): 211–244.

Mahdi, Ali Akbar. 1999. "Trading Places: Changes in Gender Roles within the Iranian Immigrant Family." In *Men and Masculinity: A Text Reader*, edited by Theodore Cohen. Sydney, Australia: Cengage Learning.

———. 2001. "Perception of Gender Roles among Female Iranian Immigrants in the United States." In *Women, Religion, and Culture in Iran*, edited by Sarah Ansari and Vanessa Martin, 185–210. London: Curzon Press.

Mahdi, Behrad. 2005. "Months after Immigration Forum, Congressman Meehan
    Continues to Set an Example for Iranian American Political Engagement."
    Iranian American Political Action Committee, IAPAC, March 28. http://www.
    iranianamericanpac.org/news/detail.php?str=wZ6soJdG2j5A5FoH.

Matin-Asgari, Afshin. 2001. *Iranian Student Opposition to the Shah.* Costa Mesa,
    California: Mazda.
McConatha, Jasmin Tahmaseb, Paul Stroller, and Fereshte Oboudiat. 2001. "Reflections
    of Older Iranian Women Adapting to Life in the United States." *Journal of Aging
    Studies* 15:369–381.
McGill, Douglas. 2002. "Iranian-Americans Protest New Law Barring Their Relatives
    from Visiting U.S." *McGill Report,* May 2.
McLemore, S. Dale, and Harriett D. Romo. 2005. *Racial and Ethnic Relations in America.*
    Boston: Allyn and Bacon.
Merton, Robert, and Elinor Barber. 1976. *Sociological Ambivalence and Other Essays.* New
    York: Free Press.
Mills, C. Wright. 1959. *The Sociological Imagination.* New York: Oxford University Press.
Mobasher, Mohsen. 1996. "Class, Ethnicity, Gender, and the Ethnic Economy: The Case
    of Iranian Immigrants in Dallas." Ph.D. dissertation, University of Michigan. Ann
    Arbor: University Microfilms International Dissertation Services.
———. 2004. "Ethnic Resources and Ethnic Economy: The Case of Iranian
    Entrepreneurs in Dallas." In *Migration, Globalization, and Ethnic Relations: An
    Interdisciplinary Approach,* edited by Mohsen Mobasher and Mahmoud Sadri,
    297–306. Upper Saddle River, New Jersey: Prentice Hall.
———. 2006. "Cultural Trauma and Ethnic Identity Formation among Iranian
    Immigrants in the United States." *American Behavioral Scientist* 50 (1): 100–117.
———. 2007. "Iranian Immigrant Entrepreneurs in the United States." In *The Handbook
    of Research on Ethnic Minority Entrepreneurship,* edited by Leo-Paul Dana, 228–248.
    Cheltenham, England: Edward Elgar.
Moghissi, Haideh. 1999. "Away from Home: Iranian Women, Displacement Cultural
    Resistance, and Change." *Journal of Comparative Family Studies* 30 (2): 207–217.
Mostofi, Nilou. 2003. "Who We Are: The Perplexity of Iranian-American Identity."
    Sociology Quarterly 44:681–703.
Mottahedeh, Roy. 1985. *The Mantle of the Prophet: Religion and Politics in Iran.* Oxford,
    England: Oneworld.
Naficy, Hamid. 1998. "Identity Politics and Iranian Exile Music Videos." *Iranian Studies*
    31:51–64.
Nagel, J. 1994. "Constructing Ethnicity: Creating and Recreating Ethnic Identity and
    Culture." *Social Problems* 41:152–176.
Nassehy-Behnam, Vida. 1985. "Change and the Iranian Family." *Current Anthropology* 26
    (5): 557–562.
National Iranian American Council. 2003. *Iran Census Report. Strength in Numbers: The
    Relative Concentration of Iranian Americans across the United States.* Washington,
    D.C.: National Iranian American Council.
Niknia, Zohreh. 2002. "The Intersection of Immigration and Gender: The
    Socioeconomic Integration of Iranian Immigrant Women in the Kansas City

Metropolitan Area." Ph.D. dissertation, University of Missouri–Kansas City. Ann
Arbor, Michigan: Bell and Howell Information and Learning.

Park, Robert E. 1928. "Human Migration and the Marginal Man." *American Journal of Sociology* 33:881–893.

———. 1939. "The Nature of Race Relations." In *Race Relations and the Race Problem*, edited by Edgar T. Thompson, 3–45. Durham, North Carolina: Duke University Press.

Portes, Alejandro, and Ruben G. Rumbaut. 2006. *Immigrant America: A Portrait*. Third edition. Berkeley: University of California Press.

Portes, Alejandro, and Min Zhou. 1993. "The New Second Generation: Segmented Assimilation and Its Variants." *Annals of the American Academy of Political and Social Sciences* 530:74–96.

Purkayastha, Bandana. 2002. "Rules, Role, and Realities: Indo-American Families in the U.S." In *Minority Families in the United States: A Multicultural Perspective*, edited by Ronald L. Taylor, 212–224. Upper Saddle River, New Jersey: Prentice Hall.

Rubin, Barry. 1980. *Paved with Good Intentions: The American Experience in Iran*. New York: Oxford University Press.

Sabagh, Georges, and Mehdi Bozorgmehr. 1987. "Are the Characteristics of Exiles Different from Immigrants? The Case of Iranians in Los Angeles." *Sociology and Social Research* 71 (2): 77–83.

———. 1994. "Secular Immigrants: Religiosity and Ethnicity among Iranian Muslims in Los Angeles." In *Muslim Communities in North America*, edited by Y. Haddad and J. Smith, 445–473. Albany: State University of New York.

Sabagh, Georges, Ivan Light, and Mehdi Bozorgmehr. 1986. "Emerging Ethnicity: Iranians in Los Angeles." *Institute for Social Science Research* 3:7–10.

Said, Edward. 1997. *Covering Islam: How the Media and the Experts Determine How We See the Rest of the World*. New York: Vintage.

Saunders, H. 1985. "Diplomacy and Pressure, November 1979–May 1980." In *American Hostages in Iran*, edited by Christopher and Kreisberg, 72–142.

Schiller Glick, Nina, Linda Basch, and Cristina Blanc-Szanton. 1992. "Towards a Transnational Perspective on Migration: Race, Class, Ethnicity, and Nationalism Reconsidered." *Annals of the New York Academy of Science* 645.

Scott, C. 2000. "Bound for Glory: The Hostage Crisis as Captivity Narrative in Iran." *International Studies Quarterly* 44:177–188.

Shavarini, Mitra K. 2004. *Educating Immigrants: Experience of Second-Generation Iranians*. New York: LFB Scholarly Publishing.

Sick, Gary. 2001. "The Clouded Mirror: The United States and Iran, 1979–1999." In *Iran at the Crossroads*, edited by J. Esposito and K. Ramazani, 191–210. New York: Palgrave.

Smelser, Neil J. 2004. "Psychological Trauma and Cultural Trauma." In *Cultural Trauma and Collective Identity*, ed. Jeffrey Alexander, Ron Eyerman, Bernhard Giesen, Neil J. Smelser, and Piotr Sztompka. Los Angeles: University of California Press.

Sparrow, Kathleen H., and David M. Chretien. 1993. "The Social Distance Perceptions of Racial and Ethnic Groups by College Students: A Research Note." *Sociological Spectrum* 13, no. 2 (April–June): 277–288.

Suarez-Orozco, Carola, and Desiree Baolian Qin. 2006. "Psychological and Gender Perspectives on Immigrant Origin Youth." *International Migration Review* 40 (1): 165–199.

Sullivan, Zohreh. 2001. *Exiled Memories: Stories of Iranian Diaspora*. Philadelphia: Temple University Press.

Sztompka, P. 2004. *Cultural Trauma and Collective Identity*. Los Angeles: University of California Press.

Tohidi, Nayereh. 1993. "Iranian Women and Gender Relations in Los Angeles." In *Irangeles: Iranians in Los Angeles*, edited by Kelley, Friedlander, and Colby, 175–183.

Turner, Jonathan H. 2006. *Sociology*. Upper Saddle River, New Jersey: Prentice Hall.

U.S. Census Bureau. 2008. *The 2006–2008 American Community Survey 3-Year Estimates*. Washington, D.C.

U.S. Committee for Refugees and Immigrants. 1988. *World Refugee Survey Report 1988*. Washington D.C.

U.S. Department of Homeland Security (DHS). *Statistical Yearbook of the Immigration and Naturalization Service 1986–2008*. Washington, D.C.

U.S. Department of Justice, Immigration and Naturalization Service (INS). 1970–1977. Annual reports. Washington, D.C.

———. 1978–1986. Statistical yearbooks. Washington, D.C.

Zahedi, Dariush. 2008. *Political Attitudes and Patterns of Political Participation of Iranian Americans in California*. Berkeley: Institute of Government Studies, University of California.

Index